ANTI-OPPRESSIVE COUNSELING AND PSYCHOTHERAPY

In *Anti-Oppressive Counseling and Psychotherapy*, Jason D. Brown examines the impact of structural inequality on mental health and provides a framework for an anti-oppressive practice that recognizes privilege and challenges systemic barriers. Incorporating theory, research and detailed case studies, readers will learn how to implement intervention techniques that take into consideration the diverse social identities of both therapist and client. The text also teaches students and practicing psychotherapists how to use anti-oppressive practices to effect social change within their communities and society at large.

Jason D. Brown, PhD, is a professor of counseling psychology at Western University in London, Ontario. He is the coauthor of the first and second editions of *Community Development* and of *Counseling Diversity in Context*.

ANTI-OPPRESSIVE COUNSELING AND PSYCHOTHERAPY

Action for Personal and Social Change

Jason D. Brown

NEW YORK AND LONDON

First published 2019
by Routledge
52 Vanderbilt Avenue, New York, NY 10017

and by Routledge
2 Park Square, Milton Park, Abingdon, Oxon, OX14 4RN

Routledge is an imprint of the Taylor & Francis Group, an informa business

© 2019 Jason D. Brown

Library of Congress Cataloging-in-Publication Data
A catalog record for this book has been requested

ISBN: 978-1-138-08735-4 (hbk)
ISBN: 978-1-138-08734-7 (pbk)
ISBN: 978-1-315-11009-7 (ebk)

Typeset in Bembo
by Apex CoVantage, LLC

To Kobe, Jenna, Kaylee and Shelley

CONTENTS

TABLES

PREFACE

There are many diversity texts in counseling and psychotherapy. However, few specifically consider professional practice from an anti-oppressive perspective. In this text it is assumed that problems individuals bring to counseling and psychotherapy are influenced by living in an unjust society. It considers structural forces as the context of political, economic and social life affecting ourselves and clients as well as the profession. It also offers practical possibilities for personal and local change.

I chose counseling psychology as a career because I wanted to help others. Later I came to the realization that I must first know myself to have any hope of being helpful to someone else. This has been—and continues to be—a very humbling journey. I have become aware of the interconnected forms of privilege I hold as a white male who is heterosexual, from a working-class family, able and middle-aged. The academic tradition in which I trained to be a psychologist is deeply rooted in this privilege. I have found that privilege is often ignored by those who possess it. Some deny its existence and others claim they are harmed by "reverse" discrimination.

It is argued herein that political, social and economic disparities reproduce unequal opportunities and have clear effects on population health, including mental health. These structural forces themselves are not directly accessible by individuals but can be altered with the power of groups. Counselors and psychotherapists addressing mental health needs in contexts of structural disadvantage, can, from an anti-oppressive perspective, be progressive forces of change with individuals and communities. These changes make counseling and psychotherapy more accessible and effective for those who are presently underrepresented and underserved. They also contribute to a more equitable and just society.

This book is intended for graduate counseling and psychotherapy students in helping professions such as psychology, education, social work, nursing and health studies. It is designed to be a main or companion text for courses on multiculturalism, diversity and anti-oppressive practice.

INTRODUCTION

Arguments in Support of an Anti-Oppressive Perspective in Counseling and Psychotherapy

Trouble in the Global Village

In 1991, Sarah Conn from the Center for Psychological Studies in the Nuclear Age at Harvard Medical School wrote about the self–world connection as

> connecting personal pain and global crises. If we apply this model of the self–world connection to the practice of psychotherapy, then the goal of psychotherapy will of necessity be the healing of the world as part of the healing of the self.
>
> *(Miller & Surrey, 1997, p. 210)*

In a 2017 *Lancet* article titled "What will Donald Trump's presidency mean for health?", health professions were challenged to "understand sources of political unrest that are fuelling widespread discontent, and especially worsening health and living conditions, which pave the way for the rise of populism and extreme nationalism" (p. 752).

Inequality Makes Us Unwell

Inequality is rooted in distributions of power and privilege (Lenski, 2013). In *The Spirit Level*, UK epidemiologists Richard Wilkinson and Kate Pickett (2010) used international data to link inequality with social outcomes across developed nations. The frequency of mental health problems, including illness and addiction, are highest in nations with the greatest social inequality (Perlman, Hunter, & Stewart, 2015).

Social Problems Are Historically Driven

Each of us is born within an existing hierarchy. Legacies of colonization and slavery (Walls, 2015) are evident in economic, political and social disparities that today reproduce the privilege that male European descendants, as a group, have over others living in what has become North America. Government policies (e.g. land, citizenship, voting rights, reproductive rights, marriage, housing) have always advantaged some groups over others, favoring dominant groups of the time and place to keep themselves in power (House, 2014).

We Choose to Either Perpetuate or Challenge Privilege

The emergence of psychology as distinct from philosophy, situated itself within the natural sciences, and, subsequently, practitioners in medicine (Brennan & Houde, 2017). Counseling and psychotherapy have become increasingly standardized and focused. There is emphasis on short-term manualized symptom-specific and measurable, cognitive or behavioral change (McGuinty, Nelson, Carlson, Crowther, Bednar, & Foroughe, 2016). For those with privilege, opportunities and odds of success require little reflection on political, social and economic contributors to mental health. Successful treatment is personal adaptation to the norms they, as members of the dominant culture, have set. However, to those facing structural oppression, the "success" of adaptation to a status quo where they remain disadvantaged is misguided at best.

It Is Expected of Professionals Providing Counseling and Psychotherapy

Professionals are required to act in accordance with a concept of justice. According to the American Counseling Association (2014, p. 3), "promoting social justice" is a "core professional value" of the profession. Indeed, "justice or treating individuals equitably and fostering fairness and equality" is a "fundamental principle of ethical behavior". The Canadian Counseling and Psychotherapy Association (2007, p. 2) note that "justice is respecting the dignity and just treatment of all persons" and "societal interest is respecting the need to be responsible to society". In the Canadian Code of Ethics for Psychologists (2000, 2007, p. 4), "Respect for the Dignity of Persons and Peoples. . . (places) . . . emphasis on inherent worth, non-discrimination, moral rights, distributive, social and natural justice", and "all persons are entitled to benefit equally from the contributions of psychology and to equal quality in the processes, procedures, and services being conducted by psychologists, regardless of the person's characteristics, condition, or status". Equal benefit in an unfair society is not possible through equal treatment, only equitable treatment.

Advocacy Is a Professional Responsibility

According to the American Counseling Association (2014, p. 5), in "The Counseling Relationship", "where appropriate, counselors advocate at individual, group, institutional and societal levels to address potential barriers and obstacles that inhibit access and/or growth and development of clients". The Canadian Psychological Association's Practice Guidelines for School Psychologists (2007, p. 6), include District/System-Wide Intervention and Advocacy as "the school psychologist advocates for children and adolescents with learning, developmental, socio-emotional and behavioral exceptionalities".

The "Fifth Force" in Psychology Is a Call to Social Justice

Multicultural psychology has been termed the fourth force in psychology. Social justice is becoming recognized as the fifth force (Chen, 2018). Like multicultural psychology, it is a macro-level perspective that may be used to inform the purposes, methods and outcomes of professional activities. It does not dismantle or prescribe but rather suggests consideration of the place of counseling and psychotherapy in society and, professionally, why and how we practice. It makes privilege and disadvantage visible with formal recognition of processes of oppression and liberation.

References

American Counseling Association. (2014). *Codes of ethics and standards of practice*. Alexandria, VA: Author.

Brennan, J. F., & Houde, K. A. (2017). *History and systems of psychology*. Cambridge, UK: Cambridge University Press.

Canadian Counselling Psychotherapy Association. (2007). *Code of ethics*. Ottawa, ON: Author.

Canadian Psychological Association. (2000). *Canadian psychological association code of ethics*. Ottawa, ON: Author.

Canadian Psychological Association. (2007). *Professional practice guidelines for school psychologists in Canada*. Ottawa, ON: Author.

Chen, J. C. (2018). The role of critical theory in the development of multicultural psychology and counseling. In *Critical theory and transformative learning* (pp. 259–281). Hershey, PA: IGI Global.

House, F. (2014). *Freedom in the world 2014: The annual survey of political rights and civil liberties*. Lanham, MD: Rowman & Littlefield Publishers.

Lenski, G. E. (2013). *Power and privilege: A theory of social stratification*. Chapel Hill, NC: UNC Press Books.

McGuinty, E., Nelson, J., Carlson, A., Crowther, E., Bednar, D., & Foroughe, M. (2016). Redefining outcome measurement: A model for brief psychotherapy. *Clinical Psychology & Psychotherapy, 23*(3), 260–271.

McKee, M., Greer, S. L., & Stuckler, D. (2017). What will Donald Trump's presidency mean for health? A scorecard. *The Lancet, 389*(10070), 748–754.

Miller, J. B., & Surrey, J. L. (1997). Rethinking women's anger: The personal and the global. In *Women's growth in diversity: More writings from the stone center*. New York, NY: Guilford.

Perlman, D., Hunter, A. G., & Stewart, A. J. (2015). Psychology, history, and social justice: Concluding reflections. *Journal of Social Issues, 71*(2), 402–413.

Walls, D. S. (2015). *Community organizing*. Cambridge, UK: John Wiley & Sons, Inc.

Wilkinson, R., & Pickett, K. (2010). *The spirit level: Why equality is better for everyone*. London, UK: Penguin.

1

OPPRESSION AND MENTAL HEALTH

This chapter introduces the topic of global inequality and presents some evidence of its existence with social, economic and political examples across Canada and the United States. A colonial analysis of historical relations between original Indigenous peoples and European immigrants to North America explores the beginnings of oppression. The arrival and establishment of settler societies represented the views of white, European, Christian males. This analysis illustrates concepts of diversity, privilege and disadvantage. It is followed by an introduction to psychological studies of stigma, prejudice and micro-aggressions.

Why is social inequality relevant to professional counseling and psychotherapy?

- We live in an unequal society. Each of us is born within a hierarchy. Position in the hierarchy is advantageous to some and disadvantageous to others. Social positions have a substantial lifelong effect on individuals.
- Inequality produces oppression. Problems exist at both the structural level and the personal level as well as in between. Social problems manifest as personal problems (e.g. gender differences in employment position and income). Personal problems manifest as social problems (e.g. employment and income opportunities and outcomes differ by gender).
- Oppression is reflection of a group's and individual's status relative to others. It puts one member of a particular group at a distinct advantage over members of another group. Differences exist in power, influence and control. These differences manifest as unequal opportunities and unequal outcomes.
- Forces of oppression are structural (e.g. market, globalization, colonization) and reflected in policies and practices between nations. These forces are national (e.g. government policy, ownership, participation) and reflected in

policies and practices within nations. The forces are also local (e.g. location, services, capital) and reflected in policies and practices within communities. These forces are personal (e.g. esteem, agency, identity) and reflected in personal meaning.

- Counseling and psychotherapy focus on individuals. The practices operate from the basis that problems exist or are accessible within the individual. Such problems manifest as imbalances, excesses or deficiencies of known properties of the mind.
- An anti-oppressive (AO) perspective broadens the view of individuals to the forces that exist outside and recognizes the profession and the professional positioned within systems of oppression.
- From an AO perspective, mental health is personally and structurally determined. Personal problems manifest as imbalances, excesses or deficiencies of known aspects of a community or society.
- AO Counseling and Psychotherapy (AOCP) locates a portion of the responsibility on context that can be influenced by a collective. AOCP views interpersonal circumstances and the social context as legitimate targets for change. The professional and client engage in both internal and external change to address the problem.

Chapter Outline

Inequality

In 2017, Oxfam reported that "8 men owned the same wealth as the poorest half of the world", and Credit Suisse reported that those in the top 1% of global wealth together owned more than the rest of the globe (Anand & Segal, 2017). Today, the United States holds 33% of global wealth, while Canada holds 3%. There is clear evidence of global economic inequality. The country one is born in and the income distribution of that country are highly predictive (Milanovic, 2015). However, differences within nations are widening to a greater extent than the gaps between nations (Milanovic, 2016).

Within nations, an index known as the **Gini coefficient** reflects the income distribution. It is one of the most widely used measures of inequality. On this measure, a score of 0 represents maximum equality and 100 represents maximum inequality. In Canada, the Gini coefficient for 2010–2015 (United Nations, 2016) was 33.7 and the US was 41.1 (Bogliacino & Maestri, 2016). According to the World Bank (2015), the nation with the highest Gini, of 176 ranked nations, was South Africa at 63.4 and the nation with the lowest Gini was Ukraine at 25.5. Internationally, Canada ranked 68th and the United States 117th, reflecting a major gap between their least and most wealthy citizens.

The relationship between inequality and social problems is linear and positive, such that the greater the inequality, the greater the indices of violent crime, obesity, mental illness, imprisonment and teen births (Wilkinson & Pickett, 2010). With greater equality, there is a greater sense of cohesion, trust, cooperation and social stress (Wilkinson & Pickett, 2017).

The connections between low population and personal health status are evident in developmental trajectories (Pless, Hodge, & Evans, 2017), as well as within regional and local communities with higher concentrations of risk factors (Fazel, Geddes, & Kushel, 2014). There is ample evidence that policies associated with improved access to education, health care, housing, employment and other services within disadvantaged or underserviced areas and populations have a positive leveling effect (Allen, Balfour, Bell, & Marmot, 2014). In the sections that follow, connections between economic, social and political inequality are described.

Economic

The *Vertical Mosaic* (Porter, 1965) was coined to reflect the prominent layers of social arrangement. While the book was written 50 years ago, the concept remains and is the subject of discussion and debate. Recently (Porter, 2015), scholars have written about the vertical mosaic in relation to gender and race inequality, citizenship and social justice as well as social class and power. To illustrate, poverty lines in Canada and the United States reflect significant differences between individuals and families along the continuum from least to most wealth.

Low Income Cut Offs (LICO) in Canada are relative measures of poverty that identify the threshold at which families are spending more than 20% of their income than the average on food, clothing and shelter. They are calculated by number of people in a family and by community size. According to the LICO measure, there are several demographic groups that are overrepresented and therefore at risk for poverty (Canada, 2010; Tweddle, Battle, & Torjman, 2015):

1. Children

    • 9.1% nationally
    • 23.4% of lone parent
    • 39.3% in recent immigrant families

2. Women

    • 9.9% nationally
    • 29% of all unattached
    • earn 71.4% of what full-time men earn on average

3. Unattached adults

    • 58.1% of 18–24 years
    • 31.6% of 45–54 years
    • 39.3% of 55–64 years

4. Indigenous peoples

    • 42.8% of all unattached
    • 25% of adults in urban families
    • 27.5% under 15 with family
    • 63% for 16–24 years

5. People with disabilities

    • lower average income, $28,503 vs. $37,309 (national average)
    • 43.9% 15–64 NOT in labor force vs. 19.8% (national average)

6. Recent immigrants

    • 32.6% of families
    • 58.3% of unattached
    • 54.7% of refugees

The **US poverty line** is based on pre-tax income and proportion spent on cost of a minimum diet, adjusted annually for inflation and reported based on family size, composition and age. The US (Department of Health and Human Services, 2015) poverty rate is quite restrictive but still includes 14.5% (45.3 million people).

- The child poverty rate was 19.9%: for African-American children 36.9%, Hispanic 30.4% and white children 10.7%.
- Nearly half of all female-headed lone-parent families (45.8%) lived in poverty.
- Working age individuals with and without disabilities had discrepant poverty rates of 28.4% vs. 12.4%.
- Women were 35% more likely to live in poverty than men.
- 19% of immigrants vs. 13.5% non-immigrants live in poverty.
- Among 18–44-year-olds, 15.3% of males and 21.1% of females live in poverty, with rates increasing among those who identify as gay or lesbian, at 20.5% and 22.7%, higher for individuals who identify as bisexual, at 25.9 and 29.4%, compared to 20.1% and 21.5% for those who do not identify as a member of the LGBTQ2+ community.
- About 40% of homeless youth identify as LGBTQ2+ (Macartney, Bishaw, & Fontenot, 2013).
- In the UK, poverty rates for Muslims are 50%, relative to those who are Jewish (13%), Sikh (27%), Hindu (22%), Anglican (14%) or Catholic (19%), with 18% as the national average (Heath & Li, 2015).

Social

Social indices of inequality are reflected in victimization statistics. In Canada (Statistics Canada, 2017), hate crimes occurred most frequently based on race or ethnicity targeting—in order of occurrence: Black, East Asian and South Asian individuals. Religion was the second most frequent target of hate crimes, with individuals who were Jewish or Muslim most frequently the targets. Sexual orientation was the third most frequent target of hate crime. In the United States, hate crimes reported to police, in order of frequency (Federal Bureau of Investigations, 2016), occurred on the basis of race/ethnicity, religion, sexual orientation, gender identity and, finally, disability.

In another illustration of social inequality, approximately 70% of incidents of abuse of woman go unreported, and of those that are, one-third are sexual assaults and beatings. Women with disabilities in Canada are 1.4× more likely than women without a disability to experience abuse. In 2013 (US), the rate of serious violent victimization for persons with disabilities (14 per 1,000) was more than three times higher than the age-adjusted rate for persons without disabilities (4 per 1,000).

Political

Political indices of inequality are reflected in voting behavior and representation of elected officials. In the United States, voting rates vary by ethnicity. In the last presidential election (2016), 65.3% of eligible white voters voted, 59.6% of Black voters and 47.6% of Hispanic voters (US Census, 2017). Canada is closer to the goal of building a diverse parliament that represents its population. A cabinet ratio of 48.3% women, 16.1% visible minorities and 6.5% Indigenous comes close to matching a Canadian population that was 50.9% women, 22.3% visible minorities and 4.9% Indigenous (Wherry, 2015).

Positions Against Social Inequality

An argument upon which this text is based is that unequal opportunities and outcomes diminish population and personal mental health. This context creates conditions in which mental health problems are more likely to be triggered, exacerbated and maintained. Three additional arguments against inequality are reflected in the following moral, economic and political positions.

A **moral argument against inequality** is that it is unfair and therefore unjust (Marquez, 2018). This is a value position that begins with the idea that no life is worth more than any other life. However, unequal life chances, unequal opportunities and unequal outcomes exist and must be addressed.

An **economic argument against inequality** is that few have the means to purchase enough to keep the economy functioning. According to the OECD (2014), economic growth decreases when inequality increases (Dabla-Norris, Kochhar, Suphaphiphat, Ricka, & Tsounta, 2015). The poorest 40% of the population are most affected when inequality rises. Greater inequality leads to less education by those at the lower end of the distribution, which diminishes economic potential.

A **political argument against inequality** is that it reduces political interest and involvement in elections. The most well off do not have the voting numbers to continue to lead democratic systems. However, those who are not represented in political office and have no candidates may choose not to vote.

Legacies of the Settler Societies

Social inequality in the United States and Canada is reflected in colonial history following the arrival of Europeans and creation of settler societies. At the time of contact, Europeans arrived within nations that were self-sufficient and connected to the land. It has been noted that

> archaeological evidence is mounting to the point where it can now be argued with growing conviction, if not absolute proof, that the pre-Columbian

Americas were inhabited in large part to the carrying capacities of the land for the ways of life that were being followed and the types of food preferred.

(Dickason, 1992, pp. 26–27)

England and France were the primary colonizers in North America during the 1600s. This European expansion led to white **settler societies** in what became Canada and the United States.

Colonial views included a belief that the existing inhabitants "had no real history" and that the land was "empty of mankind and its works". In this view, the people of the Americas "lived in an eternal, unhistorical state" (Mann, 2005, p. 9). Land ownership and a lucrative fishery and fur trade, as well as timber, tobacco, wheat and potash, were imposed for the benefit of the colonies and colonists (Rosenbloom, 2018). Although assimilation efforts were made in multiple ways, there has been consistent effort by Indigenous peoples to partner with and, eventually, resist colonial influences.

There was some diversity among the European settlers. For example, the need for cheap labor opened immigration to the colonies, but at a lower status than the proletariat in the colonies. Following British defeat of the French in 1760, French subordination began to emerge. Those "at the helm of the colonial, then dominion states, and those shaping civil society drew from imperial and home-grown philosophies about the appropriate character, physical appearance, roles and behavior of settler women and men" (Stasiukis & Jhappan, 1995, p. 97). These ideas were evident in colonial beliefs of racial and ethnic superiority, rigid gender and sexual roles, and the need for a young, Christian workforce.

Race and Ethnicity

In race and ethnicity, "settler and post-settler society citizenship is best conceptualized and described by examining the linked processes of what is called the aboriginalization (of indigenous minorities), the ethnification (of immigrant minorities) and the indigenization (of settler majorities)" (Pearson, 2002). Loyalists from the United States included European, Indigenous and Black soldiers who, in return for their freedom, supported the British. Nova Scotia was the first place in Canada where the experiences of racism and segregation were documented. The underground railroad provided a means from the US to Canada, where individuals would be inexpensive labor, but "free". Over time, communities of those who fled the United States developed. Newcomers in the late nineteenth and early twentieth centuries arrived from Europe, China, Japan and India. The minister and politician JS Woodsworth, in his book *Strangers Within Our Gates*, described these immigrants as "non-assailable elements that are clearly detrimental to our highest national development, and vigorously excluded" (1909, p. 279).

Gender and Sexuality

Men "founded" North America. They held top positions in production and decision-making. The Company of One Hundred Associates (New France) claimed all land and took over all but fishing industries. To do this, they needed management and skilled labor, who were male. "Women were represented as little more than breeders to reproduce the nation, the empire and the future of the race" (Stasiukis & Jhappan, 1995, p. 99). For example, the "Daughters of the King" were women from France who came to marry settlers. **Nuclear families** formed the basis of settler societies. Laws and customs regulated male–female sex and marriage to shape these units with clearly defined gender roles and purposes (Wells, 2015). Individuals without family membership could be relegated to the margins of a settler society (Phillips, 2009).

Employment and Ability

The **British "poor laws"** of the late 1500s distinguished between those who were worthy and unworthy of assistance (Roberts, 2016). In the colonies, this responsibility was transferred, and those who could not work were left to live in the margins, while any who could work were put to work. The Charity Aid Act assigned responsibility for the poor to charity and churches. Ability determined whether one was capable of working or not. Those who were capable of working were "able", and those who were not were "disabled" (Martel, 2016). While they were provided with some assistance, their value to the colony was limited.

> The person naturally disabled, either in wit or member, as an idiot, lunatic, blind, lame etc., not being able to work . . . all these . . . are to be provided for by the overseers of necessary relief and are to have allowances . . . according to . . . their maladies and needs.
>
> *(Ward & Flynn, 1994, p. 30)*

Age

At the time, depending on their parents' wealth, children were either protected and educated or became part of the workforce (McCusker & Menard, 2014). Workers that became too old or experienced injury became liabilities and were replaced. For women, who needed only be 13 years old to legally marry in England in 1875, their roles as child-bearers and parents began early. There were no protections for children from the workforce or regarding their treatment until the Society for Prevention of Cruelty to Animals was created in 1824 and in 1891 the Society for Prevention of Cruelty to Children (Flegel, 2016).

Religion

Missionaries were sent by the colonizers to convert the Indigenous peoples (Fisher, 2018). This effort brought new hierarchies. Beliefs in God and church extended into rites of passage and Christian ceremonies such as marriage, baptism and burial (Woolford, 2013). Interestingly, it was the submissive role of women within the church that met the greatest resistance among Indigenous women (Smith, 2015). Values of self-reliance and hard work were viewed positively and as a means to economic reward (Bayley, 2008).

Colonialism Today

The legacies of the settler societies are evident today. A fundamental driver of colonial interest was and continues to be control. Efforts to control movement of Indigenous peoples through the reserve system and forced relocations; spirituality through the outlawing of traditional practices; families and parenting through adoptions and residential schools; and governance through the Indian Agents were applied (Smylie & Firestone, 2016). Other methods have been used and are still practiced today (Moane, 2014), including violence (via law enforcement), political exclusion (via scrutiny of voters), economic means (via ownership and taxes), sexuality (via motherhood, marriage, birth control), education (via access, content omissions, media control) and ethnic fragmenting (e.g. competition, tokenism and immigration). Stages of colonization in the United States and Canada include 1) denial and withdrawal, 2) destruction and eradication, 3) denigration, belittlement and insults, 4) composure under the surface, accommodate and tokenize, 5) transformation and exploitation (Laenui, 2000, p. 1).

Social Privilege

The notion of inequality confers both privilege and disadvantage. Many of us, as students and beneficiaries of higher education, possess some level of privilege. Many of us also experience levels of disadvantage. It is important to recognize the complexity of these ideas and that each person as well as each group has experience with both. The degree to which one is more or less advantaged or disadvantaged is of limited value in this discussion because accumulations and intersections of identity and social group membership exist. What is important is to make the concept of privilege explicit.

What is privilege? It has been defined as four qualities (Lucal, 1996; Robinson & Walker, 1999), including: 1) special advantage that is not universal, 2) something bestowed and not earned, 3) something related to a preferred status and 4) something that benefits only those who possess it and no others. An adapted version of a "check your privilege" (Holm, Gorosh, Brady, & White-Perkins, 2017) activity follows. It is important as a learning opportunity to reflect on your own and others' experiences and to recognize the effects each of us has on others.'

Privilege and Responsibility Exercise (Holm et al., 2017)
*Modified for therapists

- If I want to move, I can rent or buy in an area I can afford and want to live.

Race/ethnicity, religion, SES, sexual orientation

- If I ask to talk to the person in charge, I will be facing a person similar to me.

Race/ethnicity, gender, sexual orientation

- If I walk towards a security checkpoint in the airport, I can feel that I will not be looked upon as suspect.

Race/ethnicity, religion

- If I walk into a restaurant I can expect to be treated with dignity and respect.

Race/ethnicity, physical/mental ability, SES, sexual orientation

- When I enter my workplace, it is a familiar layout and furnishings to what I'm used to.

Race/ethnicity, SES

- I have no trouble getting to and from work and in and out of my office.

Physical/mental ability, SES

- I have never seen vandalism or had someone say something to me in public that was offensive.

Race/ethnicity, physical/mental ability, SES, sexual orientation

- If I walk through a parking garage at night, I don't have to feel vulnerable.

Gender, age

- I can buy posters, postcards, picture books, greeting cards, dolls, toys and magazines featuring people who look like me.

Race/ethnicity

- People like me are featured in history books that elementary school children read.

Race/ethnicity, physical/mental ability, SES, sexual orientation

- I feel confident that my clients feel that I am qualified upon first impression.

Race/ethnicity, age, gender

- My employer gives days off for the holidays that are most important to me.

Religion, ethnicity

- I can work whenever needed and know that my children will be cared for.

Gender, SES

- I can speak in a roomful of professionals and feel that I am heard.

Age, race/ethnicity, gender
- My age adds to my credibility.

Age
- My body stature is consistent with an image of success.

Gender, ethnicity/race
- I can bring my partner to a professional or community gathering without thinking about it.

Sexual orientation
- I can feel confident that if a family member requires counseling they would be treated with dignity and respect even if they don't mention my profession.

Race/ethnicity, physical/mental ability, SES, sexual orientation
- I have no medical conditions or cultural/religious dietary restrictions that require special arrangements or that makes others see me as different.

Religion, physical/mental ability

Oppression

Oppression is the result of unchecked "entitlement, sanction, power, immunity and advantage or right granted or conferred by the dominant group to a person or group solely by birthright membership or prescribed identities" (Black & Stone, 2005, p. 245). It happens through force or deprivation, and at primary (e.g. personal), secondary (e.g. beneficiaries of oppression) or tertiary (e.g. oppressed group seeks approval from dominant by victimizing members of own group) levels (Hanna, Talley, & Guindon, 2000). Types of oppression include **exploitation** (e.g. using the efforts of some for another group's benefit), **marginalization** (e.g. pushing a group to the margins, as not valued enough to exploit), **powerlessness** (e.g. the haves and the have nots), **cultural imperialism** (e.g. making the culture of the ruling class the "norm") and **violence** (e.g. fear of themselves or their property being attacked) (Romney, Tatum, & Jones, 1992).

Power differences are integral to the creation and experience of oppression. The "matrix of domination", for instance, includes four domains of power: structural, disciplinary, hegemonic and interpersonal (Mosedale, 2003). **Structural power** is the power of the institutions and laws that are prominent within a society. **Disciplinary power** is the influence held by those who act in roles created by the institutions and laws of a society. **Hegemonic power** refers to the dominance of a set of ideas or views over all others within a society. While structural, disciplinary and hegemonic power operate at a high level of influence and deal with oppression via governance and education, justice and social services as well as health systems, **interpersonal power** is what occurs between individuals within a society.

Oppression can be viewed as the "causes of the causes" of ill health, including systemic forces such as globalization, imperialism and neoliberalism. Oppression is associated with diminished health outcomes. At the level of individual experience, these forces intersect and lead to psychological distress (Pascoe & Richman, 2009; Williams & Mohammed, 2009). For example, internal and external sexism and racism among African-American women is associated with psychological distress (Szymanski & Stewart, 2010). In another example, stressors including heterosexist events, racist events, heterosexism in communities of color, racism in sexual minority communities, race-related dating and relationship problems, internalized heterosexism or homophobia, 'outness' to family and 'outness' to the world accounted for one-third of the distress experienced by LGBTQ Asian Americans (Ray, 2016).

Stigma and Prejudice

Stigma and prejudice are "societal-level conditions, cultural norms, and institutional policies that constrain . . . opportunities, resources, and well-being" (Hatzenbuehler & Link, 2014, p. 2). They produce similarly negative psychological effects but for different reasons. Stigma concerns conditions that are not commonly experienced, such as HIV or Fetal Alcohol Spectrum Disorder, while prejudice is based on more 'usual' issues like race, gender or class. Two psychological consequences of stigma are: 1) anticipation of reaction to self (e.g. vigilance and anxiety) and 2) internalization of stigma—directing negative attitudes from society toward self, which is also called "appropriated" stigma. Prejudice occurs as a result of interpersonal treatments of individuals who are marginalized by another who is not marginalized. There are multiple studies of the negative psychological effects (e.g. Bostwick, Boyd, Hughes, West, & McCabe, 2014; Velez, Campos, & Moradi, 2015; Calabrese, Meyer, Overstreet, Haile, & Hansen, 2016).

In an important study linking social policy to mental health (Hatzenbuehler, 2014), it was found that diagnosed psychiatric disorders in the LGBTQ community were higher in states with no protection versus those with legal marriage, even after perceived discrimination was controlled for. In the state of Massachusetts before and after same-sex marriage was legalized in 2003, there was: 1) a reduction in depression and hypertension for gay and bisexual men from 12 months before to 12 months after and 2) less health care demand as well as 3) health care cost savings. A comparison on prejudicial attitudes showed higher mortality in high stigma communities, with a 12-year difference between these and the lowest stigma communities. Among LGBTQ youth in neighborhoods with higher rates of hate crimes, there were higher rates of suicide ideation and attempts than among LGBTQ youth in lower hate crime neighborhoods (Hatzenbuehler, 2014).

Stigma and prejudice affect mental health in five ways. First, the effect may manifest as an activation of stress processes among those discriminated against by others in encounters, leading to mistreatment in jobs, education and health care. Second, structural problems with access, such as denial of health services or benefits, affect mental health. Third, unconscious forms of prejudice occur without awareness of the one acting in a discriminatory manner but with the notice of the individual being discriminated against. Fourth, there may be internalized prejudice and stigma by those who are discriminated against. Fifth, mental health may be affected due to vigilance by individuals fearing discrimination, leading to stress and compromised social interactions (Stuber, Meyer, & Link, 2008).

Micro-Aggressions

Sue (2010) distinguishes between modern and aversive racism. Modern racism is right wing, conservatives who talk about traditional values or family values. Aversive racism is what liberals practice when they are conflicted between values of equality but harbor negative feelings. Aversive racism is not conscious. It is difficult to identify, yet very harmful. It is also not apparent to those holding the beliefs so difficult to address by others and self. One way that aversive racism manifests is through micro-aggressions. Indeed, the personal, structural and relational are all interconnected; "inasmuch as a person who is constantly exposed to hearing language which stigmatizes him/her is distressed by that experience, this is as real a form of oppression as structural discrimination" (Hopton, 1997).

As defined by Sue et al. (2007, p. 273).

> Microaggressions are the everyday verbal, nonverbal, and environmental slights, snubs, or insults, whether intentional or unintentional, which communicate hostile, derogatory, or negative messages to target persons based solely upon their marginalized group membership. In many cases, these hidden messages may invalidate the group identity or experiential reality of target persons, demean them on a personal or group level, communicate they are lesser human beings, suggest they do not belong with the majority group, threaten and intimidate, or relegate them to inferior status and treatment.

Three forms of micro-aggressions can be identified (Sue, 2010): **micro-assault**, **microinsult** and **microinvalidation**. Micro-assault is explicit denigration that is deliberate and conscious, held and expressed when the person feels safe to do so or is just overwhelmed. Microinsult is subtler and not recognized by the person doing it but is apparent to the other, such as talking over someone or diverting one's attention when they speak. Microinvalidation is communication that invalidates another's experience.

The examples below focus on color blindness and denial of individual racism (Sue et al., 2007, p. 276).

> *Color blindness: Statements that indicate that a White person does not want to acknowledge race. For example, "When I look at you, I don't see color." In effect, this is denying a person of color's racial/ethnic experiences.*

Denial of individual racism: A statement made when Whites deny their racial biases. "As a woman, I know what you go through as a racial minority." The meaning of this is that your racial oppression is no different than my gender oppression. I can't be a racist. I'm like you.

Conclusion

Social inequality is a major cause of compromised mental health and wellness. Each individual is located within groups of differences that have a legacy in the settler societies of North America. These groupings, including sex and gender, race and ethnicity, age, religion, class and ability, refer to characteristics that are organized hierarchically. This social hierarchy is largely a European import that has produced categories of difference within which each of us is embedded. AOCP is situated in this unequal environment, and its practitioners are mindful of the ways that social categories operate in their own professional and personal lives, the lives of their clients and on their interactions. This awareness creates understanding of contextual and interpersonal forces that affect mental health and the necessity of challenging oppression at different levels.

Web Links

Joe Gone—Historical Trauma, Therapy Culture, and the Indigenous Boarding School Legacy
https://vimeo.com/104030869

Canada Continues to Be a Settler Society
http://newcanadianmedia.ca/item/5199-canada-continues-to-be-a-settler-society

Psychotherapy and Traditional Intervention Strategies: Being an Effective Helper
www.ccpa-accp.ca/wp-content/uploads/2015/06/2014conf.PeterMenzies.pdf

Strategies for Responding to Colonization and Oppression
www.ohtn.on.ca/strategies-for-responding-to-colonization-and-oppression/

Temptations of Power and Certainty
www.kennethstewart.com/temptations-of-power-and-certainty.html

Key Terms

Gini coefficient   7
Low Income Cut Offs   8
US poverty line   9

References

Allen, J., Balfour, R., Bell, R., & Marmot, M. (2014). Social determinants of mental health. *International Review of Psychiatry, 26*(4), 392–407.

Anand, S., & Segal, P. (2017). Who are the global top 1%? *World Development, 95,* 111–126.

Bayley, S. (2008). *Victorian values: An introduction.* Montreal: Dawson College.

Black, L. L., & Stone, D. (2005). Expanding the definition of privilege: The concept of social privilege. *Journal of Multicultural Counseling and Development, 33*(4), 243–255.

Bogliacino, F., & Maestri, V. (2016). Wealth inequality and the great recession. *Intereconomics, 51*(2), 61–66.

Bostwick, W. B., Boyd, C. J., Hughes, T. L., West, B. T., & McCabe, S. E. (2014). Discrimination and mental health among lesbian, gay, and bisexual adults in the United States. *American Journal of Orthopsychiatry, 84*(1), 35.

Calabrese, S. K., Meyer, I. H., Overstreet, N. M., Haile, R., & Hansen, N. B. (2016). Exploring discrimination and mental health disparities faced by Black sexual minority women using a minority stress framework. *Psychology of Women Quarterly, 39*(3), 287–304.

Canada. (2010). *Federal poverty reduction plan: Working in partnership towards reducing poverty in Canada.* Ottawa, ON: House of Commons.

Dabla-Norris, M. E., Kochhar, M. K., Suphaphiphat, M. N., Ricka, M. F., & Tsounta, E. (2015). *Causes and consequences of income inequality: A global perspective.* International Monetary Fund. Retrieved November 9, 2018, from https://www.imf.org/external/pubs/ft/sdn/2015/sdn1513.pdf

Department of Health and Human Services. (2015). *Further resources on poverty measurement, poverty lines, and their history.* Retrieved April 16, 2018, from https://aspe.hhs.gov/further-resources-poverty-measurement-poverty-lines-and-their-history

Dickason, O. P. (1992). *Canada's first nations: A history of founding peoples from the earliest times.* Norham, OK: University of Oklahoma Press.

Fazel, S., Geddes, J. R., & Kushel, M. (2014). The health of homeless people in high-income countries: Descriptive epidemiology, health consequences, and clinical and policy recommendations. *The Lancet, 384*(9953), 1529–1540.

Federal Bureau of Investigation. (2016). *Hate crime statistics.* Washington, DC: US Department of Justice.

Fisher, L. (2018). Natives, religion, and race in colonial America. *The Oxford Handbook of Religion and Race in American History*, 323.

Flegel, M. (2016). *Conceptualizing cruelty to children in nineteenth-century England: Literature, representation, and the NSPCC.* London: Routledge.

Hanna, F. J., Talley, W. B., & Guindon, M. H. (2000). The power of perception: Toward a model of cultural oppression and liberation. *Journal of Counseling & Development, 78*(4), 430–441.

Hatzenbuehler, M. L. (2014). Structural stigma and the health of lesbian, gay, and bisexual populations. *Current Directions in Psychological Science, 23*(2), 127–132.

Hatzenbuehler, M. L., & Link, B. G. (2014). Introduction to the special issue on structural stigma and health. *Social Science & Medicine, 103*, 1–6.

Heath, A., & Li, Y. (2015, January). *Review of the relationship between religion and poverty.* An analysis for the Joseph Rowntree Foundation. CSI Working paper. Retrieved from http://csi.nuff.ox.ac.uk/

Holm, A. L., Gorosh, M. R., Brady, M., & White-Perkins, D. (2017). Recognizing privilege and bias: An interactive exercise to expand health care providers' personal awareness. *Academic Medicine, 92*(3), 360–364.

Hopton, J. (1997). Anti-discriminatory practice and anti-oppressive practice: A radical humanist psychology perspective. *Critical Social Policy, 17*(52), 47–61.

Stasiukis, D., & Jhappan, R. (1995). The fractious politics of a settler society: Canada. In D. Stasiulis & N. Youval-Davis (Eds.), *Unsettling Settler Societies* (pp. 95–131). London, UK: Sage.

Sue, D. W., Capodilupo, C. M., Torino, G. C., Bucceri, J. M., Holder, A., Nadal, K. L., & Esquilin, M. (2007). Racial microaggressions in everyday life: Implications for clinical practice. *American Psychologist, 62*(4), 271.

Laenui, P. (2000). Processes of decolonization. *Reclaiming Indigenous Voice and Vision*, 150–160.

Lucal, B. (1996). Oppression and privilege: Toward a relational conceptualization of race. *Teaching Sociology*, 245–255.

Macartney, S., Bishaw, A., & Fontenot, K. (2013). *Poverty rates for selected detailed race and Hispanic groups by state and place: 2007–2011.* Washington, DC: US Department of Commerce, Economics and Statistics Administration, US Census Bureau.

Mann, C. (2005). *1491: New revelations of the Americas before Columbus.* New York, NY: Knopf.

Marquez, X. (2018). Is income inequality unjust? Perspectives from political philosophy. *Policy Quarterly, 7*(2).

Martel, G. (2016). *For the glory of the nation: Eugenics, child-saving and the segregation of the "Feeble-Minded"* (Doctoral dissertation).

McCusker, J. J., & Menard, R. R. (2014). *The economy of British America, 1607–1789.* Chapel Hill, NC: UNC Press Books.

Milanovic, B. (2015). Global inequality of opportunity: How much of our income is determined by where we live? *Review of Economics and Statistics, 97*(2), 452–460.

Milanovic, B. (2016). *Global inequality.* Cambridge, MS: Harvard University Press.

Moane, G., & Sonn, C. (2014). Postcolonial psychology. In *Encyclopedia of critical psychology* (pp. 1444–1448). New York, NY: Springer.

Mosedale, S. (2003). Towards a framework for assessing empowerment. *New Directions in Impact Assessment for Development: Methods and Practice Manchester, UK*, 24–25.

OECD. (2014). *Does income inequality hurt economic growth?* Retrieved November 9, 2018, from https://www.oecd.org/social/Focus-Inequality-and-Growth-2014.pdf

Oxfam. (2017). *An economy for the 99%*. Retrieved April 16, 2018, from https://d1tn3vj7xz9fdh.cloudfront.net/s3fs-public/file_attachments/bp-economy-for-99-percent-160117-en.pdf

Pascoe, E. A., & Smart Richman, L. (2009). Perceived discrimination and health: A meta-analytic review. *Psychological Bulletin, 135*(4), 531.

Pearson, D. (2002). Theorizing citizenship in British settler societies. *Ethnic and Racial Studies, 25*(6), 989–1012.

Phillips, R. (2009). Settler colonialism and the nuclear family. *The Canadian Geographer/Le Géographe canadien, 53*(2), 239–253.

Pless, I. B., Hodge, M., & Evans, R. G. (2017). If not genetics, then what? Biological pathways and population health. In *Why are some people healthy and others not?* (pp. 161–188). London: Routledge.

Porter, J. (1965). *The vertical mosaic: An analysis of social class and power in Canada*. Toronto, ON: University of Toronto Press.

Porter, J. (2015). *The vertical mosaic: An analysis of social class and power in Canada*. Toronto, ON: University of Toronto Press.

Ray, J. M. (2016). *Minority stress and substance use in lesbian, gay, bisexual, queer, and questioning adults: An exploration of outness and family attachment* (Doctoral dissertation), Bowling Green State University.

Roberts, F. D. (2016). *Paternalism in early Victorian England*. London: Routledge.

Robinson, V. M. J., & Walker, J. C. (1999). Theoretical privilege and researchers' contribution to educational change. *Stirring the Waters: The Influence of Marie Clay*, 239–259.

Romney, P., Tatum, B., & Jones, J. (1992). Feminist strategies for teaching about oppression: The importance of process. *Women's Studies Quarterly, 20*(1–2), 95–110.

Rosenbloom, J. L. (2018). *The colonial American economy*. Retrieved November 9, 2018, from https://lib.dr.iastate.edu/econ_ag_workingpapers/1/

Smith, A. (2015). *Conquest: Sexual violence and American Indian genocide*. Durham, NC: Duke University Press.

Smylie, J., & Firestone, M. (2016). The health of Indigenous peoples. In D. Raphael (3rd ed.) *Social Determinants of Health: Canadian Perspective* (pp. 434–469). Toronto, ON: Canadian Scholars Press.

Statistics Canada. (2017). *Police-reported hate crime in Canada, 2016*. Ottawa: Author.

Stuber, J., Meyer, I., & Link, B. (2008). Stigma, prejudice, discrimination and health. *Social Science & Medicine (1982), 67*(3), 351.

Sue, D. W. (2010). *Microaggressions in everyday life: Race, gender, and sexual orientation*. New York, NY: John Wiley & Sons, Inc.

Sue, D. W., & Sue, D. (2012). *Counseling the culturally diverse: Theory and practice*. New York, NY: John Wiley & Sons, Inc.

Szymanski, D. M., & Stewart, D. N. (2010). Racism and sexism as correlates of African American women's psychological distress. *Sex Roles, 63*(3–4), 226–238.

Tweddle, A., Battle, K., & Torjman, S. (2015). *Welfare in Canada 2012*. Ottawa: Caledon Institute of Social Policy.

US Census. (2017). *Reported voting rates*. Retrieved April 16, 2018, from www.census.gov/content/dam/Census/newsroom/press-kits/2017/voting-and-registration/figure02.png

United Nations. (2016). *Report on the World Social Situation*. Retrieved November 9, 2018, from https://www.un.org/esa/socdev/rwss/2016/full-report.pdf

Velez, B. L., Campos, I. D., & Moradi, B. (2015). Relations of sexual objectification and racist discrimination with Latina women's body image and mental health. *The Counseling Psychologist, 43*(6), 906–935.

Ward, L., & Flynn, M. (1994). What matters most: Disability, research and empowerment. In M. Rioux & M. Bach (Eds.), *Disability in not measles: New research paradigms in disability* (pp. 25–42). North York, ON: Roeher Institute.

Wells, R. V. (2015). *Population of the British colonies in America before 1776: A survey of census data*. Princeton, NJ: Princeton University Press.

Wherry, A. (2015). *How the federal government is slowly becoming as diverse as Canada*. Retrieved November 9, 2018, from https://www.cbc.ca/news/politics/trudeau-appointments-diversity-analysis-wherry-1.4448740

Wilkinson, R. G., & Pickett, K. E. (2010). The spirit level. In *Why equality is better for everyone*. London, UK: Penguin.

Wilkinson, R. G., & Pickett, K. E. (2017). The enemy between us: The psychological and social costs of inequality. *European Journal of Social Psychology, 47*(1), 11–24.

Williams, D. R., & Mohammed, S. A. (2009). Discrimination and racial disparities in health: Evidence and needed research. *Journal of Behavioral Medicine, 32*(1), 20–47.

Woodsworth, J. S. (1909). *Strangers within our gates: Or, coming Canadians* (No. 5). FC Stephenson. Retrieved November 9, 2018, from https://archive.org/details/strangerswithino00wooduoft/page/n5

Woolford, A. (2013). Nodal repair and networks of destruction: Residential schools, colonial genocide, and redress in Canada. *Settler Colonial Studies, 3*(1), 65–81.

World Bank. (2015). *World development indicators 2013*. Washington, DC: World Bank. Retrieved October 2013, from http://data.worldbank.org

Discussion Questions

1. In what ways have you and your family experienced social disadvantage and advantage? Do you believe that these have changed over time or across generations? Why or why not?

2. Take a walk through your community or neighborhood and a commercial or retail establishment. In what ways is diversity reflected? What is absent? What are the messages about who is "in" and "out"?

3. In what ways is being a professional a privileged position? How could this have an effect on clients who already face significant social disadvantage? How could you counteract this?

2
PSYCHOLOGIES OF LIBERATION

In this chapter, the origins of liberation psychology in Latin America are presented as a background to other psychologies of liberation. Each of these psychologies offers a representation of the psyche as contextually embedded within worldviews that differ from dominant cultures. Each therefore engages explicitly with the topics of oppression and liberation. Oppression exists both outside of and within individuals. Critical consciousness is essential to the development of an awareness of political, social and economic forces associated with identity and power relations at individual and group levels. Approaches to the development of competencies for counseling and psychotherapy with their own and their clients' critical consciousness are presented.

Why are psychologies of liberation relevant to professional counseling and psychotherapy?

- From an AO perspective, each of us is both the oppressed and the oppressor. We have advantaged statuses. We have disadvantaged statuses. We oppress others by not challenging what is unequal and unfair, as well as by deliberately benefitting from that advantage. We also oppress ourselves by accepting a disadvantaged position as well as believing messages that I am "lesser than".
- Social justice is an essential concept in counseling and psychotherapy. AOCP poses a view of personal problems as social problems. Social problems are rooted in inequality. Equity for both opportunities and outcomes is liberating.
- AOCP identifies power differentials that are embedded in society and in counseling and psychotherapy. They exist within the profession and our personal lives. They exist in the lives of clients and the communities with which they intersect.
- In ACOP, liberation is important as both an end and a means to that end. True freedom is rooted in equity. This includes freedom to choose, freedom

from personal judgments and freedom from social judgments. Without equity, freedom eludes us.

Chapter Outline

Liberation Psychologies

Liberation psychology first emerged in Latin America during the 1960s through intellectual and political movements representing the experiences of those living in poverty. A philosophy, sociology and theology of liberation accompanied the psychology (Montero & Sonn, 2009). The purpose of liberation psychology was to represent those who were oppressed. It was based on a critical understanding of the circumstances that caused and maintained poverty (Burton & Gómez, 2015). It was political, conceptual and action-oriented (Adams, Dobles, Gómez, Kurtiş, & Molina, 2015). It was also revolutionary and posed a threat to those in power (Moane, 2003).

Ignacio Martin-Baro (1942–1989) was a Jesuit priest. In 1986, in "Writings for a liberation psychology", it was argued that psychology must become a psychology of the people—not a subject of itself—as a way to provide service for those in need. It was based on a bottom-up or inductive process in which theories emerge from experience and practice. It had to be practical to change reality to more favorable conditions for the oppressed (Ledwith, 2017). He was a proponent of the view that the social, political and economic context was what produced human suffering (Chen, 2018). Said another way, it was the unhealthy context that created unhealthy people (Hodgetts, Chamberlain, Tankel, & Groot, 2014). In 1989, he was murdered by the Salvadorian army for documenting the revolution and civil war (Montgomery, 2018).

Oppression is a fundamental cause of psychological distress (Giacaman et al., 2011). Oppression originates in the political, social and economic context (King, 2016). From this view, psychological problems begin as adaptive responses to abnormal circumstances (Johnstone et al., 2018). Relief from distress requires both personal and social change (Ross, 2017). This orientation is reflected in many other psychologies that have become topics of scholarly writing.

Psychologies of liberation parallel, blend or extend mainstream psychology from its largely male-oriented and positivist basis and its representation of European, heterosexual and upper-class views (Teo, 2015). With origins in the cosmologies, philosophies and worldviews or social, economic and political realities of life, liberation psychologies attend to contexts as experienced by members of particular groups (Christopher, Wendt, Marecek, & Goodman, 2014). They represent how psychologies developed to reflect the strengths and skills, histories and realities, values and practices of wellness and well-being in an increasingly divisive global context (Liu, 2015). As a result, these psychologies are political and contextual as well as emergent from cultural experiences (Abi-Hashem, 2015). Several that have become the subject of scholarly writing can be identified. Some of these are feminist, LGBTQ2+, Black, Indigenous and Latina/o psychologies.

Feminist Psychologies

Feminist psychologies emerged alongside the women's movement in North America during the 1960s (Cole, Rothblum, & Chesler, 2014). The male-dominated views prominent within psychology at the time reflected gendered perceptions of normalcy (Wilkinson, 1997). There was limited research from women's perspectives, women's roles and "work". Adherence to socially prescribed and dichotomized roles were de facto standards for treatment (Lips, 2016).

Feminist psychologies began as reactions to the psychoanalytic tradition where deviation was pathologized (e.g. aggressiveness among women, passivity among men) but emerged into its own independent and self-referential field (Unger, 1991). Inequality was the major problem. Patriarchy was the force that created and sustained it (Sidanius, Cotterill, Sheehy-Skeffington, Kteily, & Carvacho, 2016). Recognition of power differences between gendered roles was essential (Mahoney, 1996).

Development of feminist psychologies occurred in three phases (Unger, 1991. Initially, feminist psychologies began with the use of techniques from other approaches in ways that were empowering for women. The second phase of development infused feminist values and perspectives into other approaches. In the third phase, complete theories of diversity, oppression and liberation were constructed.

There are four major perspectives in contemporary feminist psychotherapy (Weedon, 1999). In liberal feminism, the purpose is for women to achieve equality to men. In cultural feminism, the purpose is to promote a feminized view of people and their relationships. Radical feminism seeks to transform gendered relationships, and in socialist feminism multiple oppressions are recognized for not only women but also others who are disadvantaged, and as a result, there is a need for social change.

Concepts within feminist psychologies that are central to psychotherapy practice include the **personal is political** and wellness as **relational**. Personal and political experiences are explicitly tied together insofar as personal problems have political conditions that contribute to their existence and their amelioration (Schuster, 2017). Wellness is located in the context of relations, insofar as one's connections to others influence the psychological health of the individual, based on their definition of self and degree of interdependence (Goodman & West-Olatunji, 2009).

Consciousness-raising efforts within feminist psychologies center on the topics of patriarchy, gender roles and relationships (Stocker, 2005). Underlying each of these notions are power relations (Allen, 2018). Patriarchy is reflected in power imbalances between genders and in roles, in favor of masculinity over femininity and in relationships where dominance and submission are embedded within people or their roles (Brannon, 2016).

LGBTQ2+ Psychologies

These psychologies began to develop alongside political change during the late 1960s and 1970s with gay rights movements in the United States and Canada (Clarke & Peel, 2007). Anti-gay sentiments underlying the criminalization of homosexuality from colonial times until 1969 were reflected in views held by the psychiatric community until the mid-1980s (Jones, 2017). During the 1970s, gay affirmative psychologies emerged and became more inclusive of lesbian and bisexual identities (Alessi, Dillon, & Kim, 2015). Presently, there are psychologies that include transgender, transsexual, two-spirited, intersex, queer and questioning as well as asexual and ally identities (Clifford & Orford, 2007).

Development occurred in response to political advocacy and professional pressure to remove homosexuality from the Diagnostic and Statistical Manual of Mental Disorders in 1987. The World Health Organization removed homosexuality from the International Classification of Diseases in 1993 (Byne, 2014). However, "conversion therapies" continued to be practiced. In 1997, the American Psychological Association stated in "Appropriate therapeutic responses to sexual orientation" that sexual orientation was not an appropriate use of professional psychology (Byne, 2014). As the community grew and diversified, unifying experiences centered on combatting heteronormative pressures (Cor & Chan, 2017).

LGBTQ2+ psychologies reflect the importance of normalizing sexuality and identity. These psychologies recognize the burden of **heteronormativity** reflected in attitudes, institutions and policies that restrict healthy development and experiences (Barker, 2007). Gay affirmative psychotherapy is a concept and practice that explicitly recognizes diversity between and within sexual minority communities, viewing sexual behavior and identity inclusively (Johnson, 2012).

Consciousness-raising efforts within LGBTQ2+ psychologies emphasize self-acceptance, with sexuality and gender as distinct but overlapping descriptors of self that represent a range of interacting identities and expressions (Milton & Coyle, 1999). There is growing recognition of the **non-binary** nature of descriptors and of fitting within as well as outside of different communities based on self-identification (Embaye, 2006).

Black Psychologies

Black psychologies emerged from experiences of individuals in the **African diaspora**. They are situated within Afrocentric philosophies and psychologies with their own values, terminology and practices (Myers, 1993). These psychologies have been defined as "African reality structure relative to psychological phenomena" (Baldwin, 1986).

The changes that followed European contact and colonial efforts into Africa were reflected in attitudes and practices of paternalism, hostility and exclusion (Vaughan, 1991). The slave trade and indentured servants created separations with traumatic treatment and effects that were felt across generations (Belgrave & Allison, 2018). In 1630, slavery was first formally legalized in a ruling within the state of Virginia. In Canada, slavery was legal until 1833 (Hou, Wu, Schimmele & Myles, 2015). The fields of anthropology, reflected in evolutionary theory and eugenics in the academy, were forms of racism under the guise of science (Paludi & Haley, 2014). Studies of physical and intellectual differences, heritability and inferiority were performed within contexts of racial segregation, voting laws and police actions (Drescher, 1990).

Traditional healing practices have been blended with Western psychotherapy approaches. One example is Ntu psychotherapy (Phillips, 1990). The approach is spiritually oriented and emphasizes authenticity and balance that is in concert with natural order (Phillips, 1990). The therapist engages with a client in a restorative approach based on principles of balance, harmony, cultural awareness, authenticity and interconnectedness (Gregory & Boston, 2016).

Black psychologies center on the reclamation of values, traditions and practices of the cultures in Africa (Stevens, 2015). Consciousness-raising efforts center on effects of history and migration, change and development of sense of self as a Black person and African person (Hall, 2014). The forces of racism in past and present, located within structures and policies as well as practices and interactions, are identified (Richeson, 2018). Pathways and processes of both personal and collective resistance and change are pursued (Ogbar, 2005).

Indigenous Psychologies

Indigenous peoples throughout the world have encountered colonial efforts to dominate through force. North America, Turtle Island, was changed in fundamental ways following European contact (Weaver, 2016). However, despite efforts to assimilate Indigenous peoples, their worldviews, experiences and traditions are now being reclaimed through collective efforts of **First Nations**, **Metis** and **Inuit** communities (Kirmayer, Brass, & Tait, 2000). While staggering differences in life chances remain between Indigenous and non-Indigenous peoples (Adelson, 2005), the Indigenous population and political power are growing.

Development of Indigenous psychologies are rooted in Indigenous ways of knowing. Traditional practices that were driven underground are re-emerging (Kovach, 2015). Contemporary healing practices exist as separate alternatives but may also blend with some Western approaches. The great diversity among Indigenous peoples is evident in the traditions and practices of each community, and with mobility and collective efforts, some similarities that inform practice are emerging (Kirmayer, Simpson, & Cargo, 2003).

Central concepts in Indigenous psychologies concern historical trauma, the need for healing and use of medicine (Hunter, Logan, Goulet, & Barton, 2006). Complex trauma has affected individuals, families and communities across generations (Bombay, Matheson, & Anisman, 2014). The forced confinement, banning of spiritual practices and forced removal of children from communities into adoptive homes and residential schools have been devastating (Haskell & Randall, 2009). Healing is ongoing and predicated on understanding of diverse and rich community traditions shared and developed long before European contact (Nutton & Fast, 2015; Whalen, Moss, & Baldwin, 2016). The idea of curative agents used by those with specific training and expertise in the Indigenous community has been a major part of treatment for sickness (Tookenay, 1996). The medicines traditionally used are not the same as Western medicine (Blignault, Hunter, & Mumford, 2018).

Consciousness-raising concepts include community history and colonial effects on families across generations (Heart et al., 2016). Efforts to reclaim traditional knowledge and sense of self as an Indigenous person are strong (Benoit, Carroll, & Chaudhry, 2003). Methods of change include political activism and investment in self-government to challenge oppressive colonial forces (Fryberg, Covarrubias, & Burack, 2018).

Latina/o Psychologies

Latina/o psychologies refer to the psychologies of people with Latin American heritage who live in North America (Fuentes, Barón, & Vásquez, 2003). Great diversity is evident in origin, timing of relocation and pre-migration experiences. Some possible similarities among Latina/o groups have been reported as aspects of shared culture, such as Spanish language, importance of family, influence of the Catholic church and traditional gender roles (Padilla & Olmedo, 2009). A major impetus for the development of a psychology rooted in Latina/o cultures was the recognition of significantly discrepant educational outcomes for children and youth (Villarruel et al., 2009).

Development of Latina/o psychologies was initiated by educational psychologists who first held interest in achievement and early school leaving. From these findings, connections were made to experiences of prejudice and discrimination (Miville et al., 2017). In 1973 the first systematic review of the literature on research with Spanish-speaking individuals was published (Padilla & Ruiz, 1973). The topics centered on mental health and psychological testing, including intelligence and performance, as well as language development in relation to bilingualism and experiences of prejudice and discrimination.

Culturally based healing practices have been integrated with Western psychological treatments (Rogler, Malgady, Costantino, & Blumenthal, 1987). An example of this is Cuento therapy. Cuento therapy is an approach used with Puerto Rican parents for teaching their children about culture through the use of folk tales. The content and delivery are culturally based and relevant; the use of folk tales traditional in healing practices provides historical evidence for its use (Malgady, Rogler, & Costantino, 1990). In their current forms, these practices in direct instruction, problem-solving and role playing have been found to assist children with anxiety and behavior challenges (Costantino & Malgady, 1996).

Concepts that are central to these psychologies attend to the importance of identity and language (Torres & Baxter Magolda, 2004). Spanish-speaking families and individuals have multiple histories across generations of migration following the first Spanish contact with the Americas in the 1500s. The topics of acculturation and biculturalism figure prominently in these psychologies, as do migration experiences. Spanish and Portuguese languages, bilingualism and language learning also appear strongly (Guyll, Madon, Prieto, & Scherr, 2010).

Consciousness-raising concerns identity, connections to family and national affiliations as well as language (Gutierrez, 1995). The development of sense of self in relation to others who are Latina/o and non-Latina/o is an important concept (Nadal, Mazzula, Rivera, & Fujii-Doe, 2014). Changes across the lifespan in educational and occupational pursuits and family life as well as in personal and collective well-being are emphasized (Koss-Chioino & Vargas, 1999).

Liberation Processes

In these psychologies, oppression is rooted in patriarchy, heteronormativity, colonization and racism. The sources are structural and interpersonal. They exist in policies that determine access, rights that determine treatment and practices that embrace cultural expectations as well as daily interactions.

Internalized views of societal judgments about self operate within and outside of acute awareness (Pheterson, 1986). They may be met with acceptance or challenge. "Internalized" suggests a self-created or imposed quality. Appropriated oppression more accurately characterizes the judgments as originating outside of the individual and borrowed from structures, practices and interactions outside of their cultural group (Tappan, 2005). Appropriated oppression is the assuming of values, beliefs and status based on another culture. As the judgments are borrowed, they are more easily challenged as impermanent, illogical or unjust (Banks & Stephens, 2018). The possibility of changing personal judgments also corresponds with a challenge to the structures and practices that sustain their societal legitimacy.

Liberation is a process of becoming free from constraints imposed by unjust forces. It is not an outcome that is fully achieved but a way of approaching change that looks for the structural contributors to illness and wellness in an individual, community or society (Tappan, 2005). As such, it is multidimensional and integrative of multiple perspectives, theories and perspectives, as well as inherently personal and structural. Liberation in psychotherapy is a process facilitated by awareness of the structural forces in play and their interrelationships with psychological phenomena (Rangel, 2014). Critical consciousness promotes insight into the connections between the uniqueness of an individual's experience and experiences that may be shared with others. Beyond insight, liberation in psychotherapy promotes agency and change (Moane, 2008).

As with oppression, liberation may be rooted in internalized views of positive social judgments that operate within and outside of acute awareness. These too are accessed through critical consciousness (Comas-Díaz, 2010). Perceptions of superiority may be challenged by members of majority cultural groups. Instead of a position of advantage, liberation flattens the structure toward a goal of equality. Those who hold advantage because of the group with which they identify, or are seen to identify, benefit from liberation to recognize their shared humanity, societal value and necessity of equity (Ford & Airhihenbuwa, 2010).

The cultural groups to which each belongs have differing values in each society. As cultural affiliations grow in number, complexity and interaction, it is increasingly likely that many individuals in psychotherapy are privileged in some contexts and oppressed in others (Croteau, Talbot, Lance, & Evans, 2002). Both professionals and clients experience privilege and oppression. Both may benefit from a process of liberation.

Critical Consciousness

The idea of critical consciousness was first written about as *conscientization* by the Brazilian educator Paulo Freire (1921–1997). In his book, *Education for Critical Consciousness* (1973), Freire was concerned about the conditions of extreme poverty faced by the majority of the population. Under such conditions, a devaluing of self emerged. He described this internalized oppression as a belief in low ability and a lack of confidence in one's self with a corresponding confidence in the power of the oppressor. This led to a **culture of silence** and allowed the ruling class to continue to benefit greatly while disadvantaging those living in poverty (1996). As an educator, Freire (1973) wrote about an approach to teaching that perpetuated these conditions.

> *the teacher teaches and the students are taught;*
> *the teacher knows everything and the students know nothing;*
> *the teacher thinks and the students are thought about;*
> *the teacher talks and the students listen—meekly;*
> *the teacher disciplines and the students are disciplined;*
> *the teacher chooses and enforces his choice, and the students comply;*
> *the teacher acts and the students have the illusion of acting through the action of the teacher;*
> *the teacher chooses the program content, and the students (who were not consulted) adapt to it;*
> *the teacher confuses the authority of knowledge with his or her own professional authority, which she and he sets in opposition to the freedom of the students;*
> *the teacher is the Subject of the learning process, while the pupils are mere objects.*
> Pedagogy of the Oppressed *(1973, pp. 54–55)*

Critical consciousness is an important vehicle through which to recognize oneself within oppressive circumstances and to analyze and transform those circumstances (Comas-Diaz, 2012). Oppression is both internal and external; political and psychological oppression do not exist without each other. Freire described the need for individuals to "read" circumstances so that they "write" their own present and future. This process necessitates the challenging of one's own "**oppressed identity**" (Glass, 2001). Transformation need not be revolutionary. The ability to interpret personal experiences as structurally imposed is itself transformational.

A conceptual model for individual therapeutic practice using critical consciousness includes an analysis of social conditions (Watts, Diemer, & Voight, 2011). A social condition analysis includes the positioning of the self in relation to human rights and responsibilities. The structural conditions or qualities that contribute to the problem are identified and noted in relation to social identity and self-judgments. Such analysis of structural oppression (i.e. social, economic and political conditions that limit opportunity and action) produced a sense of empowerment to challenge problematic conditions through personal or collective efforts. This practice has been used with youth and young adults concerning mental health and career development (Diemer & Li, 2011).

Power: Personal and Structural

Power is the force that makes change possible. It operates within and between people, communities and institutions. Power is what propels action from insight and produces external change (Overbeck, Neale, & Govan, 2010). Psychological power is reflected in a number of concepts such as **competence** and **mastery** of self and inanimate objects (White, 1959), **personal causation** (DeCharms, 1968), Heider's (1958) concept of can, autonomy ad Ryan and Deci's (2000) **agency**. For Maslow (1943), human beings strive for power to overcome feelings of powerlessness in early life (1966). Power also is evidenced in **locus of control** (Rotter, 1966), **illusions of control** (Taylor & Brown, 1988), **outcome dependency** (Erber & Fiske, 1984), **learned helplessness** (Petersen, Maier, & Seligman, 1995) and **self-efficacy** (Bandura, 1977).

Interpersonal power refers to the nature and degree of influence that an individual has with others (Kelley, Thibaut, Radloff, & Mundy, 1962). **Fate control** (another's outcomes) and behavior control (another's actions) are associated with the resources one holds (Pfeffer & Salancik, 2003) and consequences that apply (Hickson, Hinings, Lee, Schneck, & Pennings, 1971). Important aspects of interpersonal power are transparency and consent. In a psychotherapeutic context, this power is not just held but consented to and includes the responsibilities and expectations of the holder for its appropriate use (Hamilton & Biggart, 1985).

The collective power of groups is influenced by membership. **Social Identity Theory** posits that people identify with groups that provide positive identity. Conflicting identities lead to conflict and shared identities to consensus (Simon & Oakes, 2006). Groups create their own power and status hierarchies. **Self-Categorization Theory** represents how individuals decide how strongly to align with and within a group (Turner, 1985). The group grows to act with its own agency as an entity and provides a means to influence other groups.

Utility

Emphasis on perceived threats and inhibition contribute to feelings of **powerlessness** (Keltner, Gruenfeld, & Anderson, 2003; Kraus, Piff & Keltner, 2011). Powerlessness is also "holding back" personal expression in favor of normative opinions (Galinsky, Magee, Gruenfeld, Whitson & Liljenquist, 2008). It looks for obstacles lying in the path of goal attainment. Risk tolerance is low and safety is a primary concern affecting how one thinks, acts and feels (Richman & Lattanner, 2014).

When feeling **powerful**, one is able to perceive potential rewards (Whitson et al., 2013) and tolerate more risk (Côté et al., 2011). Power increases authenticity and the expression of opinions that are not the norm (Galinsky et al., 2008). However, being powerful does emphasize the self, puts less attention and effort on others and reduces willingness to compromise. It increases the likelihood of using mental shortcuts and stereotypes to make decisions (Lammers, Stoker, Rink, & Galinsky, 2016). Being powerful is also associated with the greater likelihood of viewing others as means to reach one's own goals.

Power is neither inherently bad nor good. Its application may be for the benefit of a particular interest or group while simultaneously at the cost to another. Theories of Freud and Adler have attended to power as dominance. Its use can be coercive and exploitative (Lenski, 1966). Maslow and Horney characterize personal power as a positive development and necessary for self-actualization.

Personal bases of power include awareness (i.e. knowledge of oneself), values (i.e. what is right and wrong), skills (i.e. specific techniques), information (i.e. knowledge of others) and purpose (i.e. motives and expectations) (Sakamoto & Pitner, 2005). Group bases of power include coercion (i.e. punishment), reward (i.e. praise), legitimation (i.e. social sanction), referents (i.e. connections), being expert (i.e. specialized knowledge) and information (i.e. access and use of information) (Hinkin & Schriesheim, 1989). A critical consciousness of one's power can be handled in one of three basic ways: 1) avoid recognition of awareness, knowledge and potential, 2) change self or others, institutions or policies or 3) accept forces and context as is. If change is selected, action may be taken: to oneself, with others and against others.

Therapist Competencies

Privilege is associated with the influence of the profession and its practitioners. The power of the therapist includes the privilege bestowed on one as a professional, within a structure that protects that role, within a society that legitimizes that position with specific expertise, skills and status (Guilfoyle, 2003). Use of privilege in the interest of client growth and a fair society necessitates attention to forces that oppress (Hertlein & Weeks, 2017). This requires work both within and outside of the office.

Due to the power differences between clients and professionals, it is essential for therapists to be aware of the assumptions we make and expectations we hold (D'Arrigo-Patrick, Hoff, Knudson-Martin, & Tuttle, 2017). It is also essential to recognize the power that clients already access as well as what they may access (Knudson-Martin et al., 2015). Empowerment refers to the cultivation and use of power within an individual as a member of a community (De La Cancela, Chin, & Jenkins, 2016).

Teaching for Critical Consciousness

From an AO perspective, psychotherapists are critically conscious of racism, classism, patriarchy, heteronormativity and white privilege and accept accountability for their roles and empower themselves and others to challenge oppression and seek social justice (Brown & Perry, 2011). This sensitivity affects therapist style and professional identity as well as potential for alliance and advocacy, which are discussed in detail in Chapter 8. There is often a connection to be made between personal clinical problems and social, economic or political disadvantage. However, there is also a substantial gap between this awareness and professional, clinical and personal action to combat oppression and privilege. The following are ways that may assist with the connection between awareness of societal injustice and taking action to promote fairness.

One possibility to connect therapeutic practice with community action is to inject values of fairness and extend the reach of theories used. For example, one may explore implicit and explicit connections to societal structure and function with questions such as: Who benefits? Who suffers? How has the status quo been maintained? How has it been successfully challenged? Another possibility is to explore voices in psychotherapy with questions such as: What vision of the good society is reflected? Which perspectives are evident? Which are not? Additionally, it may be useful to explore a focal issue from different disciplinary perspectives with questions such as: What is the problem? How did it start? Why does it continue? How can it be resisted, diminished or stopped?

A second possibility for connecting knowledge with action is to explore personal values and beliefs associated with their practice. Knowing one's biases (i.e. prejudgments based on categories) and stereotypes (i.e. applications of knowledge from one person to a whole group) helps by avoiding the imposition of personal values and beliefs on clients. Colby and Damon's (1994) **Social Responsibility** interview can be a helpful framework for questions that explore this topic based on personal experiences and their prominence in an interpretation of the client's experiences. In relation to a particular issue, the process explores the relationships that define self. This includes critical events and people that shape their lives and, additionally, one's sense of responsibility in areas of work, family, volunteering and politics as well as priorities, motives and meaning making. Sense of self in relation to others, connection to spiritual/personal philosophy and community participation are also considered.

A third possibility is through formal training (Sakamoto & Pitner, 2005). It is important to locate one's social identity (i.e. who I am is in part determined for me and in part by the groups of which I am a member). While groups and their members change over time, they are also historically and culturally situated. Importantly, identities have status—power—that is played out with a client. These locations direct attention and processing of information. Standpoints vary, and where one is located in any given situation relative to others is highly influential (Sakamoto & Pitner, 2005).

Honest exploration of biases and stereotypes may force one to see oneself negatively and challenge one's worldview, which means letting go of power, and that creates anxiety (Fang, 2017). The cognitive load from heightened critical consciousness can be very demanding. To avoid that pressure, it is easier to rely on stereotypical thinking, retain the same worldview unaltered and exercise the power at one's disposal (Prati, Vasiljevic, Crisp, & Rubini, 2015). Countertransference may be a defensive stance as protection from the anxiety of viewing self and the world differently (Sharma & Fowler, 2016). It has been found that less personalized analysis via stories, movies and emphasis on concepts (e.g. power and control wheels) while remaining aware of the dissonance and disequilibrium created in the process is a potentially less threatening way to address this highly sensitive material (Ehrke, Berthold, & Steffens, 2014).

In research with practicing psychotherapists, Goodman and West-Olatunji (2009) asked them to reflect on their biases with clients. The sequence of development included: 1) awareness (i.e. recognition that I bring my own biases into a situation), 2) respect (i.e. valuing community members' knowledge), 3) context (i.e. recognition of sociopolitical context), 4) integration (i.e. incorporating this understanding into clinical conceptualization), 5) empowerment (i.e. intervention with empowerment), 6) praxis (i.e. advocacy and action) and 7) transformation (i.e. integrating experience into identity both personal and professional). The process drew therapists out of the "banking" approach with clients. It also required taking a one-down position to understand a client, appreciate the narrative and engage with it in a collaborative way.

Ali and Sichel (2014) described the resulting insight and practice as a "**structural competency**". Structural competency concerns the "downstream implications of upstream decisions". It is predicated on the notion that inequitable institutional, social and political forces cause disease and suffering. The essential component for learning is to get those in power to free themselves from their assumptions. More simply stated, it means to embark on a process of "othering" oneself by putting oneself in unfamiliar places to begin to experience what others encounter. By engaging in this process of learning, participants activate what Jemal (2017) calls **transformative potential**. The two dimensions are transformative consciousness (denial, blame and critical levels) and transformative action (which is destructive, avoidant and critical).

Conclusion

Liberation draws attention to systemic disadvantage and the need for efforts to address those forces. Psychologies developed in response to the recognition of social hierarchies offer perspectives through which mainstream psychology can be viewed and used to promote equitable practice in a diverse society. Critical consciousness may be enhanced among practitioners. It may be a challenge that is uncomfortable but necessary to be aware of forces of oppression and the power that creates and sustains them. Liberation is the use of power for fairness. Counselors and psychotherapists can use this understanding and skills as a means to promote equity in their practice, the profession and society.

Web Links

Liberation Psychology
https://thepsychologist.bps.org.uk/volume-27/edition-11/liberation-
psychology-history-future

What Is Liberation Psychology?
www.pacifica.edu/degree-program/community-liberation-ecopsychology/
what-is-liberation-psychology/

Is Inequality Natural?
www.psychologytoday.com/us/blog/busting-myths-about-human-nature/
201210/is-inequality-natural

The Kind of Racism You Don't Even Know You Have
https://medium.com/@martiesirois/the-kind-of-racism-you-dont-even-
know-you-have-44b053cf0c80

Five Stereotypes About Poor Families and Education
www.washingtonpost.com/news/answer-sheet/wp/2013/10/28/five-stere-
otypes-about-poor-families-and-education/?noredirect=on&utm_term=.
cfef47ad81f1

Tarana Burke
www.businessinsider.com/how-the-metoo-movement-started-where-its-
headed-tarana-burke-time-person-of-year-women-2017–12
www.theguardian.com/world/2018/jan/15/me-too-founder-tarana-burke-
women-sexual-assault
www.theglobeandmail.com/news/investigations/unfounded-37272-sexual-
assault-cases-being-reviewed-402-unfounded-cases-reopened-so-far/
article37245525/

Key Terms

References

Abi-Hashem, N. (2015). Revisiting cultural awareness and cultural relevancy. *American Psychologist, 70*(7), 660–661.

Adams, G., Dobles, I., Gómez, L. H., Kurtiş, T., & Molina, L. E. (2015). Decolonizing psychological science: Introduction to the special thematic section. *Journal of Social and Political Psychology, 3*(1), 213–238.

Adelson, N. (2005). The embodiment of inequity: Health disparities in aboriginal Canada. *Canadian Journal of Public Health/Revue Canadienne de Sante'e Publique*, S45–S61.

Alessi, E. J., Dillon, F. R., & Kim, H. M. S. (2015). Determinants of lesbian and gay affirmative practice among heterosexual therapists. *Psychotherapy, 52*(3), 298.

Ali, A., & Sichel, C. E. (2014). Structural competency as a framework for training in counseling psychology. *The Counseling Psychologist, 42*(7), 901–918.

Allen, A. (2018). *The power of feminist theory*. London: Routledge.

Baldwin, J. A. (1986). African (Black) psychology: Issues and synthesis. *Journal of Black Studies, 16*(3), 235–249.

Bandura, A. (1977). Self-efficacy: Toward a unifying theory of behavioral change. *Psychological Review, 84*(2), 191.

Banks, K. H., & Stephens, J. (2018). Reframing internalized racial oppression and charting a way forward. *Social Issues and Policy Review, 12*(1), 91–111.

Barker, M. (2007). Heteronormativity and the exclusion of bisexuality in psychology. *Out in Psychology: Lesbian, Gay, Bisexual, Trans, and Queer Perspectives*, 86–118.

Belgrave, F. Z., & Allison, K. W. (2018). *African American psychology: From Africa to America*. New York: Sage Publications.

Benoit, C., Carroll, D., & Chaudhry, M. (2003). In search of a healing place: Aboriginal women in Vancouver's downtown eastside. *Social Science & Medicine, 56*(4), 821–833.

Blignault, I., Hunter, J., & Mumford, J. (2018). Integration of Indigenous healing practices with western biomedicine in Australia, Canada, New Zealand and the United States of America: A scoping review protocol. *JBI Database of Systematic Reviews and Implementation Reports, 16*(6), 1354–1360.

Bombay, A., Matheson, K., & Anisman, H. (2014). The intergenerational effects of Indian residential schools: Implications for the concept of historical trauma. *Transcultural Psychiatry, 51*(3), 320–338.

Brannon, L. (2016). *Gender: Psychological perspectives.* London: Taylor & Francis.

Brown, A. L., & Perry, D. (2011). First impressions: Developing critical consciousness in counselor training programs. *Journal of Feminist Family Therapy, 23*(1), 1–18.

Burton, M., & Gómez, L. (2015). Liberation psychology. *Handbook of Critical Psychology,* 348.

Byne, W. (2014). Forty years after the removal of homosexuality from the DSM: Well on the way but not there yet. LGBT Health, *1*(2), 67–69.

Chen, J. C. (2018). The role of critical theory in the development of multicultural psychology and counseling. In *Critical theory and transformative learning* (pp. 259–281). Hershey, PA: IGI Global.

Christopher, J. C., Wendt, D. C., Marecek, J., & Goodman, D. M. (2014). Critical cultural awareness: Contributions to a globalizing psychology. *American Psychologist, 69*(7), 645–655.

Clarke, V., & Peel, E. (Eds.). (2007). *Out in psychology: Lesbian, gay, bisexual, trans and queer perspectives.* Hoboken, NJ: John Wiley & Sons, Inc.

Clifford, C., & Orford, J. (2007). The experience of social power in the lives of trans people. *Out in Psychology: Lesbian, Gay, Bisexual, Trans and Queer Perspectives,* 195–216.

Colby, A., & Damon, W. (1994). *Some do care: Contemporary lives of moral commitment.* New York, NY: Free Press.

Cole, E., Rothblum, E. D., & Chesler, P. (2014). *Feminist foremothers in women's studies, psychology, and mental health* (Vol. 17, No. 1–4). London: Routledge.

Comas-Díaz, L. (2010). On being a Latina healer: Voice, consciousness, and identity. *Psychotherapy: Theory, Research, Practice, Training, 47*(2), 162.

Comas-Diaz, L. (2012). Humanism and multiculturalism: An evolutionary alliance. *Psychotherapy, 49*(4), 437.

Cor, D. N., & Chan, C. D. (2017). Intersectional feminism and LGBTIQQA+ psychology: Understanding our present by exploring our past. *LGBT Psychology and Mental Health: Emerging Research and Advances,* 109.

Costantino, G., & Malgady, R. G. (1996). *Culturally sensitive treatment: Cuento and hero/heroine modeling therapies for Hispanic children and adolescents.* Washington, DC: American Psychological Association.

Côté, S., Kraus, M. W., Cheng, B. H., Oveis, C., Van der Löwe, I., Lian, H., & Keltner, D. (2011). Social power facilitates the effect of prosocial orientation on empathic accuracy. *Journal of Personality and Social Psychology, 101*(2), 217.

Croteau, J. M., Talbot, D. M., Lance, T. S., & Evans, N. J. (2002). A qualitative study of the interplay between privilege and oppression. *Journal of Multicultural Counseling and Development, 30*(4), 239–258.

D'Arrigo-Patrick, J., Hoff, C., Knudson-Martin, C., & Tuttle, A. (2017). Navigating critical theory and postmodernism: Social justice and therapist power in family therapy. *Family Process, 56*(3), 574–588.

DeCharms, R. (1968). *Personal causation.* New York, NY: Academic Press.

De La Cancela, V., Chin, J. L., & Jenkins, Y. (2016). *Community health psychology: Empowerment for diverse communities.* London: Routledge.

Diemer, M. A., & Li, C. H. (2011). Critical consciousness development and political participation among marginalized youth. *Child Development, 82*(6), 1815–1833.

Drescher, S. (1990). The ending of the slave trade and the evolution of European scientific racism. *Social Science History, 14*(3), 415–450.

Ehrke, F., Berthold, A., & Steffens, M. C. (2014). How diversity training can change attitudes: Increasing perceived complexity of superordinate groups to improve intergroup relations. *Journal of Experimental Social Psychology, 53*, 193–206.

Embaye, N. (2006). Affirmative psychotherapy with bisexual transgender people. *Journal of Bisexuality, 6*(1–2), 51–63.

Erber, R., & Fiske, S. T. (1984). Outcome dependency and attention to inconsistent information. *Journal of Personality and Social Psychology, 47*(4), 709.

Fang, N. (2017). On (not) listening for theory: The trainee's use of theory as defence against the stress of beginning psychodynamic practice. *Psychodynamic Practice, 23*(3), 269–281.

Ford, C. L., & Airhihenbuwa, C. O. (2010). Critical race theory, race equity, and public health: Toward antiracism praxis. *American Journal of Public Health, 100*(S1), S30–S35.

Freire, P. (1973). *Education for critical consciousness* (Vol. 1). London, UK: Bloomsbury Publishing.

Freire, P. (1996). *Pedagogy of the oppressed* (revised). New York, NY: Continuum.

Fryberg, S. A., Covarrubias, R., & Burack, J. A. (2018). The ongoing psychological colonization of North American Indigenous people: Using social psychological theories to promote social justice. *The Oxford Handbook of Social Psychology and Social Justice*, 113.

Fuentes, C. D. L., Barón, A., & Vásquez, M. J. (2003). *Teaching Latino psychology*. Washington, DC: American Psychological Association.

Galinsky, A. D., Magee, J. C., Gruenfeld, D. H., Whitson, J. A., & Liljenquist, K. A. (2008). Power reduces the press of the situation: Implications for creativity, conformity, and dissonance. *Journal of Personality and Social Psychology, 95*(6), 1450.

Giacaman, R., Rabaia, Y., Nguyen-Gillham, V., Batniji, R., Punamäki, R. L., & Summerfield, D. (2011). Mental health, social distress and political oppression: The case of the occupied Palestinian territory. *Global Public Health, 6*(5), 547–559.

Glass, R. D. (2001). On Paulo Freire's philosophy of praxis and the foundations of liberation education. *Educational Researcher, 30*(2), 15–25.

Goodman, R. D., & West-Olatunji, C. A. (2009). Applying critical consciousness: Culturally competent disaster response outcomes. *Journal of Counseling & Development, 87*(4), 458–465.

Gregory, H., & Boston, D. (2016). *NTU psychotherapy: An African-centered approach to healing and wellness*. Office of Diversity and Inclusion Lectures. 7. https://digitalcommons.ciis.edu/diversityandinclusion-lectures/7

Guilfoyle, M. (2003). Dialogue and power: A critical analysis of power in dialogical therapy. *Family Process, 42*(3), 331–343.

Gutierrez, L. M. (1995). Understanding the empowerment process: Does consciousness make a difference? *Social Work Research, 19*(4), 229–237.

Guyll, M., Madon, S., Prieto, L., & Scherr, K. C. (2010). The potential roles of self-fulfilling prophecies, stigma consciousness, and stereotype threat in linking Latino/a ethnicity and educational outcomes. *Journal of Social Issues, 66*(1), 113–130.

Hall, S. (2014). Cultural identity and diaspora. In *Diaspora and visual culture* (pp. 35–47). London: Routledge.

Hamilton, G. G., & Biggart, N. W. (1985). Why people obey: Theoretical observations on power and obedience in complex organizations. *Sociological Perspectives, 28*(1), 3–28.

Haskell, L., & Randall, M. (2009). *Disrupted attachments: A social context complex trauma framework and the lives of Aboriginal peoples in Canada*. Retrieved November 9, 2018, from http://vawlearningnetwork.ca/sites/default/files/Haskell-Randall.pdf

Heart, M. Y. H. B., Chase, J., Elkins, J., Martin, M. J., Nanez, M. J. S., & Mootz, J. J. (2016). Women finding the way: American Indian women leading intervention research in Native communities. *American Indian and Alaska Native Mental Health Research (Online)*, *23*(3), 24.

Heider, F. (1958). *The psychology of interpersonal relations*. New York, NY: John Wiley & Sons, Inc.

Hertlein, K. M., & Weeks, G. R. (2017). The logical and clinical argument for the concept of meta-schema in cognitive therapy. *Journal of Family Psychotherapy*, *28*(1), 4–22.

Hickson, D. J., Hinings, C. R., Lee, C. A., Schneck, R. E., & Pennings, J. M. (1971). A strategic contingencies' theory of intraorganizational power. *Administrative Science Quarterly*, 216–229.

Hinkin, T. R., & Schriesheim, C. A. (1989). Development and application of new scales to measure the French and Raven (1959) bases of social power. *Journal of Applied Psychology*, *74*(4), 561.

Hodgetts, D., Chamberlain, K., Groot, S., & Tankel, Y. (2014). Urban poverty, structural violence and welfare provision for 100 families in Auckland. *Urban Studies*, *51*(10), 2036–2051.

Hou, F., Wu, Z., Schimmele, C., & Myles, J. (2015). Cross-country variation in interracial marriage: A USA—Canada comparison of metropolitan areas. *Ethnic and Racial Studies*, *38*(9), 1591–1609. Retrieved from www.theglobeandmail.com/news/investigations/unfounded-sexual-assault-canada-main/article33891309/

Hunter, L. M., Logan, J., Goulet, J. G., & Barton, S. (2006). Aboriginal healing: Regaining balance and culture. *Journal of Transcultural Nursing*, *17*(1), 13–22.

Jemal, A. (2017). Critical consciousness: A critique and critical analysis of the literature. *The Urban Review*, *49*(4), 602–626.

Johnson, S. D. (2012). Gay affirmative psychotherapy with lesbian, gay, and bisexual individuals: Implications for contemporary psychotherapy research. *American Journal of Orthopsychiatry*, *82*(4), 516–522.

Johnstone, L., Boyle, M., Cromby, J., Dillon, J., Harper, D., Kinderman, P., . . . Read, J. (2018). *The power threat meaning framework: Towards the identification of patterns in emotional distress, unusual experiences and troubled or troubling behaviour, as an alternative to functional psychiatric diagnosis*. Leicester: British Psychological Society.

Jones, O. (2017). Putting LGBTQ people back on the canvas of history. *The Lancet*, *390*(10092), 352–353.

Kelley, H. H., Thibaut, J. W., Radloff, R., & Mundy, D. (1962). The development of cooperation in the "minimal social situation". *Psychological Monographs: General and Applied*, *76*(19), 1.

Keltner, D., Gruenfeld, D. H., & Anderson, C. (2003). Power, approach, and inhibition. *Psychological Review*, *110*(2), 265.

King, D. K. (2016). Multiple jeopardy, multiple consciousness: The context of a Black feminist ideology. In *Race, gender and class* (pp. 36–57). London: Routledge.

Kirmayer, L. J., Brass, G. M., & Tait, C. L. (2000). The mental health of aboriginal peoples: Transformations of identity and community. *The Canadian Journal of Psychiatry*, *45*(7), 607–616.

Kirmayer, L., Simpson, C., & Cargo, M. (2003). Healing traditions: Culture, community and mental health promotion with Canadian aboriginal peoples. *Australasian Psychiatry*, *11*(S1), S15–S23.

Knudson-Martin, C., Huenergardt, D., Lafontant, K., Bishop, L., Schaepper, J., & Wells, M. (2015). Competencies for addressing gender and power in couple therapy: A socio emotional approach. *Journal of Marital and Family Therapy*, *41*(2), 205–220.

Koss-Chioino, J. D., & Vargas, L. A. (1999). *Working with Latino youth: Culture, development, and context.* San Francisco, CA: Jossey-Bass Publishers.

Kovach, M. (2015). Emerging from the margins: Indigenous methodologies. *Research as Resistance: Revisiting Critical, Indigenous, and Anti-Oppressive Approaches,* 43.

Kraus, M. W., Piff, P. K., & Keltner, D. (2011). Social class as culture: The convergence of resources and rank in the social realm. *Current Directions in Psychological Science, 20*(4), 246–250.

Lammers, J., Stoker, J. I., Rink, F., & Galinsky, A. D. (2016). To have control over or to be free from others? The desire for power reflects a need for autonomy. *Personality and Social Psychology Bulletin, 42*(4), 498–512.

Ledwith, M. (2017). Emancipatory action research as a critical living praxis: From dominant narratives to counternarrative. In *The Palgrave international handbook of action research* (pp. 49–62). New York, NY: Palgrave Macmillan.

Lenski, G. E. (1966). *Power and privilege* (Vol. 96). New York, NY: McGraw-Hill.

Lips, H. M. (2016). *A new psychology of women: Gender, culture, and ethnicity.* Long Grove, IL: Waveland Press.

Liu, J. (2015). Globalizing Indigenous psychology: An East Asian form of hierarchical relationalism with worldwide implications. *Journal for the Theory of Social Behaviour, 45*(1), 82–94.

Mahoney, M. A. (1996). The problem of silence in feminist psychology. *Feminist Studies, 22*(3), 603–625.

Malgady, R. G., Rogler, L. H., & Costantino, G. (1990). Culturally sensitive psychotherapy for Puerto Rican children and adolescents: A program of treatment outcome research. *Journal of Consulting and Clinical Psychology, 58*(6), 704.

Martin-Baro, I. (1986). *Writings for a liberation psychology.* Cambridge, MA: Harvard University Press.

Maslow, A. H. (1943). A theory of human motivation. *Psychological Review, 50*(4), 370.

Maslow, A. H. (1966). *The psychology of science a reconnaissance.* New York: Harper & Row.

Milton, M., & Coyle, A. (1999). Lesbian and gay affirmative psychotherapy: Issues in theory and practice. *Sexual and Marital Therapy, 14*(1), 43–59.

Miville, M. L., Arredondo, P., Consoli, A. J., Santiago-Rivera, A., Delgado-Romero, E. A., Fuentes, M. A., . . . Cervantes, J. M. (2017). Liderazgo: Culturally grounded leadership and the national Latina/o psychological association. *The Counseling Psychologist, 45*(6), 830–856.

Moane, G. (2003). Bridging the personal and the political: Practices for a liberation psychology. *American Journal of Community Psychology, 31*(1–2), 91–101.

Moane, G. (2008). Applying psychology in contexts of oppression and marginalisation: Liberation psychology, wellness, and social justice. *The Irish Journal of Psychology, 29*(1–2), 89–101.

Montero, M., & Sonn, C. C. (Eds.). (2009). *Psychology of liberation: Theory and applications.* New York: Springer, Science & Business Media.

Montgomery, T. S. (2018). *Revolution in El Salvador: From civil strife to civil peace.* London: Routledge.

Myers, L. J. (1993). *Understanding an Afrocentric world view: Introduction to an optimal psychology.* Dubuque; IA: Kendall, Hunt Publishing Company.

Nadal, K. L., Mazzula, S. L., Rivera, D. P., & Fujii-Doe, W. (2014). Microaggressions and Latina/o Americans: An analysis of nativity, gender, and ethnicity. *Journal of Latina/o Psychology, 2*(2), 67.

Nutton, J., & Fast, E. (2015). Historical trauma, substance use, and Indigenous peoples: Seven generations of harm from a "Big Event". *Substance Use & Misuse, 50*(7), 839–847.

Ogbar, J. O. (2005). *Black power: Radical politics and African American identity*. Baltimore, MD: Johns Hopkins Press.

Overbeck, J. R., Neale, M. A., & Govan, C. L. (2010). I feel, therefore you act: Intrapersonal and interpersonal effects of emotion on negotiation as a function of social power. *Organizational Behavior and Human Decision Processes, 112*(2), 126–139.

Padilla, A. M., & Ruiz, R. A. (1973). *Latino mental health: A review of literature*. Retrieved November 9, 2018, from https://eric.ed.gov/?id=ED088246

Padilla, A. M., & Olmedo, E. (2009). Synopsis of key persons, events, and associations in the history of Latino psychology. *Cultural Diversity and Ethnic Minority Psychology, 15*(4), 363.

Paludi, M. A., & Haley, S. (2014). Scientific racism. In *Encyclopedia of critical psychology* (pp. 1697–1700). New York, NY: Springer.

Peterson, C., Maier, S. F., & Seligman, M. E. P. (1995). *Learned helplessness: A theory for the age of personal control*. Oxford: Oxford University Press.

Pfeffer, J., & Salancik, G. R. (2003). *The external control of organizations: A resource dependence perspective*. Stanford: Stanford University Press.

Pheterson, G. (1986). Alliances between women: Overcoming internalized oppression and internalized domination. *Signs: Journal of Women in Culture and Society, 12*(1), 146–160.

Phillips, F. B. (1990). NTU psychotherapy: An Afrocentric approach. *Journal of Black Psychology, 17*(1), 55–74.

Prati, F., Vasiljevic, M., Crisp, R. J., & Rubini, M. (2015). Some extended psychological benefits of challenging social stereotypes: Decreased dehumanization and a reduced reliance on heuristic thinking. *Group Processes & Intergroup Relations, 18*(6), 801–816.

Rangel, R. (2014). *The appropriated racial oppression scale development and initial validation*. New York: Columbia University.

Richeson, J. A. (2018). The psychology of racism: An introduction to the special issue. *Current Directions in Psychological Science, 27*(3), 148–149.

Richman, L. S., & Lattanner, M. R. (2014). Self-regulatory processes underlying structural stigma and health. *Social Science & Medicine, 103*, 94–100.

Rogler, L. H., Malgady, R. G., Costantino, G., & Blumenthal, R. (1987). What do culturally sensitive mental health services mean? The case of Hispanics. *American Psychologist, 42*(6), 565.

Ross, C. E. (2017). *Social causes of psychological distress*. New York: Routledge.

Rotter, J. B. (1966). Generalized expectancies for internal versus external control of reinforcement. *Psychological Monographs: General and Applied, 80*(1), 1.

Ryan, R. M., & Deci, E. L. (2000). Self-determination theory and the facilitation of intrinsic motivation, social development, and well-being. *American Psychologist, 55*(1), 68.

Sakamoto, I., & Pitner, R. O. (2005). Use of critical consciousness in anti-oppressive social work practice: Disentangling power dynamics at personal and structural levels. *The British Journal of Social Work, 35*(4), 435–452.

Schuster, J. (2017). Why the personal remained political: Comparing second and third wave perspectives on everyday feminism. *Social Movement Studies, 16*(6), 647–659.

Sharma, S., & Fowler, J. C. (2016). When countertransference reactions go unexamined due to predetermined clinical tasks: How fear of love can keep us from listening. *Psychotherapy, 53*(3), 302.

Sidanius, J., Cotterill, S., Sheehy-Skeffington, J., Kteily, N., & Carvacho, H. (2016). Social dominance theory: Explorations in the psychology of oppression. In *Cambridge handbook of the psychology of prejudice* (pp. 149–187). Cambridge: Cambridge University Press.

Simon, B., & Oakes, P. (2006). Beyond dependence: An identity approach to social power and domination. *Human Relations, 59*(1), 105–139.

Stevens, G. (2015). Black psychology. *Handbook of Critical Psychology*, 182–185.

Stocker, S. S. (2005). The ethics of mutuality and feminist relational therapy. *Women & Therapy*, *28*(2), 1–15.

Tappan, M. B. (2005). Domination, subordination and the dialogical self: Identity development and the politics of "ideological becoming". *Culture & Psychology*, *11*(1), 47–75.

Taylor, S. E., & Brown, J. D. (1988). Illusion and well-being: A social psychological perspective on mental health. *Psychological Bulletin*, *103*(2), 193.

Teo, T. (2015). Critical psychology: A geography of intellectual engagement and resistance. *American Psychologist*, *70*(3), 243–254.

Tookenay, V. F. (1996). Improving the health status of aboriginal people in Canada: New directions, new responsibilities. *CMAJ: Canadian Medical Association Journal*, *155*(11), 1581.

Torres, V., & Baxter Magolda, M. B. (2004). Reconstructing Latino identity: The influence of cognitive development on the ethnic identity process of Latino students. *Journal of College Student Development*, *45*(3), 333–347.

Turner, J. C. (1985). Social categorization and the self-concept: A social cognitive theory of group behavior. *Advances in Group Processes*, *2*, 77–122.

Unger, R. (1991) *Resisting gender: Twenty-five years of feminist psychology*. Thousand Oaks, CA: Sage Publications, 1998.

Vaughan, M. (1991). *Curing their ills: Colonial power and African illness*. Palo Alto, CA: Stanford University Press.

Villarruel, F. A., Carlo, G., Grau, J. M., Azmitia, M., Cabrera, N. J., & Chahin, T. J. (Eds.). (2009). *Handbook of US Latino psychology: Developmental and community-based perspectives*. Thousand Oaks, CA: Sage Publications.

Watts, R. J., Diemer, M. A., & Voight, A. M. (2011). Critical consciousness: Current status and future directions. *New Directions for Child and Adolescent Development*, *134*, 43–57.

Weaver, H. N. (Ed.). (2016). *Social issues in contemporary native America: Reflections from Turtle Island*. New York: Routledge.

Weedon, C. (1999). *Feminism, theory, and the politics of difference*. Hoboken, NJ: Wiley.

Whalen, D. H., Moss, M., & Baldwin, D. (2016). Healing through language: Positive physical health effects of Indigenous language use. *F1000Research*, *5*.

White, R. W. (1959). Motivation reconsidered: The concept of competence. *Psychological Review*, *66*(5), 297.

Whitson, J. A., Liljenquist, K. A., Galinsky, A. D., Magee, J. C., Gruenfeld, D. H., & Cadena, B. (2013). The blind leading: Power reduces awareness of constraints. *Journal of Experimental Social Psychology*, *49*(3), 579–582.

Wilkinson, S. (1997). *Feminist psychology*. Thousand Oaks, CA: Sage.

Discussion Questions

1. Consider some assumptions that might be made within mainstream counseling and psychotherapy. Is neutrality possible? Is there a mind–heart divide? What others can you think of? Are some advantaged and others disadvantaged by acting on those assumptions?

2. What about power in counseling and psychotherapy? Is it normal or problematic? Is it theoretical or empirical or both? Is it in individuals or systems or both? Is it a possibility or an execution or both? Is it zero sum?

3. What roles might a counselor or psychotherapist play in the lives of clients (e.g. facilitator of Indigenous healing methods, facilitator of Indigenous support systems, adviser, advocate, agent of change, consultant)? How do we know which roles are appropriate (e.g. clients' level of acculturation, internal versus external etiology of the client's problem, goals of intervention)?

3

ANTI-OPPRESSIVE PRACTICE

In this chapter, this idea of justice is applied to social issues. Both structural and postmodern theoretical perspectives are considered. A description of historical events that led to the development of progressive and radical ideas about human services in response to postwar economic and social policies is presented. These ideas emerged in psychiatry and psychotherapy in the context of civil rights. It is the field of counseling in which professional psychology's social justice interests have most often embraced and reflected anti-oppressive practice. The chapter concludes with a description of anti-oppressive practice and its applications through subsequent chapters of this text.

Why is anti-oppressive practice relevant to professional counseling and psychotherapy?

- There is no neutral context within which we work. Either we are working to change the status quo, or we are working to accept it. It is necessary to reflect on and understand our professional practice in a racist, homophobic, classist, ablest, sexist, ageist and exclusivist society. Practice rooted in a sense of fairness and justice can counteract these forces.
- Each of us has human rights according to the United Nations Declaration (1948). Universal rights are dignity, liberty and security, recognition as a person, fairness and honor, nationality, opinion and expression, peaceful assembly, participation in governance, social security and employment, standard of living to sustain health, education and participation in community life.
- These rights apply to counselors and psychotherapists as professionals and citizens. They concern how we view problems within the person and the context, what we do inside and outside the office, what we say we do and what we actually do, how we are individuals and part of the community and

system, how we are the oppressed and the oppressor and how we are the privileged and the disadvantaged.

Chapter Outline

Western psychology emerged during the Enlightenment. It was the age of reason and scientific revolution (Brennan & Houde, 2017). Academic scholarship emerged with the first journals as well as scientific books (Lillis & Curry, 2015). Socially, it was the time of a rising middle class (Johansen, 2014) and politically, it was the time of the development of ideas about economic freedom as well as separation of church and state (Ferrari, 2017). Progressive voices concerning gender and class were also present. For example, Mary Wollstonecraft (1759–1797) wrote about women as human beings, not objects, with a need for education and challenged the hereditary privilege of the ruling classes (Janes, 2017).

During the industrial revolution, the factory system benefitted owners over workers (Gilboy, 2017). It divided those who owned the means of production from those who worked within it (Mokyr, Vickers, & Ziebarth, 2015). For Hegel (1770–1831), civil society was a network of economic relationships in capitalist systems, with conflict and inequality as both inevitable from and influential on choices people make about their roles (Burbidge, 1981). Rather than function to close growing social divisions, Marx (1818–1883) viewed the state as a vehicle for the interests of the bourgeoisie (Rubinštejn, 1987). He wrote that resource distribution should be based on need rather than class status.

"Capitalism came in the first ships" (Degler, 1959). Imperialism is the expansion of a nation's territory. **Colonialism** is occupation of the territory and use for the benefit of the nation (Mamdani, 2015). Cultural imperialism is the value of all cultural aspects of the expanding nation over the cultures within the territory expanded upon (Inglis, 2017). European colonization of the Americas began with Columbus' arrival in the "new world". The colonial economy benefitted from the cheap goods and labor available for use in the colonized nation (Madrigal Muñoz, 2015). In strong contrast to the prevailing sentiments of colonial interests of the time, Denis Diderot (1713 —1784) argued that the Indigenous were the civilized ones and that each Indigenous society (unlike the Europeans) created rules without creating injustices and cruelties (Krippner, 2002). Culture, not reason, according to Diderot, was the defining human quality. To flourish, societies balanced individual and collective interests to address the challenges of each physical environment (Muthu, 2003).

Progressive voices of opposition continued. Through their analyses, Gramici, Kautsky and Said have made major contributions to a contemporary anti-oppressive perspective. Antonio Gramsci (1891–1937) wrote about the state and its ruling class' use of cultural hegemony to take control of cultural institutions and exert control through ideology expressed as common-sense values (Colucci, 1999). Karl Kautsky (1854–1938) saw the capitalist interests expressed through colonialism as continuing to provide a basis for collusion between the developed nations that continued to exploit the developing nations. These efforts were not intended to "help" developing nations because their positions were necessary in the capitalist global village (Panitch & Gindin, 2004). Edward Said's (1935–2003) analysis of the global West's perceptions of the East in **Orientalism** (1979) illustrated by way of texts reinforcement of the imperialist project. The analysis located the fundamental point of reference as the West with the Other—as the Middle East, North Africa and West Asia—as primitive and inferior. Europe was defined by what it was not in the Other, and organizing knowledge about the Other self-evidenced its own superiority.

Defining Justice

Justice concerns fairness. It includes all ways that justice is understood, applied and measured through processes and outcomes. Consequently, there are many views of justice. According to **divine command**, God decides about fairness. Moral goodness is determined on whether God commanded. Morality is determined by God and moral conduct is acting in accordance with those determinations (Wierenga, 1983). From a **natural law** view, there are inherent human rights. Laws of conduct exist across people, times, governments and cultures. They are natural and immutable (Weinreb, 1987). According to **social contact**, there is a trade-off between freedoms in exchange for protections. This is a mutual agreement with obligations evidenced in the contract with the society of which one is a member (Rousseau, 1968).

According to a **utilitarian** view, actions that are just are those that lead to the best outcomes (Sandel, 1998). If the action leads to greater happiness and less pain, then it is to be pursued. For JS Mill (1806–1873), justice is "greatest good for greatest number". It is impartial. From this view, everyone's "good" is equal. Therefore, each individual has an interest in promoting the good. In contrast, a **libertarian** view stresses freedom: the greatest amount of freedom that is the same for everyone (Sterba, 1992). As related to justice, a fundamental question is: do I have my rights to myself and my property respected? **Egalitarian** justice can only exist within equality (Robeyns, 2015). This view is grounded in the belief that the worth and social status of all people are essentially the same.

Major distinctions are made between distributive and procedural justice and retributive and restorative justice. **Distributive** justice concerns what is distributed, between whom and the proper distribution. It concerns a fair process of distribution (Nozick, 2017). **Procedural** justice concerns processes of dispute resolution or resource distribution (Folger, 1977). It concerns a share of what is distributed. **Retributive** justice is based on punishment for wrongdoing, while **restorative** is about making amends with those who have been harmed (Wenzel, Okimoto, Feather, & Platow, 2008). Restorative justice places emphasis on the good and focuses on the needs of those who have been wronged as well as the wrongdoers (Zehr, 2015).

Freedom and Equality

A just and fair society embraces both equality and liberty (Vera & Speight, 2003). The American philosopher John Rawls integrated liberty and equality in his *Original Position* for a socially just society (1985). Rawls described the possibility for an integration of equal basic liberties within an appropriate political and economic structure (Rawls, 1985). In this view, freedom, or pursuit of a good life, can occur within a social structure that permits each person to live to maximum advantage. In a psychological application of this idea, Prilleltensky (1989, 2012, 2013) has argued convincingly that maximum fairness is necessary for maximum wellness, and that a lack of fairness reduces wellness at both group and personal levels. To illustrate, he described four psychological approaches: traditional, empowering, postmodern and emancipatory communitarian (Prilleltensky, 1997). From a **traditional** view, self-determination for individuals is maximally valued to strengthen individuality. From an **empowering** view, diversity is recognized, and self-determination of marginalized individuals and groups is specifically addressed to challenge disempowerment. From a **postmodern** view, both diversity and self-determination are emphasized to strengthen identity and challenge dogma. In an **emancipatory communitarian** view, there is a balance struck between self-determination and distributive justice to promote both community wellness and personal emancipation.

Both structural and postmodern thought have been highly influential to the understanding of freedom and equality (Fraser & Nicholson, 1988). A structural approach emphasizes social structures and relations manifested between personalities, families and communities (Gewirtz, 1998). It attends to the racist, homophobic, classist, ablest, sexist, ageist and exclusivist society and how individuals and groups are affected. These dynamics shape everyday experience. They are social in nature and can therefore be dismantled. Finally, there is a right and wrong judgment implicit and a direction to pursue that will reduce both oppression and privilege (Hatch, 2018). A postmodern approach emphasizes multiple oppressions, including identity, social location, voice, diversity borders, inclusion, exclusion and difference (Lundy, 2004). From this view, the focus is on the reproduction of oppression. All knowledge is equally valid. The emphasis on relationships and the assumptions and knowledges underlie their meaning (Pease & Fook, 2016). It is about ways of knowing and not a theory for moral action. The outcome is improved ways of understanding existence and the operation of oppression rather than changing it.

The strengths of a structural view of fairness and equality include clear lines of responsibility for disadvantage and oppression and specific locations for social change and judgment of what is morally right and wrong. The strengths of a postmodern view of fairness and equality include more recent insights into variations of diversity illustrating its complexity and interactive nature, as well as multiple sites of power and functions of its unequal presence. Critical realism (Bhaskar, 1944–2014) offers integration for structural and postmodern views. From this perspective, science that is positivist also permits a subjective view of its explanatory power (Collier, 1994). Philosophy and social science are situated socially but not socially determined. Critique is possible and motivational toward social change in interests of freedom (Bhaskar, 1998). There are three conclusions afforded by this view: 1) identities and cultures are both manifestations of difference that are socially situated, 2) privilege and oppression are the products of hierarchical social arrangements and 3) justice is promoted by social change to maximize equality (Bhaskar, 1997).

Origins of Anti-Oppressive Practice

Anti-oppressive practice refers to the concepts that inform professional decision-making and actions as expressions of how one views social as well as economic and political justice. An AO perspective begins with awareness of internalized therapist views and attitudes (Lago, 2011). It

> requires a fundamental re-thinking of values, institutions and relationships: therapists are seen as change agents and are proactive rather than reactive. Therapists accept that they can influence at individual-to-individual level but are also aware of their contribution at structural level in terms of institutional levels of the cultural norm.
>
> *(Dhillon-Stevens, 2005, p. 47)*

This necessitates demonstrable knowledge of oppression and discrimination, critical examination of personal values and beliefs on one's work and concrete skills to work with clients experiencing different forms of oppression (Dhillon-Stevens, 2005).

It is possible to trace some events and demographic changes that have informed the development of an AO perspective. The 1920s were a time of significant economic growth, urbanization and deepening class divisions in the United States that ended with the Wall Street Crash in 1929, which had global effects (Temin, 2016). High rates of poverty and lack of jobs led to the emergence of authoritarian leaderships and territorial expansion in Africa, China and Europe (Herbst, 2014). Roosevelt's New Deal included federal initiatives to provide relief, stimulate the economy and reform the financial system (Mitchell, 2017). A Canadian version was introduced during the mid-1930s. It was World War II that lifted both Canada and the United States, providing much needed employment and economic stimulation (Reich, 2017).

The 1950s and 1960s were a period of significant population growth. Many of the ideas associated with progressive thought emerged in concert with or as a result of the civil rights movement in the United States (Morris, 1986). In response to continued African-American racial segregation and discrimination, many acts of civil disobedience and nonviolent protest appeared (Sanders, 2016). Second wave feminism emerged, focusing on women's rights related to sexuality and family (Thornham, 2004). It was also the beginning of environmentalism with the silent spring (Carson, 2009). Protests by a growing population of university students rallied against the war and more generally the status quo, challenging the role of government as a protector of business and enforcer of outdated moral standards. At the time, Vatican II (1962) represented a liberalizing and modernizing of the Catholic church (Hastings, 1991). **The New Left**, with an intellectual basis and theoretical location in Europe from existentialism (Sartre) and neo-Marxism (Fanon), represented a range of issues from women's rights, gay rights and civil rights, to social class and workers' rights, as well as drug policy reforms (Evans, 1979).

During this time, there was a current led by individuals who were not themselves **anti-psychiatry** but who rallied against psychodynamic and biomedical models to support freedom and humanity, personal vulnerability and social causes of mental illness. To Thomas Szasz (1920–2012), mental illness was incorrectly defined as a biological condition. He viewed mental illness as a metaphor for being an outlier and more properly recognized as a social problem, with the DSM as a political document (Szasz, 1972). David Cooper (1931–1986) viewed pathology as the product of living one's life with a prescribed social identity given by others and internalized, rather than one's true identity (Cooper, 2013). For RD Laing (1927–1989), madness was a sane reaction to an insane world and hospital treatment was inhumane (Crossley, 1998). A supportive environment was needed.

In humanistic psychology, whole people, with mind, body and spirit, were evidenced in person-centered (Rogers, 1902–1987) views. Existential psychology emphasized uniqueness. What mattered was one's ability to make meaning (Frankl, 2014). Therapists, to be helpful, need to understand the world as their clients see it and help them find their own answers. This enterprise is not value free. Therapists and their clients as well as the settings, communities and societies in which they live and work have an effect. George Albee (1921–2006), who served as president of the American Psychological Association between 1969 and 1970, contended that psychology had become too medical. He reminded the profession to look at the social contexts for the causes of suffering and, in addition to clinical work, to take preventive and political action to change those causes (Albee, 1982). He reacted strongly against what he viewed as the increasing emphasis in professional psychology research and practice on medical perspectives of mental disorders and medication treatment.

Albee argued in support of the distinctiveness of psychology and social causes of mental health. In a moving obituary it was written (Fryer, 2007) that

> instead of using George's death to promote all that George, radical community psychologist, stood against, George's obituary should surely be a statement of continuing indefatigable and implacable determination to continue his commitment to uncover and contest social causes of distress, illness, and community misery such as inequality, poverty, unemployment, exploitation, colonization, racism, disableism, heterosexism, and other manifestations of social injustice and to doggedly pursue, hold to account, and depower those who benefit from such injustice, especially those seeking to explain away unjust societal arrangements by use of victim-blaming, status-quo preserving, highly profitable, psychiatric, medical, and pharmaceutical models.

Dimensions of Anti-Oppressive Practice in Counseling and Psychotherapy

There are overlapping literatures on anti-oppressive practice related to counseling and psychotherapy. Some authors refer to this area as anti-discriminatory practice and others refer to it as anti-oppressive practice. The contents of these literatures are similar. The term anti-oppressive was selected for this text because of its association with the concept of power in addition to issues of fairness with the distribution of opportunities and resources in a society. In this section, authors from both social work and psychology are included to represent some of the breadth on the topic.

Clifford and Burke (2005) use the term 'anti-oppressive' to refer to social, personal and organizational dimensions of social categories and abuse of power in a context of sociohistorical complexity. Mullaly (2002) refers to this concept as "the domination of subordinate groups in society by a powerful (politically, economically, socially and culturally) group" (p. 27). A consultation participant (2009), in discussions about the development of an anti-oppressive framework for child protection, defined it as "giving up power, being inclusive of all groups, of all marginalized groups, having representation from these groups and having joint decision-making about policy, procedures and practices". The psychologists Feltham and Horton define anti-oppressive practice as "social, economic, historical, political, cultural and psychological inequalities created structurally, systematic oppression: individual and structural levels and create prejudice, discrimination and oppression" (Feltham, Hanley, & Winter, 2017).

Anti-oppressive practice may be viewed as a set of dimensions. In one conceptualization (Dominelli, 1996), there are five: **philosophical**, **value base**, **structural orientation**, **methodological** and **relational dimensions**. The philosophical dimension is reflected in a person-centered view. Values associated with this model are egalitarian. Structural effects of inequality are recognized, and actions taken to address them. Methods include both processes and outcomes. Relationally, interactions are set up as and understood to function against the negative effects of hierarchies.

Central concepts in anti-discriminatory practice include ideology, **hegemony**, **discourse**, identity and language (Lago & Smith, 2010). Ideologies are the ideas that create and sustain social relationships. Hegemony refers to the power dominance in a group whose members are supposed to be equal. Discourse is how we talk and write, including what we say and how we say it. This may include jargon and stereotypes as well as stigma, exclusion and depersonalization. Identity refers to unquestioned norms, often highly scrutinized others, and recognition of social identity groups as homogenous and heterogeneous, assigned and self-assigned and historical and contextual (Tajfel, 2010).

Central themes in the anti-oppressive practice literature have been identified (Thompson, 2016). These themes include power (which is possessed by and operates within networks of influence), diversity (social categories are positional), ideology (views about what a good society is and how it is created), oppression (power over others) and empowerment (equitable power). An important addition to the definitions and models is the idea of "no middle road". This is the suggestion that there is no way for a professional to be apolitical, value neutral or unbiased in practice. This is an important consideration. While there are theories of counseling and psychotherapy discussed in later chapters of this text that emphasize the importance of positive regard and client-focused efforts, the degree to which one is or can be neutral or fully client-centered throughout this endeavor is questionable from an anti-oppressive perspective. There is tension here from within an AO perspective as well. What if the presence of a particular orientation toward fairness and power relations that AO practitioners may endorse differs from or encroaches on a client's freedom to choose or act?

Applications of Anti-Oppressive Practice in Counseling and Psychotherapy

While there are many definitions, models and approaches, there has been far less attention to practices. This is understandable because most practice in and of itself is less important than the meaning and purpose of it. While making efforts to identify some practices associated with an AO perspective throughout this text, there are undoubtedly places where practices described may be judged as unacceptable or perhaps even oppressive. It is a calculated risk however, to move forward on these possibilities in order to promote reconsideration and discussion about professional counseling and psychotherapy in an unfair and inequitable society. The following sections describe broadly what AOP is and is not and are followed by a rationale for the major topics in subsequent chapters.

What AOP in Counseling and Psychotherapy Is

It explicitly recognizes structural advantage and disadvantage.

It is highly sensitive to power imbalances and their manifestations.

It is embedded within values of economic, social and political justice.

It necessitates that privilege be challenged to order to promote liberation from oppression.

It is the recognition that one's perspective is not necessarily generalizable to another.

It is a commitment to self-reflection and awareness in practice.

What AOP in Counseling and Psychotherapy Is Not

It is not limited to any one theory, concept or practice, nor does it exist as a prescribed sequence or combination. It can borrow from diverse schools of thought when necessary.

It is not stagnant because conditions and issues shift and require responsivity. It is constantly in process and evolving within different contexts.

It is not limited to particular settings or populations or issues.

It is not an answer to every problem. Not every counseling and psychotherapeutic issue is rooted in a structural problem.

Anti-Oppressive Counseling and Psychotherapy

AOCP necessitates an awareness of evidence for professional practice. While evidence-based practice is often held out as a means for identifying the best approach, there are some challenges with relying solely on random controlled trials given the highly controlled contexts of such studies, problem specificity and accessible populations. In Chapter 4, an alternative and complementary process of practice-based evidence is presented. It is becoming more recognized as a means by which to generate data on real world problems with underrepresented populations. Common factors provides a framework that is highly flexible to the setting, therapist and client, as well as psychotherapeutic processes that can utilize any therapy, if appropriately decontextualized and re-contextualized for a specific use. Additional challenges emerge from an AO perspective in relation to accessibility and effectiveness of counseling and psychotherapy within the constraints of social, economic and political disadvantage.

Health status varies according to population level factors. In Chapter 5, these determinants of health provide guidance for AOCP on the major contributors and barriers to accessibility and effectiveness among groups that are disadvantaged relative to others. The Centers for Disease Control has established nine factors that have substantial effects, including early development, education, employment and occupation, food security, health care, housing and income. These factors contribute to unequal opportunities and outcomes in health and mental health and invoke values and beliefs about a good society. Socioeconomic status is a population factor that has been studied extensively. Groups with relatively lower SES have a far greater likelihood of experiencing limited choices and engaging in less optimal choices, as well as accumulating a greater amount and degree of adverse experiences over time. The chronic stress this creates is associated with compromised mental health and mental health problems.

AOCP is open to practice-based evidence as well as processes to appropriately contextualize theory and practice. AOCP is also sensitized to the population level factors that function as relative privilege and disadvantage, creating barriers to access and effectiveness. Each of the remaining chapters focuses on concepts that inform typical counseling and psychotherapy practice, beginning with considerations for assessment and intervention. The subsequent chapters extend the reach of professional activities into endeavors that connect with clients in the community, such as outreach, and finally, with a view to group level change via community assessment and intervention.

Conclusion

Major developments in progressive Western thought offer insight into the notion of fairness that is prominent in AOCP. While psychology emerged from the perspectives of upper-class males, the views of women and writers who emphasized class struggle as well as those who opposed colonization were evident among scholarly contributions of the time. Such diversity was also evident in views of justice, as well as notions of freedom and equality. Modern philosophical contributions offer a theoretical basis for the simultaneous promotion of both fairness and liberty from combined structural and postmodern views of society. Critical thought in human services has been apparent within professional psychology. An AO perspective includes the recognition of social problems and their effects on the lives of individuals. It is critical in the sense that links to oppression are specifically considered. The actions are intended to empower as well as challenge forces at different levels that perpetuate disadvantage.

Web Links

'We Have to Do Better': Trudeau Reacts to Gerald Stanley Verdict
www.ctvnews.ca/canada/we-have-to-do-better-trudeau-reacts-to-gerald-
   stanley-verdict-1.3798036

How the Justice System Let Race Taint the Stanley Verdict
www.theglobeandmail.com/opinion/how-the-justice-system-let-race-taint-
   the-stanley-verdict/article37931748/

Simply Psychology: Prejudice and Discrimination
www.simplypsychology.org/prejudice.html

The 5 W's and the H's of the Anti-Oppression Framework
http://shamelessmag.com/blog/entry/the-5-ws-and-the-h-of-the-anti-
   oppression-framewo

Anti-Oppressive Practice in Counseling Psychology
https://study.sagepub.com/node/38391/student-resources/further-reading-
   and-case-studies/chapter-12-working-with-difference-a-1

Canadian Counseling and Psychotherapy Association—Social Justice Chapter
www.ccpa-accp.ca/chapters/social-justice/

Society for Community Research and Action
www.scra27.org

Key Terms

Colonialism   47
Orientalism   48
Divine command   48
Natural law   48
Social contact   48
Utilitarian   48
Libertarian   49
Egalitarian   49
Distributive   49
Procedural   49
Retributive   49
Restorative   49
Postmodern   49
Emancipatory communitarian   49
The New Left   51
Anti-psychiatry   51

References

Albee, G. W. (1982). Preventing psychopathology and promoting human potential. *American Psychologist, 37*(9), 1043.

Assembly, U. G. (1948). *Universal declaration of human rights.* New York: UN General Assembly.

Bhaskar, R. A. (1997). *A realist theory of science.* London: Verso, 1975. ISBN 1-85984-103-1.

Bhaskar, R. A. (1998). *The possibility of naturalism* (3rd ed.). London: Routledge, 1979. ISBN 0-415-19874-7.

Brennan, J. F., & Houde, K. A. (2017). *History and systems of psychology.* Cambridge: Cambridge University Press.

Burbidge, J. W. (1981). *On Hegel's logic: Fragments of a commentary* (p. 48). Atlantic Highlands, NJ: Humanities Press.

Carson, R. (2009). *Silent spring,* 1962. Greenwich, CT: Fawcett

Clifford, D., & Burke, B. (2005). Developing anti-oppressive ethics in the new curriculum. *Social Work Education, 24*(6), 677–692.

Collier, A. (1994). *Critical realism: An introduction to Roy Bhaskar's philosophy.* London: Verso.

Colucci, F. P. (1999). The relevance to psychology of Antonio Gramsci's ideas on activity and common sense. *Perspectives on Activity Theory,* 147.

Consultation Participant. (2009). *An anti-oppression framework for child welfare in Ontario.* Retrieved November 10, 2018, from http://www.oacas.org/wp-content/uploads/2017/01/Framework.pdf

Cooper, D. (Ed.). (2013). *Psychiatry and anti-psychiatry.* New York: Routledge.

Crossley, N. (1998). RD Laing and the British anti-psychiatry movement: A socio-historical analysis. *Social Science & Medicine, 47*(7), 877–889.

Degler, C. N. (1959). *Out of our past.* London: Harper Colophon Books.

Dhillon-Stevens, H. (2005). Personal and professional integration of antioppressive practice and the multiple oppression model in psychotherapeutic education. *British Journal of Psychotherapy Integration, 1*(2), 47–62.

Dominelli, L. (1996). Deprofessionalizing social work: Anti-oppressive practice, competencies and postmodernism. *The British Journal of Social Work, 26*(2), 153–175.

Evans, S. M. (1979). *Personal politics: The roots of women's liberation in the civil rights movement and the new left* (Vol. 228). New York: Vintage.

Feltham, C., Hanley, T., & Winter, L. A. (Eds.). (2017). *The SAGE handbook of counseling and psychotherapy.* Thousand Oaks, CA: Sage Publications.

Ferrari, S. (2017). Separation of church and state in contemporary European society. In *Law and religion, an overview* (pp. 125–139). London: Routledge.

Folger, R. (1977). Distributive and procedural justice: Combined impact of voice and improvement on experienced inequity. *Journal of Personality and Social Psychology, 35*(2), 108.

Frankl, V. E. (2014). *The will to meaning: Foundations and applications of logotherapy.* London: Penguin.

Fraser, N., & Nicholson, L. (1988). Social criticism without philosophy: An encounter between feminism and postmodernism. *Theory, Culture & Society, 5*(2–3), 373–394.

Fryer, D. (2007). George Wilson Albee (1921–2006), radical community psychologist: A critical obituary. *Journal of Primary Prevention, 28*(1), 15–18.

Gewirtz, S. (1998). Conceptualizing social justice in education: Mapping the territory. *Journal of Education Policy, 13*(4), 469–484.

Gilboy, E. W. (2017). Demand as a factor in the industrial revolution. In *The causes of the industrial revolution in England* (pp. 121–138). London: Routledge.

Hastings, A. (1991). *Modern Catholicism: Vatican II and after*. Oxford: Oxford University Press.

Hatch, M. J. (2018). *Organization theory: Modern, symbolic, and postmodern perspectives*. Oxford: Oxford University Press.

Herbst, J. (2014). *States and power in Africa: Comparative lessons in authority and control*. Princeton University Press. Retrieved from www.theglobeandmail.com/opinion/you-and-i-can-question-the-gerald-stanley-verdict-politicians-should-not/article37954500/

Inglis, D. (2017). Cultural imperialism. *The Wiley-Blackwell Encyclopedia of Social Theory*, 1–3.

Janes, R. M. (2017). On the reception of Mary Wollstonecraft's a vindication of the rights of woman. In *Mary Wollstonecraft* (pp. 25–34). London: Routledge.

Johansen, S. (2014). *Family men: Middle-class fatherhood in industrializing America*. London: Routledge.

Krippner, S. C. (2002). Conflicting perspectives on shamans and shamanism: Points and counterpoints. *American Psychologist, 57*(11), 962–977.

Lago, C. (Ed.). (2011). *The handbook of transcultural counseling and psychotherapy*. New York: McGraw-Hill Education.

Lago, C., & Smith, B. (2010). *Anti-discriminatory practice in counselling & psychotherapy*. Thousand Oaks, CA: Sage Publications.

Lillis, T., & Curry, M. J. (2015). The politics of English, language and uptake: The case of international academic journal article reviews. *AILA Review, 28*(1), 127–150.

Lundy, C. (2004). *Social work and social justice: A structural approach to practice*. Toronto, ON: University of Toronto Press.

Madrigal Muñoz, E. (2015). From Columbus to globalism: The construction of western hegemony. *Revista Humanidades, 5*(1).

Mamdani, M. (2015). Settler colonialism: Then and now. *Critical Inquiry, 41*(3), 596–614.

Mitchell, B. (2017). *The depression decade: From new era through new deal, 1929–41* (Vol. 9). New York: Routledge.

Mokyr, J., Vickers, C., & Ziebarth, N. L. (2015). The history of technological anxiety and the future of economic growth: Is this time different? *Journal of Economic Perspectives, 29*(3), 31–50.

Morris, A. D. (1986). *The origins of the civil rights movement*. New York: Simon and Schuster.

Mullaly, R. P. (2002). *Challenging oppression: A critical social work approach*. Oxford: Oxford University Press.

Muthu, S. (2003). *Enlightenment against empire*. Princeton, NJ: Princeton University Press.

Nozick, R. (2017). Distributive justice. In *Distributive justice* (pp. 3–61). London: Routledge.

Panitch, L., & Gindin, S. (2004). Global capitalism and American empire. *Socialist Register, 40*(40).

Pease, B., & Fook, J. (2016). Postmodern critical theory. *Transforming Social Work Practice: Postmodern Critical Perspectives*, 1.

Prilleltensky, I. (1989). Psychology and the status quo. *American Psychologist, 44*(5), 795–802.

Prilleltensky, I. (1997). Values, assumptions, and practices: Assessing the moral implications of psychological discourse and action. *American Psychologist, 52*(5), 517.

Prilleltensky, I. (2012). Wellness as fairness. *American Journal of Community Psychology*, *49*(1–2), 1–21.

Prilleltensky, I. (2013). Wellness without fairness: The missing link in psychology. *South African Journal of Psychology*, *43*(2), 147–155.

Rawls, J. (1985). Justice as fairness: Political not metaphysical. *Philosophy & Public Affairs*, 223–251.

Reich, M. (2017). *Racial inequality: A political-economic analysis*. Princeton, NJ: Princeton University Press.

Robeyns, I. (2015). On GA Cohen's "On the Currency of Egalitarian Justice". *Ethics*, *125*(4), 1132–1135.

Rousseau, J. J. (1968). *The social contract* (pp. 87–94). Hoboken, NJ: John Wiley & Sons, Inc.

Rubinštejn, S. L. (1987). Problems of psychology in the works of Karl Marx. *Studies in Soviet Thought*, *33*(2), 111–130.

Said, E. (1994). *Orientalism*. New York, NY: Vintage, 1979.

Sandel, M. J. (1998). *Liberalism and the limits of justice*. Cambridge, UK: Cambridge University Press.

Sanders, K. (2016). Black culture centers: A review of pertinent literature. *Urban Education Research & Policy Annuals*, *4*(1).

Sterba, J. P. (1992). *Justice: Alternative political perspectives*. Belmont, CA: Wadsworth Publishing Company.

Szasz, T. S. (1972). The ethics of addiction. *Journal of Drug Issues*, *2*(1), 42–49.

Tajfel, H. (Ed.). (2010). *Social identity and intergroup relations*. Cambridge, UK: Cambridge University Press.

Temin, P. (2016). Great depression. In *Banking crises* (pp. 144–153). London: Palgrave Macmillan.

Thompson, N. (2016). *Anti-discriminatory practice: Equality, diversity and social justice*. New York: Palgrave Macmillan.

Thornham, S. (2004). Second wave feminism. In *The Routledge companion to feminism and postfeminism* (pp. 36–46). London: Routledge.

Vera, E. M., & Speight, S. L. (2003). Multicultural competence, social justice, and counseling psychology: Expanding our roles. *The Counseling Psychologist*, *31*(3), 253–272.

Weinreb, L. L. (1987). *Natural law and justice*. Cambridge, MA: Harvard University Press.

Wenzel, M., Okimoto, T. G., Feather, N. T., & Platow, M. J. (2008). Retributive and restorative justice. *Law and Human Behavior*, *32*(5), 375–389.

Wierenga, E. (1983). A defensible divine command theory. *Nous*, 387–407.

Zehr, H. (2015). *The little book of restorative justice: Revised and updated*. New York: Skyhorse Publishing, Inc.

Discussion Questions

1. What are the dominant theories in counseling and psychotherapy? Who developed them? For whom? For what purpose? How do they intersect with concepts of justice and fairness, oppression and privilege?

2. Which groups are represented in the center of economic, social and political power? What does it mean to be in the center? Who is on the periphery? What does it mean to be on the periphery? How can equality be promoted?

   a. Have no center? (is this possible?)
   b. Expand the center? ("too many cooks"?)
   c. Diversify the center? ("representation": does being in the center alter the "diversity" one represents?)
   d. Replace the center? (oust and replace with another group?)
   e. Restructure the center? (change the processes and outcomes of the center?)

3. In what ways can counseling and psychotherapy practice address social inequality? In the therapy room? In the profession? In the community?

4

COMMON FACTORS

Accessible and effective approaches to counseling and psychotherapy may be top down or bottom up, technical or relational, therapist-driven or client-driven, precise or flexible, goal oriented or open ended. Which of these resonate most strongly for you? To which do you react positively and negatively? What kind of approach suits you best as a client? What kind of therapist are you? What kind of therapist do you want to be?

In this chapter, we consider the use of a common factors framework as a basis for both research-informed practice and practice-informed research in counseling and psychotherapy. This generic framework provides guidance about the forces that make counseling and psychotherapy work without predetermining a specific theory, orientation or technique as inherently superior to others by itself or in relation to a particular issue or client or therapist. It does allow for the imposition of worldview, values and beliefs and a metaphor for personal change that fits with a therapist's capacities, a client's understandings, their relationship, setting and context. It is suggested that anti-oppressive practice in counseling and psychotherapy can use this framework, which allows for explicitly culturally based approaches.

Why are common factors relevant to professional counseling and psychotherapy?

- It is essential that services are effective. It is also important that high-quality practices reach those most in need. We know far more about which treatments work for some groups than for others. To make services accessible and effective for all, it is necessary to expand treatments to include those based in diverse worldviews and knowledge.
- Evidence continues to narrow the range of "what works" for what problems and which people. For example, there is a great deal of evidence for the effectiveness of CBT for depression among white, middle-class North

Americans. From an AO perspective, factors that affect engagement and outcome include access and effectiveness, the context outside of therapy and cultural congruence of the therapist and therapy itself. These factors contain a range that opens possibilities for other ways of working with members of groups not as extensively studied.

- An AO perspective also allows for evidence to be generated from both the top down and the bottom up. Evidence-informed practice (EIP) is top down, isolates elements, is based on populations and norms and has robust evidence for majority populations. Practice-informed evidence (PIE) is bottom up, contextualizes elements, is based on experiences and commonalities and has evidence of effectiveness for non-majority groups. It does not matter the direction from which evidence is collected. Common factors—client, therapist, relationship and context—are consistent but also specific to the application.

Chapter Outline

Politics and Evidence

Evidence is a product of process and outcome research. **Process research** is the study of what goes on during counseling and psychotherapy, while **outcome research** is what the end result of the counseling and psychotherapy is (Orlinsky, Grawe, & Parks, 1994). Clinical judgment is what clinicians use to interpret and use the evidence. Clinical judgment is informed by personal, professional and institutional experiences (Chin-Yee & Fuller, 2018).

There is an increasing reliance on **evidence** in psychotherapy to determine effectiveness and value. Providing a helpful service is an ethical responsibility (Jacobson & Truax, 1991). There has been tension, however, regarding the use of evidence-based practice standards in psychotherapy, particularly in consideration of diversity and disadvantage (Persons & Silberschatz, 1998). One challenge has been the definition of evidence that is used (Lilienfeld, McKay, & Hollon, 2018). If evidence is only the product of **Randomized Controlled Trials** (RCTs), then it has limited use for the work of diverse therapists with diverse clients, providing different therapies within an unfair and inequitable society (Stuart, Bradshaw, & Leaf, 2015).

Effectiveness

RCTs report the effect of a therapy on a particular disorder. The conditions are theoretically neutralized to isolate the effect of the intervention on the problem (Kennedy-Martin, Curtis, Faries, Robinson, & Johnston, 2015). This information is helpful as a guide for a type of therapist working with a type of client on a type of disorder (Carey & Stiles, 2016). However, therapists and clients vary. If the therapy works, it does so under whatever conditions were present in the study that reported the results. Results of treatment effectiveness across studies are influential and, if diversity is specifically sought and reported, lend support to its applicability with different populations and therapists in different settings within different communities (Weiss, Westerhof, & Bohlmeijer, 2016). However, because the emphasis in this line of research is on the treatment itself and claims about its general effectiveness, relatively less attention is paid to the participants, their challenges and the contexts of living and treatment or characteristics of the therapists themselves (Mulder et al., 2018).

Research Funding

It is important to consider the degree to which government-sponsored or privately sponsored (e.g. pharmaceutical) decision-makers elect to allocate and specify the topics and approaches for research, and in what ways counseling and psychotherapy are fundable (Lieb, von der Osten-Sacken, Stoffers-Winterling, Reiss, & Barth, 2016). It is also important to consider the views of those funding counseling and psychotherapy research and what they believe to be the most important evidence to collect for what therapy and disorder (Levitt, 2015). This connects to the types of proposals that will be requested. Those who review the proposals decide what of the limited funding available will go to which project. As such, their views about what is credible evidence as well as how it is best generated factor heavily in decisions about who and what issues get funding.

For example, is the purpose to find ways to support an RCT on the effectiveness of medication among those most likely to purchase it, or is it to do a qualitative study with community leaders to engage positively with inner city youth for crime reduction? There is far more research on the former than the latter given its clear profit potential. So, there are different political forces at play that determine not only what provides the best evidence, but also what clinical, as well as economic, social and political, ends the research is a means to.

Evidence-Based Practice

There are some issues to consider when basing clinical decisions on RCT evidence in psychotherapy. First, is there enough evidence about an intervention with the specific population to support its use with that population? Second, therapists vary, so is adherence a reflection of ability in general or ability to do therapy the way it was specified in the protocol? Third, are problems that may not fit within the diagnostic categories and outcomes other than reduction of diagnostic symptoms explored? From an anti-oppressive perspective, the problems people bring to counseling and psychotherapy, such as emotional responses to discrimination, for example, reflect a personal experience of a social problem.

Practice-Based Evidence

Practice-based evidence (PBE) may be defined as

> a range of treatment approaches and supports that are derived from, and supportive of, the positive cultural attributes of the local society and traditions. Practice-based evidence services are accepted as effective by the local community, through community consensus, and address the therapeutic and healing needs of individuals and families from a culturally-specific framework.
>
> *(Isaacs, Huang, Hernandez, & Echo-Hawk, 2005)*

Types of PBE practices include: "(a) community valued, (b) culturally and socially embedded, (c) heretofore unaddressed community/population conditions, and (d) emergent issues" (Lieberman et al., 2010, p. 4). Types of evidence for these PBEs include the circumstances, data sources, type of evidence, population and dissemination efforts.

Practice-based evidence may be distinguished from evidence-based practice (EBP). In PBE, the emphasis is on the client, and in EBP, the emphasis is on the treatment. One might argue that a major difference is that EBP is strong at internal validity (i.e. how well a particular intervention A causes an effect in a target B), while PBE is strong at external validity (i.e. under what conditions A is associated with B). Moving outside of an experimental research design, differences between PBE and EBP also center on views of knowledge creation. PBE is bottom up and EBP is top down, or inductive and deductive, respectively. This is reflected in differences between quantitative and qualitative data, their collection and analysis.

Gone (2015) distinguishes evidence-based practice from **cultural competence** in psychology. EBP is based on intervention science, which is exclusively quantitative. The purpose of this research is to standardize treatment. Cultural competence, in contrast, is based on cultural analysis, which is exclusively qualitative. The purpose of this research is to diversify treatment. Gone introduces a concept of **cultural equivalence** as a process of bringing evidence-based practice and practice-based evidence to a meeting point. Establishment of cultural equivalence is a concept that has not been well studied but offers a way to connect evidence and practice in a reciprocal relationship. The determination of equivalence between groups in relation to diversity and disadvantage may permit the applicability of practice-based to evidence-based and vice versa. He further challenges researchers to create "novel metaphors for representing cultural difference that better represent and appreciate fluency, dexterity, and hybridity across multiple cultural domains" (p. 143). Essentially, the argument he makes is a pragmatic one. There are major differences in evidence generation and use between evidence-based practice and cultural competence. From an AO perspective on counseling and psychotherapy, RCTs without practice-based evidence represent a limited range of people, problems and conditions. Those people, problems and conditions overrepresent majority cultural groups.

Theory and Practice

When psychology emerged as a discipline separate from philosophy, it followed a path based on the scientific method. The scientific method rests on a philosophy of science that is rooted on an empirical view of reality (i.e. what is real is what can be directly sensed) (Kaplan, 2017). Psychological phenomena are best studied through observable data and its systematic collection, frequency analysis and relationships. A high value is placed on causal relationships between measures, such that A causes B. Theory means, from this perspective, a set of phenomena that exist in relationship to one another. These relationships can be tested. Researchers generate hypotheses to make an informed estimation of what relationships are expected between some constructs and not others. Practitioners base clinical decisions on relationships for which there is evidence of a causal relationship.

Theoretical psychology is a discipline that, from an AO perspective, opens up additional possibilities for considering what knowledge is and what it means (Stam, 2013). Defining reality via Rationalism (i.e. what is real occurs through intellect and logic) and Skepticism (i.e. what is real is unknown and perhaps unknowable) allows for the generation of possibilities that are not necessarily linked to existing theories (rational) or that look for alternative explanations in existing theories (skeptic). **Theory** may then be defined as of phenomena that coexist. Theories may be discovered or created via logical (and empirical) processes that directly challenge or completely ignore existing theories. Researchers may begin with some ideas about the phenomenon or perhaps a formal framework or maybe even a complete theory from which they recognize and make meaning of data and its interconnections. Practitioners base clinical decisions on what others have found or argued, what they themselves observe and what it all means in that context.

Theory from an AO perspective can be represented in many ways. Four possibilities include absent, emergent, relational and causal (Denzin, 2017). An **absent** theoretical basis for one's practice is difficult to justify ethically and professionally. However, and despite the many theories in psychology, there are inevitably times where existing theories do not apply well. Oftentimes, practitioners interpret these experiences according to some combined basis of experience, logic and intuition. An **emergent** theoretical basis builds in coverage and strength over time and can be at any point in its development. While emergent theories do not have a strong support base in the existing scholarly literature (descriptive or causal), they may be informed by practice experience and preliminary data. **Relational** theories are complete theories that have scholarly support. They do not however, lead to measurable directional relationships. Their major sources of support are practice and descriptive research. Finally, **causal** theories are complete and supported by empirical data of causality. From an AO perspective, there is value in each of these sources, and particularly among the underrepresented sources of intuition, as well as emergent and relational theories.

There are many theories of change to draw from and inform an AO perspective on counseling and psychotherapy. These can be divided into problem-solving, empowerment and social change (Turner, 2017). **Problem-solving theories** are those that address an issue of concern for an individual and their immediate context. Theories in this category include psychodynamic, systems and ecological, crisis and task centered and cognitive behavioral. This category of theories has limited to high research support. Insight is central for change to occur. One's childhood and immediate environment are important forces in personality. Personal change probability ranges from low to very high. The duration of intervention ranges from short to long term. Among these theories, the therapist is the expert.

Empowerment theories are those that emphasize the strengths of an individual to address matters within self and environment. Theories in this category include macro practice, humanist/existential/spiritual, strengths/solutions/narratives and advocacy. These theories have moderate research support. Personal agency is central for change to occur. The major shaping forces in personality development are one's human potential in their context. Personal change is a gritty process that has a high probability for change. The duration of intervention ranges from short to moderate term. For these theories, the client is the expert.

Finally, **social change theories** emphasize the social, political and economic societal structures as fundamental causes of individual problems. In this category, the theories include critical, feminist and anti-discriminatory. These theories have limited to moderate research support. Collective personal and social action is central for change to occur. The forces that shape personality concern the efforts to promote and achieve justice in an oppressive context. Personal change is taking from privilege to distribute power evenly to the oppressed and has a moderate probability for change. The duration of intervention is long term, and in these theories the client and therapist are experts with each possessing different expertise.

Common Factors

Common factors leverages knowledge from intervention science while maintaining openness and flexibility to different views of the healing process (Duncan et al., 2010). CF offers a theory about the structure (not content) of counseling and psychotherapy. CF is open to various theories about how psychotherapy works, evidenced by the diversity within and between problem-solving, empowerment and social change theories. Each, from a CF view, possesses similar explanatory powers about change. CF does not privilege one therapy above the others. The choice of therapy is made on the basis of fit for the therapist and client as well as the purpose within a context. Common factors represent elements that are necessary for therapeutic change to occur (Fife, Whiting, Bradford, & Davis, 2014). It is not a recipe for counseling and psychotherapy but rather a structure that can include diverse theories of change.

Common factors can be justifiable as evidence-based practice while remaining open to practice-based evidence. From a CF perspective, more than the therapeutic encounter contributes to change (i.e. what goes on outside of the office). It permits the use what of makes cultural sense to therapist and client. It is not necessary to reproduce the same therapy in the same way every time. It allows for change in response to feedback.

The study of common factors began in 1936 with Saul Rosenzweig's (1907–2004) publication, "Some implicit common factors in diverse methods of psychotherapy". In this paper, he wrote the often-quoted line "At last the Dodo said, 'Everybody has won, and all must have prizes'". This reference to the Dodo character in *Alice in Wonderland* spoke to the similarities across counseling and psychotherapy theories and practice. In 1950, Dollard and Miller argued that those factors were actually principles of learning. The humanizing view of Carl Rogers was reflected in his 1957 paper, "The necessary and sufficient conditions of therapeutic personality change". For Rogers, the only essential factors for therapeutic change were therapist empathy, respect and positive regard.

Jerome Frank's 1973 book, titled *Persuasion and Healing*, described four factors that were required for a healing relationship. These factors have remained highly influential in CF. For Frank, all effective healing required an emotional, trusting relationship; a setting for healing; a reason/theory/myth that explains symptoms and a procedure for healing; and a procedure/ritual that both therapist and client believe is helping. To further clarify types of factors, Goldfried and Padawer (1982) described different levels of interventions in psychotherapy, including theories (philosophical understanding), principles and techniques (different ways of using the sample principle). In a *Generic Model of Psychotherapy* (Orlinsky & Howard, 1986), it was posited that the contract, activities, bond, relatability and understanding were key ingredients in any effective psychotherapy.

In a *Transtheoretical Model of Change* (Prochaska & Diclemente, 2005), the process in counseling and psychotherapy required the following: **consciousness raising** (new information that supports change), **dramatic relief** (negative emotions that accompany the current status), **self-re-evaluation** (importance of change to personal identity) and **environmental re-evaluation** (change viewed as positive, status quo as negative). Additionally, the process included **self-liberation** (commitment is made to change), **counterconditioning** (replacement of old with new), stimulus control (cues to support change and challenge old status) and **social liberation** (change in keeping with social norms).

A review of published studies concluded that there were four common factors: 1) therapeutic alliance, 2) **catharsis**, 3) acquisition and practice of new behavior and 4) client expectancies for positive change (Grencavage & Norcross, 1990). Proportions of therapeutic effect were calculated, including extra-therapeutic change (40%), those qualities in context and client that change regardless of participation in psychotherapy, and common factors (30%), the qualities of different therapies that are similar, such as warmth and positive regard. The remaining two factors include expectancy (15%), which reflected clients' belief in the process, and techniques (15%), which were specific acts that reflected each client's uniqueness and the therapist's response (Lambert, 1992). In 2001, Wampold proposed "areas of agreement in psychotherapy" that included similar purposes, centrality of relationship, client choice and the responsibility for and broadening of clients' self-understandings (Norcross & Wampold, 2011).

In response to criticisms of CF as an incomplete type of counseling or psychotherapy, "a common factors framework is not a model, psychotherapy or specific set of techniques. As such it cannot be 'manualized' but informs the immediate therapeutic encounter one client at a time" (Sparks, Duncan, & Miller, 2008, p. 454). The specific client, issue and therapist are variable but tend to operate through a set of factors making all therapy "specific" in the strictest sense. When there is enough diversity in the client, therapist and issue, the judgment of "common" may be applied.

The notion of "different thinks for different shrinks" is one way to characterize the CF model (Laska & Wampold, 2014). CF presupposes that counselors and psychotherapists select therapeutic models that fit their own worldview, experience and particular challenges for different client groups. The point of significance for an AO perspective in counseling and psychotherapy is that any approach derives its power from a belief in its utility and effectiveness. Having confidence as a therapist in your approach—one that also makes sense to clients in their social, economic and political world—is essential.

CF opens possibilities for therapies that are responsive to clients and communities as well as that fit with the therapist's strengths. Practice-based evidence offers a view of the place of emergent theory of change. This combination allows for the development of understanding about what works for a particular therapist and client in a particular setting according to five major factors: bond between client and therapist; the healing setting; therapist with an explanation of the distress; an explanation that is believable and accepted by the client; and rituals or procedures that lead the client to do something helpful or adaptive or positive.

Conceptual Models for Cultural Equivalence

Cultural equivalence is an important concept and process for AOP in relation to theory, principles and techniques. There are many possible ways to employ CF with some well validated, culturally explicit approaches to practice. Some of these include Sue and colleagues' tripartite model, Helms' interactional process model, Atkinson and colleagues' three-dimensional process model, and Neville and Mobley's ecological process model. These provide guidance about applying CF in ways that are sensitive to power differentials for the client as well as the therapist in their own personal, professional and civic lives and how the two intersect in a therapeutic relationship.

In the **tripartite model** (Sue & Sue, 2003), which overlaps substantially with the CF framework, the onus is on the therapist to have an understanding of the setting and client as well as the nature of client concerns. In order to develop this understanding, therapists cultivate self-awareness of their own beliefs, values and biases that affect how they view therapy and the dynamics within it. This approach requires that the therapist be understanding of a client's view of the world, with history and current events affecting experience. Additionally, the therapist has skills for creating and using strategies relevant to client values, beliefs and expectations. This view speaks about therapist preparation and flexibility for diverse clientele and little to the dynamics of the therapeutic encounter.

In the **interactional process model** (Helms, 1984), the emphasis is on similarities and differences in racial consciousness between the therapist and client. Identity is collective sense of self within a racial group. Race is a social construct that represents diverse experiences with oppression and privilege. Development is a maturational process that evolves with intellectual change and social experience. Stages are not mutually exclusive. Each individual may be connected to qualities of different stages simultaneously with aspects that are dominant in some situations and less so in others. Attitudes about whites and people of color with a transcendent non-racist identity means connections with other marginalized groups.

White identity development (Helms, 1990) includes several stages. In **contact**, there is no recognition of racism and unawareness of whiteness. In **disintegration**, there is recognition of racism and awareness of whiteness but use of suppression to avoid anxiety. In **reintegration**, one idealizes their own group and explains differences in terms of getting what is deserved. **Pseudo-independence** includes commitment to one's own group and verbal tolerance of other groups. **Immersion/emersion** recognizes the need for change of others like self to become non-racist. Finally, **autonomy** is a commitment to leave the benefits of racism behind.

People of color identity development (Helms, 1995) includes **conformity** (i.e. aligning with white society), **dissonance** (i.e. suppressing anxiety because of tension between white and people of color belonging) and **immersion/emersion** (i.e. favoring own group and rejecting white). Subsequent stages of development include **internalization** (i.e. becoming flexible in determination of whiteness and be more objective in dealings) and **integrative awareness** (i.e. valuing one's own oppressed group and connections with other oppressed groups).

Racial identity interaction statuses (Ladany, Brittan-Powell, & Pannu, 1997) include progressive, regressive and parallel. In **progressive**, the counselor has high racial identity development that is positive. In **regressive**, the counselor has low racial identity development. **Parallel** is when counselor and client have similar racial identity development.

The **three-dimensional process model** (Atkinson, Thompson, & Grant, 1993) refers to the selection of an appropriate therapist role and strategies for working across cultures. Appropriateness is based on client **acculturation** (extent to which an individual has adopted mainstream or dominant cultural identity with bicultural orientation as an apex of development) and the **locus of source of problem** (internal and external sources associated with oppression). Different roles the therapist may function in are: **advisor** (assisting low acculturated individuals on what to expect), **advocate** (helping clients with low acculturation who have a problem stemming from oppression or discrimination), **facilitator of Indigenous support systems** (aiding clients with adjusting and coping with a new culture by making connections) and **facilitator of Indigenous healing systems** (connecting clients with traditional persons or by helping the client from such a worldview). Practitioners may also act as **consultant** (assisting high acculturated clients to *prevent* problems due to oppression or discrimination), **change agent** (aiding high acculturated clients to *address* problems due to oppression or discrimination), **counselor** (helping with the prevention of intrapsychic problems) and **psychotherapist** (addressing intrapsychic problems resulting from oppression and discrimination).

The **ecological process model** (Neville & Mobley, 2001) is based on ecological theory in its contextual emphasis on individuals and their relationships. However, the EPM differs from the pure forms of ecological models in three ways: personal qualities influence social experience, culture affects all behavior and there are hierarchies that inform self- and other perceptions. There are connections between personal values and social structures, but the circular model does not point to causal relationships between them. In addition to the personal experiences of identity and association with dominant culture, there is an awareness of community agencies, social policies and hierarchies that are present at the highest levels of society. Within a dyad, sociocultural positions differ and inform worldview and views of others as well as a particular helping environment with policies and practices sophistication in recognizing these dynamics.

The multicultural literature was organized according to common factors evidence to illustrate culturally specific frameworks (Fischer, Jerome, & Atkinson, 1998). The review centered on relationship factors as well as shared worldview, client expectations and interventions. It was concluded that "the skeleton of universal healing factors requires the flesh of cultural knowledge" (p. 525). The cultural analysis found literature and support for the idea that there are groups of clients who benefit from explicitly culturally relevant metaphors and interventions with particular therapists.

However, therapists who are effective with diverse clientele are more effective in general, not just in cross-cultural dyads (Hayes, McAleavey, Castonguay, & Locke, 2016). Therapeutic process was found to be more sensitive to therapist competence among the more effective therapists with diverse clientele. In a meta-analysis, multicultural competencies of therapists had r = .29 relationship to outcome and r = .75 to process (Tao, Owen, Pace, & Imel, 2015). It is also noteworthy that while cultural insensitivity has been associated with client dissatisfaction, sensitivity is not a major contribution to client satisfaction. Stylistic contributions carried greater weight for client satisfaction; therapists who were more active, engaged, directive and disclosing were favored in cross-race therapeutic relationships (Chang & Berk, 2009).

Differential Access

Several reasons for not accessing counseling and psychotherapy services have been studied. Issues reported in the literature include stigma, fears about what treatment is, fear of emotion, expected benefits/risks, self-disclosure, norms and self-esteem (Blake, 2008). Ethnic considerations concern the degree to which therapy and seeing a therapist are inconsistent with culture. For example, concerns (Watkins, 2017) may include privacy, someone outside family/faith community knowing one's personal information, avoidance rather than disclosure as a preferred way to handle problems, the existence of problems being taboo, value of prayer over treatment and potential of losing face. Paradoxically, the greater the experience of oppression and discrimination, the lower the likelihood of utilizing health and mental health care, including counseling and psychotherapy (Vogel, Wester, & Larson, 2007). Demographic data indicate that young adults who attend school (and can enter counseling for academic purposes) (Olfson, Druss, & Marcus, 2015), and adults with low incomes who are people of color are less likely to access counseling and psychotherapy services (Kim et al., 2017).

One approach to make counseling and psychotherapy more inclusive is to consider the barriers to service. Barriers include availability, accessibility, acceptability, appropriateness and adequacy (Gallagher & Truglio-Londrigan, 2004). **Availability** concerns whether the service is available or perceived to be available. **Acceptability** refers to the degree to which potential clients feel that they can use the services. **Affordability** includes the costs—financial and otherwise—of services. **Appropriateness** is about the degree to which the service is the right kind. **Adequacy** refers to the quality and completeness of service for the level of diversity and need.

Differential Effectiveness

There are various combinations of common factors concerning which therapist for which client is most appropriate and effective. However, there has been relatively little attention paid to the circumstances of one's life outside of therapy and the extent to which oppression and discrimination, as well as other social, political and economic conditions, limit the effectiveness of counseling and psychotherapy (Bonnie, Stroud, Breiner, & National Research Council, 2015). Client factors can be understood to include internal (i.e. what is present during the therapy encounter) as well as external (i.e. what is present for a client outside of the therapeutic encounter). For example, the external factor of **social support** is an understudied and important component of the existing model. Family and neighborhood factors may also be considered (Robinson et al., 2015).

Contextualization

General principles cannot, nor should they, always be contextualized for specific populations; some therapies are culturally rooted and based and not applicable to others. However, interventions developed within a particular cultural context may be relevant to other contexts if appropriately decontextualized and re-contextualized. It is important to note that there is always a context. Indeed, without context, what remains is meaningless.

For any counseling or psychotherapy approach, it is valuable to know why it was developed, by whom and for whom. All were developed for a particular type of client, often one who is young, attractive, verbal, intelligent and successful (**YAVIS**) (Moodley & Sunderani, 2015). All therapies use jargon, including terminology that is specific to the profession of mental health, as well as the therapy itself. All therapies have a social and political context for their history and applications. Most are silent on privilege.

Ways to consider context for the use of a particular approach with a particular client for a particular problem may begin with recognition of some assumptions embedded within it as well as the process of seeking it (Elliott, Westmacott, Hunsley, Rumstein-McKean, & Best, 2015). For example, some issues to consider associated with the context include expectations of the therapeutic relationship and expectations about counseling (Patterson, Anderson, & Wei, 2014); clients' use of rituals; values (relationships, time, activity, nature and human nature); national values (power distance, uncertainty avoidance, masculinity and individualism); personal identity (fixed qualities, acquired experiences); historical context; mental health beliefs/practices; health care practices; defining the "problem"; arrival to therapy (self or mandated); and agency philosophy and practices. What remains important from a CF view is that the therapist and client have confidence in the approach (Quintana & Atkinson, 2002).

Another conceptualization is that the therapy is the product of the context and relationship between individuals. Most of this is done 'on the fly' within therapy itself. It has been suggested that the meaning of a phenomenon is due to both the history of the context (culture, society, group, situation) and the history of the person and their previous life experiences (Pascual-Leone, Paivio, & Harrington, 2016). Consequently, meaning is something that, often spontaneously and without reflection, originates from the interaction between phenomena, the person and the culture. In language learning (Szmrecsanyi, 2015), there is a process of using knowledge generated in one context and re-contextualizing it for another setting. To re-contextualize language requires the replacement of familiar words and labels for particular things with others that describe similar, the same or possibly different qualities within another context.

Conclusion

All counseling and psychotherapy must have a basis in theory and research. From an AO perspective, theories that address social inequality with values on freedom and fairness are necessary. There should be evidence upon which our professional work is based. Evidence, from an AO perspective, need not be useful only if generated from a Randomized Clinical Trial. Practice-based evidence is a means by which to represent the knowledge base for working with groups underrepresented in the published research. Common factors is a well-supported framework for counseling and psychotherapy that is open to theory development and diversity as well as research on emerging or traditional healing practices. A practice that increases cultural competence is the decontextualization and recontextualization of a therapy for a particular problem, group and setting.

Web Links

Theories in Psychology and Social Sciences
http://changingminds.org/explanations/theories/a_clusters.htm

Cultural Sensitivity Can Improve Health Care
www.youtube.com/watch?v=8uAL4WzPhd0

Centre for Diversity in Counseling and Psychotherapy
www.oise.utoronto.ca/cdcp/

Diversity—What Is It and What Does It Mean?
www.apa.org/about/division/officers/dialogue/2011/03/diversity.aspx

Diversity in Action
https://psychologyfoundation.org/Public/Programs/Diversity_in_Action/
    Public/Programs/Diversity_in_Action.aspx?hkey=445d04d5-c4ab-4623-
    8fa8-11636ed4e47b

Key Terms

References

Atkinson, D. R., Thompson, C. E., & Grant, S. K. (1993). A three-dimensional model for counseling racial/ethnic minorities. *The Counseling Psychologist, 21*(2), 257–277.

Blake, J. P. (2008). *Psychological distress, masculinity ideology, and self-threat: A model of men's attitudes toward help seeking.* New York: Fordham University.

Bonnie, R. J., Stroud, C., Breiner, H., & National Research Council. (2015). *Diversity and the effects of bias and discrimination on young adults' health and well-being.* Washington, DC: National Academies Press.

Carey, T. A., & Stiles, W. B. (2016). Some problems with randomized controlled trials and some viable alternatives. *Clinical Psychology & Psychotherapy, 23*(1), 87–95.

Chang, D. F., & Berk, A. (2009). Making cross-racial therapy work: A phenomenological study of clients' experiences of cross-racial therapy. *Journal of Counseling Psychology, 56*(4), 521.

Chin-Yee, B., & Fuller, J. (2018). Clinical judgement: Multidisciplinary perspectives. *Journal of Evaluation of Clinical Practice, 24*, 635–637.

Denzin, N. K. (2017). *The research act: A theoretical introduction to sociological methods*. London: Routledge.

Duncan, B. L., Miller, S. D., Wampold, B. E., & Hubble, M. A. (2010). *The heart and soul of change: Delivering what works in therapy*. Washington, DC: American Psychological Association.

Elliott, K. P., Westmacott, R., Hunsley, J., Rumstein-McKean, O., & Best, M. (2015). The process of seeking psychotherapy and its impact on therapy expectations and experiences. *Clinical Psychology & Psychotherapy, 22*(5), 399–408.

Fife, S. T., Whiting, J. B., Bradford, K., & Davis, S. (2014). The therapeutic pyramid: A common factors synthesis of techniques, alliance, and way of being. *Journal of Marital and Family Therapy, 40*(1), 20–33.

Fischer, A. R., Jerome, J. M., & Atkinson, D. R. (1998). Reconceptualizing multicultural counsel- ling: Universal healing conditions in a culturally specific context. *Counseling Psychologist, 26*.

Frank, J. D. (1973). *Persuasion and healing: A comparative study of psychotherapy (Rev. ed.)*. Oxford, England: Schocken.

Gallagher, L. P., & Truglio-Londrigan, M. (2004). Community support: Older adults' perceptions. *Clinical Nursing Research, 13*(1), 3–23.

Goldfried, M. R., & Padawer, W. (1982). Current status and future directions in psychotherapy. *Converging Themes in Psychotherapy*, 3–49.

Gone, J. P. (2015). Reconciling evidence-based practice and cultural competence in mental health services: Introduction to a special issue. *Transcultural Psychiatry, 52*(2), 139–149.

Grencavage, L. M., & Norcross, J. C. (1990). Where are the commonalities among the therapeutic common factors? *Professional Psychology: Research and Practice, 21*(5), 372.

Hayes, J. A., McAleavey, A. A., Castonguay, L. G., & Locke, B. D. (2016). Psychotherapists' outcomes with white and racial/ethnic minority clients: First, the good news. *Journal of Counseling Psychology, 63*(3), 261.

Helms, J. E. (1984). Toward a theoretical explanation of the effects of race on counseling a black and white model. *The Counseling Psychologist, 12*(4), 153–165.

Helms, J. E. (1990). *Black and white racial identity: Theory, research, and practice*. Westport, CN: Greenwood Press.

Helms, J. E. (1995). An update of Helm's White and people of color racial identity models. In J. G. Ponterotto, J. M. Casas, L. A. Suzuki, & C. M. Alexander (Eds.), *Handbook of multicultural counseling* (pp. 181–198). Thousand Oaks, CA: Sage Publications.

Isaacs, M. R., Huang, L. N., Hernandez, M., & Echo-Hawk, H. (2005). *The road to evidence: The intersection of evidence-based practices and cultural competence in children's mental health*. Report of the National Alliance of Multi-ethnic Behavioral Health Associations.

Jacobson, N. S., & Truax, P. (1991). Clinical significance: A statistical approach to defining meaningful change in psychotherapy research. *Journal of Consulting and Clinical Psychology, 59*(1), 12.

Kaplan, A. (2017). *The conduct of inquiry: Methodology for behavioural science*. London: Routledge.

Kennedy-Martin, T., Curtis, S., Faries, D., Robinson, S., & Johnston, J. (2015). A literature review on the representativeness of randomized controlled trial samples and implications for the external validity of trial results. *Trials, 16*(1), 495.

Kim, G., Dautovich, N., Ford, K. L., Jimenez, D. E., Cook, B., Allman, R. M., & Parmelee, P. (2017). Geographic variation in mental health care disparities among racially/ethnically diverse adults with psychiatric disorders. *Social Psychiatry and Psychiatric Epidemiology, 52*(8), 939–948.

Ladany, N., Brittan-Powell, C. S., & Pannu, R. K. (1997). The influence of supervisory racial identity interaction and racial matching on the supervisory working alliance and supervisee multicultural competence. *Counselor Education and Supervision, 36*(4), 284–304.

Lambert, Michael J. (1992). Psychotherapy outcome research: Implications for integrative and eclectic therapists. In J. C. Norcross & M. R. Goldfried (Eds.), *Handbook of psychotherapy integration* (1st ed., pp. 94–129). New York, NY: Basic Books. ISBN 0465028799. OCLC 25547822.

Laska, K. M., & Wampold, B. E. (2014). Ten things to remember about common factor theory. *Psychotherapy, 51*(4), 519–524.

Levitt, H. M. (2015). Qualitative psychotherapy research: The journey so far and future directions. *Psychotherapy, 52*(1), 31.

Lieb, K., von der Osten-Sacken, J., Stoffers-Winterling, J., Reiss, N., & Barth, J. (2016). Conflicts of interest and spin in reviews of psychological therapies: A systematic review. *BMJ Open, 6*(4), e010606.

Lieberman, R., Zubritsky, C., Martinez, K., Massey, O., Fisher, S., Kramer, T., . . . Obrochta, C. (2010). *Issue brief: Using practice-based evidence to complement evidence-based practice in children's behavioral health.* Atlanta, GA: ICF Macro, Outcomes Roundtable for Children and Families.

Lilienfeld, S. O., McKay, D., & Hollon, S. D. (2018). Why randomised controlled trials of psychological treatments are still essential. *The Lancet Psychiatry, 5*(7), 536–538.

Moodley, R., & Sunderani, S. (2015). Diversity in counseling and psychotherapy. *The Beginner's Guide to Counseling & Psychotherapy,* 387.

Mulder, R., Singh, A. B., Hamilton, A., Das, P., Outhred, T., Morris, G., . . . Lyndon, B. (2018). The limitations of using randomised controlled trials as a basis for developing treatment guidelines. *Evidence-Based Mental Health, 21*(1), 4–6.

Neville, H. A., & Mobley, M. (2001). Social identities in contexts: An ecological model of multicultural counseling psychology processes. *The Counseling Psychologist, 29*(4), 471–486.

Norcross, J. C., & Wampold, B. E. (2011). What works for whom: Tailoring psychotherapy to the person. *Journal of Clinical Psychology, 67*(2), 127–132.

Olfson, M., Druss, B. G., & Marcus, S. C. (2015). Trends in mental health care among children and adolescents. *New England Journal of Medicine, 372*(21), 2029–2038.

Orlinsky, D. E., Grawe, K., & Parks, B. K. (1994). Process and outcome in psychotherapy: Noch einmal. In A. E. Bergin & S. L. Garfield (Eds.), *Handbook of psychotherapy and behavior change* (pp. 270–376). Oxford, England: John Wiley & Sons.

Orlinsky, D. E., & Howard, K. I. (1986). The psychological interior of psychotherapy: Explorations with the Therapy Session Reports. In L. S. Greenberg & W. M. Pinsof (Eds.), *Guilford clinical psychology and psychotherapy series. The psychotherapeutic process: A research handbook* (pp. 477–501). New York, NY, US: Guilford Press.

Pascual-Leone, A., Paivio, S., & Harrington, S. (2016). Emotion in psychotherapy: An experiential–humanistic perspective. In D. J. Cain, K. Keenan, & S. Rubin (Eds.), *Humanistic psychotherapies: Handbook of research and practice* (pp. 147–181). Washington, DC, US: American Psychological Association.

Patterson, C. L., Anderson, T., & Wei, C. (2014). Clients' pretreatment role expectations, the therapeutic alliance, and clinical outcomes in outpatient therapy. *Journal of Clinical Psychology, 70*(7), 673–680.

Persons, J. B., & Silberschatz, G. (1998). Are results of randomized controlled trials useful to psychotherapists? *Journal of Consulting and Clinical Psychology, 66*(1), 126.

Prochaska, J. O., & DiClemente, C. C. (2005). The transtheoretical approach. *Handbook of Psychotherapy Integration, 2*, 147–171.

Quintana, S. M., & Atkinson, D. R. (2002). A multicultural perspective on principles of empirically supported interventions. *The Counseling Psychologist, 30*(2), 281–291.

Robinson, B. A., Winiarski, D. A., Brennan, P. A., Foster, S. L., Cunningham, P. B., & Whitmore, E. A. (2015). Social context, parental monitoring, and multisystemic therapy outcomes. *Psychotherapy, 52*(1), 103.

Sparks, J. A., Duncan, B. L., & Miller, S. D. (2008). Common factors in psychotherapy. In J. L. Lebow (Ed.), *Twenty-first century psychotherapies: Contemporary approaches to theory and practice* (pp. 453–497). Hoboken, NJ: John Wiley & Sons Inc.

Stam, H. J. (2013). Theoretical psychology. In *Encyclopedia of sciences and religions* (pp. 2259–2262). Dordrecht, Netherlands: Springer.

Stuart, E. A., Bradshaw, C. P., & Leaf, P. J. (2015). Assessing the generalizability of randomized trial results to target populations. *Prevention Science, 16*(3), 475–485.

Sue, D. W., & Sue, D. (2003). *Counseling the culturally diverse: Theory and practice* (4th ed.). New York, NY: John Wiley & Sons, Inc.

Szmrecsanyi, B. (2015). Recontextualizing language complexity. *Change of Paradigms-New Paradoxes: Recontextualizing Language and Linguistics*, 347–360.

Tao, K. W., Owen, J., Pace, B. T., & Imel, Z. E. (2015). A meta-analysis of multicultural competencies and psychotherapy process and outcome. *Journal of Counseling Psychology, 62*(3), 337.

Turner, F. J. (2017). *Social work treatment: Interlocking theoretical approaches*. Oxford: Oxford University Press.

Vogel, D. L., Wester, S. R., & Larson, L. M. (2007). Avoidance of counseling: Psychological factors that inhibit seeking help. *Journal of Counseling & Development, 85*(4), 410–422.

Wampold, B. E. (2001). *The great psychotherapy debate: Models, methods, and findings*. Mahwah, NJ: Lawrence Erlbaum.

Watkins, T. A. (2017). *"We Don't Talk about That": Mental health promotion by parents in African American communities* (Doctoral dissertation).

Weiss, L. A., Westerhof, G. J., & Bohlmeijer, E. T. (2016). Can we increase psychological well-being? The effects of interventions on psychological well-being: A meta-analysis of randomized controlled trials. *PloS One, 11*(6), e0158092.

Discussion Questions

1. What does cultural sensitivity mean to you? In what ways does the concept apply to counseling and psychotherapy theory and practice? Are there limits to cultural equivalence? For example, can psychodynamic concepts of ego and transference be used, if appropriately recontextualized, with clients who are not white males?

2. Using the common factors framework, what theory or theories of change can you construct for yourself? What has been an effective process for your own personal change? Could this process apply to others? If so, what are the limits of generalizability? Why?

3. How could you assist a client in constructing and using their own experience and expertise as a guide, a theory of change that makes sense for them? Is this necessary? Does it need to be made explicit? If the "theory" is yours and not shared explicitly, is this problematic?

5

SOCIAL DETERMINANTS

In this chapter, the interconnections between social issues and personal mental health are described. There are a small but impactful number of social determinants that distinguish groups with more frequent and serious mental health challenges. These factors include lack of emotional/social support, financial strain, discrimination, loneliness, social status, older age and more negative life events. Because mental health disparities are heavily influenced by social inequity, government policy and action play an important role in its resolution.

Why are social determinants relevant to professional counseling and psychotherapy?

- There is a great deal of evidence about population level factors associated with individual health status. Social conditions are profound forces on mental health. Each of us exists in relation to these conditions.
- Each of us makes choices in relation to the conditions of life. These decisions may be deliberate or automatic, conscious or preconscious. They are based on perceived and evident opportunities. In response to challenging circumstances, combinations of adapting to, resisting, accepting and changing circumstances may be pursued.
- Choices are as much sociopolitical as psychotherapeutic (e.g. the demands of a racist landlord). Sociopolitical choices are, however, not typically attended to in psychotherapy but could be (e.g. making a human rights complaint). A sociopolitical choice would, similarly to a psychotherapeutic act, draw upon personal and cultural strengths, taking energy and effort from which some benefit is derived.
- What we believe about the influence of social determinants affects what we view to be the problem. The problem may be the context, the relationship to it

or the perception of it. Some problems brought to therapy may well be adaptive responses to an inequitable society. Typically, counseling and psychotherapy begin with viewing the problem as an individual's unhealthy response to a healthy or unalterable society. From an AO perspective, change in the person, society and relationship between person and community are viable options.

Chapter Outline

Determinants of Health

Contemporary public health has its origins in the sanitary campaigns of the nineteenth century (Stone, 1979). This period of increasing urbanization and poverty co-occurred with the spread of disease (Richardson, 2017). Science found that a lack of hygiene caused and transmitted disease (Prüss-Üstün & Neira, 2016). Sanitation was necessary to improve conditions. Public health offered a scientific basis for social influence and political decisions regarding which problems were caused by which factors and how those would be addressed through social hygiene measures (Irwin & Scali, 2007). Community-based health programs began to develop in the 1960s and 1970s, in part in response to growing awareness that top-down medication approaches were not helping those who were the most in need (Shediac-Rizkallah & Bone, 1998).

Social determinants of health offer a view of population-level forces associated with varied health outcomes. Shared factors (Rosenfield, 1985) underlying the creation of social determinants were that: social aspects of health were of fundamental importance, a welfare approach to development was necessary, the participation of communities in health decisions was necessary, universal coverage to increase equity was essential, and making connections between sectors was the way forward. In 1986, the First National Conference on Health Promotion was organized by the World Health Organization (Baum, 2016). From this event, the

Ottawa Charter was drafted (Gagné & Lapalme, 2017). The Charter is an international agreement about the social causes of illness. The "fundamental drivers of these conditions include unequal distributions of power, money and resources" (Marmot & Bell, 2012, p. S7).

According to the World Health Organization (2015), social determinants of health are "the conditions in which people are born, grow, work, live and age, and the wider set of forces and systems shaping the conditions of daily life". According to the National Academies of Sciences, Engineering, and Medicine (2017), there are nine areas that have a major influence on health disparities. These areas include early childhood development, educational achievement, employment, occupation, food security, access to quality health care, affordable housing and income. Finally, the degrees of discrimination faced and social support held also determine health.

Social determinants influence population and individual health in several ways (Barer, 2017). One prominent means is the transmission of resources that meet basic physical and social needs. For example, low income is associated with food insecurity and inadequate nutrition. Another prominent view is that the lack of met needs causes stress that is health-damaging. For example, housing vulnerability because of family poverty is a source of stress for parents. A third view is that the determinants affect choices and opportunities and also form barriers to positive changes in behavior, which accumulate negative effects over time (Whitehead, Judge, & Benzeval, 1995). For example, poor nutrition during the prenatal period, infancy and early childhood contribute to educational challenges, early leaving and low job prospects.

Routes through which social determinants operate may be latent, pathway or cumulative transmissions in nature (Hertzman, 2012). **Latent transmission** refers to the appearance of risk at a particularly sensitive time in development that has an effect later in life (e.g. prenatal exposure to alcohol and learning problems). **Pathway transmission** is the experience of a particular risk that places an individual on a particular trajectory (e.g. early school leaving and job choice). **Cumulative transmission** is a build-up over time of risks throughout experience that are a combination of latent and pathway outcomes (e.g. prenatal exposure, learning problems, early school leaving and economic disadvantage).

Two theories of disadvantage account for differential health status. These theories include **cultural/behavioral** and **materialist/structuralist** views (Petersen, 1990). From a cultural/behavioral perspective, individual decisions determine health. Poor health, from this view, is a personal choice. Groups of people who face poor health share the unhealthy decisions. From a materialist/structuralist perspective, the distribution of necessary resources determines health. Living conditions and the availability of resources in those conditions directly contribute to health by deprivation or excess. Also, self-perceptions relative to those with greater access to necessary resources that are negative determine health.

Health disparities are heavily influenced by unequal opportunities (Braveman & Gruskin, 2003). Inequality is embedded within the conditions of life and therefore invokes the need for equity. Policies and programs need to address fundamental issues such as employment, education and income. The degree to which disparities are addressed in public policy (legislation that affects social equality) and social norms (cultural biases, public opinions) are important forces on group as well as personal health (Phelan, Link, & Tehranifar, 2010).

The role of government, as a site of formal public policy, varies considerably (Jacobs & Mettler, 2018) There have been studies of population health in relation to inequity and state sponsored intervention (Mackenbach et al., 2008). However, it is not clear which types are the most effective to promote equity (Bergqvist, Yngwe, & Lundberg, 2013). In one comparative study of unemployment policies and benefits, higher benefits were associated with better health, but only when coverage was already relatively high (Alber, 2017). This result suggests a more universalized approach to provision is more effective for improving health (Lundberg, Yngwe, Bergqvist, & Sjoberg, 2016). The notion of a "welfare state" represents a package of social programs that government may provide or delegate in accordance with public policy. Application of the concept of "welfare state" reflects degrees and types of large-scale social investment (Morel, Palier, & Palme, 2012).

Welfare State

The welfare state may be defined as a program of coordinated efforts by government to intervene in the social and economic lives of citizens to enforce a minimum standard quality of life (Ringen, 2017). Development of the welfare state in North America followed from the challenges of Great Depression with measures meant to build upon the economic momentum fueled by World War II (Porter, 2005). While it has been argued that the German welfare state was undertaken to build a nation state and the Canadian welfare state was built upon the British model in the postwar period, the United States came closest to a welfare state during its Great Society reforms of the 1960s (Ferrera & Rhodes, 2013).

Otto von Bismarck (1815–1898), German Chancellor, created a system of government supports for members of the working class to prevent their migration to the US in the nineteenth century. At the time, laborers were leaving for America with the promise of better wages. The introduction of accident and unemployment insurance made the relatively lesser wages in Germany more attractive because of the social benefits (Streeck & Trampusch, 2005). The development of social programs was not intended to make legislative changes that undermined economic development but rather to offset some potential risks to workers. The purpose was also not to flatten the hierarchically arranged society and its classes but rather to engender support of the working class to make the state stronger and resist change from other interests (Flora, 2017).

Franklin Roosevelt's (1882–1945) **New Deal reforms** in the mid-1930s represented the beginning of a welfare state in the United States (Sherraden & Gilbert, 2016). While the policies promoted capitalism and increased government power, their impact was diminished during WWII when there was a great deal of work (Skocpol, 1987). Old age pensions and widows' benefits, unemployment and disability insurance were added to respond to the social effects of soldiers returning from war.

In 1942 William Beveridge (1879–1973), a British economist, authored the *Social Insurance and Allied Services*. These were a series of reforms based on full employment and the intention of not allowing any citizen to fall below set minimum living standards. The measures were introduced to help industry by ensuring a productive workforce with benefits centralized in government and not paid by industry (Abel-Smith, 1992). The purpose was to promote fairness through legislation and government programs.

Leonard Marsh (1906–1983) was a student of Beveridge's at the London School of Economics. He moved to Canada in 1930 to work on major research projects out of McGill University. Following the release of the **Beveridge Report**, Prime Minister Mackenzie King (1874–1950) was eager to capitalize on the positive reception it had in Canada and hired Marsh to write a similar report for postwar reconstruction. The *Report on Social Security for Canada* was produced in 1943. It formed the basis of policies and programs that comprise the Canadian welfare state (Baker, 1997).

Great Society legislation of the 1960s by President Lyndon Johnson (1908–1973) was intended to address poverty and racial injustice (Zelizer, 2015). The series of reforms attended to civil rights and declared a "war on poverty", including changes to policy in education, health, welfare, cultural institutions, transportation, consumer protection, housing, rural development and labor (Schulman, 2001). In 1996, the Temporary Assistance to Needy Families legislation was passed, providing income support to single parents with children (Ziliak, 2015).

Values Underlying Types

Government programs designed to protect minimum standards and create equity provide a framework from which to identify problems and gaps as well as policy achievements. In a democracy, policies should reflect public opinion. The degree to which each of us identifies with a particular purpose and approach to government intervention influences the votes we cast (Vecchione et al., 2015). These values connect to actions in support of the society, its communities and its families as well as those we encounter directly in our psychotherapy work (Schwartz et al., 2014). It is important to recognize our personal values on these issues because of their connection to all aspects of our work with and on behalf of clients.

Major principles in public policy concern liberty, equality and solidarity (Saint-Arnaud & Bernard, 2003). They exist in tension with one another. More liberty is reflected in low market intervention, low social equality and sense of community. More equality is associated with the move to totalitarianism, limits to political freedom and the failure of community programs to involve residents. More solidarity moves toward ideological indoctrination, limiting freedom and separating those who control the movement from those who do not.

Welfare states can be characterized similarly by three types, including **social democratic**, **conservative** and **liberal** (Arts & Gelissen, 2002). In social democratic welfare state, the level of support is universal and generous. In a conservative welfare state, the support is general but focuses on males as primary income earners. In a liberal welfare state, support is modest and used as a last resort, for which access is means-tested.

	Ideology	Principle	Program Focus	Main Institution
Social democracy	equity	universal	resources	state
Liberalism	liberty	residual	needs	market
Conservatism	solidarity	insurance	risks	family

Using 2016 OECD Data, a comparison between benefits for a single parent with two children in Canada, the United States and the United Kingdom illustrates different orientations to support provision. In Canada, social benefits amount to about 50% of the average wage in the nation, of which 23% is social assistance, 5% is tax credits and 22% is family benefits. In the UK, social benefits amount to about 52% of the average wage, of which 11% is social assistance, 20% is housing benefits and 21% is family benefits. In the US, social benefits amount to about 23% of the average wage, where 11% is social assistance and 12% is family benefits. The UK and Canadian models emphasize the social democracy approach, while the United States reflects a more liberal approach to social welfare.

More generous social benefits result in less inequality (Raphael, 2006) between class, gender and racial groups. In a more progressive political climate, there is better public access to income and services, unions protect wages and conditions for workers and there is more even participation in elections (Allen, Balfour, Bell, & Marmot, 2014). **Neoliberal** policies, in contrast, promote inequality and weaken social institutions, cohesion and civil society (Giroux, 2018). For example, in Russia between 1992 and 2001, after the collapse of the Soviet Union, there were 2–3 million more deaths than expected resulting from to cardiovascular disease and injury due to high alcohol consumption (Uutela, 2010). In the European Union between 1970 and 2007, for every 1% rise in unemployment there was an 8% rise in suicides of the population under 65 years. In Spain and Sweden between 1980 and 2005, unemployment and increased suicides in Spain but not in Sweden because of its higher levels of labor market protection via social benefits (Schrecker & Bambra, 2015).

Social Determinants of Mental Wellness

Mental health includes both wellness and illness. One can simultaneously have illness as well as wellness. A deficit-oriented approach has as its goal the minimization of illness and its effects. A promotion-oriented approach has as its goal the maximization of wellness. In Canada, the development of the **positive mental health surveillance indicator framework** includes positive mental health factors (Orpana et al., 2016). Positive mental health is defined as self-rated mental health, happiness, life satisfaction, psychological well-being and social well-being.

Individual factors include self-rated mental health and presence of chronic conditions, healthy living/personal health practices, addiction, parent's prenatal health status, personality (i.e. self-esteem, sense of mastery, sense of coherence, optimism/pessimism, emotional intelligence, spirituality and religiosity), adverse childhood experiences and current stressful life. Family factors include parental contact and relationships, parental health and caring for family members.

Community factors include social support and social networks, such as interpersonal relationships, inclusion and belonging, school environment and school achievement or workplace characteristics/environment. Access to health services includes mental health services, neighborhood satisfaction and community connectedness and trust and safety (e.g. neighborhood safety/crime/violence). Societal factors include equality analysis in physical environment (i.e. built and natural environments, overcrowding, noise), politics and governance, laws and policies (e.g. victimization, discrimination) and culture and values.

Socioeconomic Status and Mental Illness

According to the World Health Organization and Calouste Gulbenkian Foundation (2014, p. 9), "many common mental disorders are shaped to a great extent by the social, economic, and physical environments in which people live".

There are associations between individual- and family-level factors and mental illness with the accumulation of adverse experiences leading to mental illness (Fisher & Baum, 2010). **Adverse experiences** and conditions build over time, and chronic repetitive stress system arousal is implicated in compromised mental health (Reuben et al., 2016). These experiences include low income, poor housing, low education, unemployment, demanding or low control work, abuse/neglect, unsafe neighborhood and low social support. These interact with individual vulnerabilities that vary with genetic contributions, childhood experiences, resources for management and current conditions of life (Bartolomucci et al., 2005).

Socioeconomic status refers to

> social standing, typically comprised of employment, education and income levels as well as illuminating inequities in resource access as well as issues of power, control and privilege . . . associated with greater threat to personal

mental health via lower levels of trust and diminished status as well as unemployment, increased risk of experience with trauma, isolation and discrimination.

(American Psychological Association, 2018)

There are three theories that explain the connections between income inequality and mental illness (Layte, 2011). These theories include **social capital, status anxiety** and **neo-materialism**. According to social capital theory, the greater the social inequality, the greater the social segregation. Increased segregation leads to decreased social capital, which is associated with less trust, less collective action, less support and less respect. Research in support of this theory finds that nations with low average incomes and high inequality have higher rates of traumatic events and psychological distress (Myer et al., 2009). Low social capital and traumatic events occur more frequently among those with low SES and social support, and distress is more often reported among those with the lowest social capital and SES. Unemployment is associated with isolation, depression and suicide and has the greatest effects on those already disadvantaged (Uutela, 2010). Unemployment has particularly isolating effects on five demographic groups: male manual workers, single moms, women who are primary earners, manual workers without unemployment benefits (men and women) (Puig-Barrachina, Malmusi, Martínez, & Benach, 2011).

According to status anxiety theory, it is the response of individuals to their position in the power hierarchy with stress, shame, distrust that is associated with personal problems. Research in support of this theory finds that the more inequality within a nation, the greater the status anxiety (Pickett & Wilkinson, 2010). There are more mental health problems in more unequal nations because of greater status competition and status insecurity, creating conditions of chronic stress that activate biological stress processes and accumulate to compromise both physical and mental health. Low interpersonal and political trust are associated with psychological distress. It has been found that in conditions of relative economic hardship, political and interpersonal trust are separately associated with psychological distress and together offer better predictive ability (Ahnquist, Wamala, & Lindstrom, 2012).

According to neo-materialist theory, income inequality differentially affects the value of possessions within one's reach. Those at the top can buy most anything available to purchase, while those at the bottom cannot. A line of research in support of this theory is associated with limited options. Fewer options exist among those with lower SES and those choices are less optimal (Compton & Shim, 2015). Mental health service access is determined by SES and insurance status relative to race (Carson, Cook, & Alegría, 2010).

Social Determinants of Depression

Mental disorder variance between nations suggests social determinants have a great deal of influence. Depression rates are associated with gender, education and income.

There has been attention to the effects of differential exposure to stressful life events, which is far more common for some groups (Rosenquist, Fowler, & Christakis, 2011). Such events and experiences include discrimination, poor land, bad working conditions, neighborhood instability, crime, food and overcrowding (Wilkinson & Marmot, 2003). Differential vulnerability has also been explored and includes poor physical health, being a young adult and ethnicity (because of its overrepresentation in lower SES) (Mawani, 2008). Differential consequences of depression include effects on other health problems, other problems affecting depression and depression affecting treatment outcomes for other problems (Barnett & Gotlib, 1988).

Stigma

Stigma may be defined as "the co-occurrence of labeling, stereotyping, separation, status loss, and discrimination in a context in which power is exercised" (Hatzenbuehler, Phelan, & Link, 2013, p. 813). It encompasses several advantaged/ disadvantaged statuses and includes stereotyping, labeling and discrimination. Psychological effects are direct and synergistic on **concealment** and **rejection sensitivity**. Stigma also moderates efficacy of psychological interventions and has multiple adverse health outcomes (Hatzenbuehler, 2016). Major personal effects include **social isolation** and **social discrimination**. **Social distance** refers to willingness to have ranging levels of relationships with those affected with whatever condition or quality is stigmatized. High social distance is associated with fear. Low social distance is associated with familiarity (Van Lente et al., 2012). Wellness, in contrast, is associated with low loneliness and high social support (Bell, Thorpe & LaVeist, 2010).

It has been argued that stigma is a cause of the social determinants of mental health. (Hatzenbuehler et al., 2013). **Structural stigma** is expressed through a variety of mechanisms but is also responsive to public policy. It has been defined as "societal-level conditions, cultural norms, and institutional policies that constrain the opportunities, resources, and well-being of the stigmatized" (Hatzenbuehler, 2014, p. 2). There are two ways to consider the effects of public policy on those who are affected by stigma. The first of these is the degree to which policies specifically identify and include members of these groups in a way that is protective or supportive. The second is the degree to which members of these groups are excluded and ignored. The effect of this approach is to render group members as less important, valued, worthy and deserving of support. This devaluation is a stance that supports the avoidance of policy change that would address those needs and is strongly in support of the status quo (Link & Hatzenbuehler, 2016).

Conclusion

Health status is influenced by social conditions. Disadvantaged status compromises health and mental wellness. Social programs make a substantial difference through their equalizing effects. However, government involvement in social welfare is largely a matter of belief and power. Political values that promote social equality also support social investment and programs. Such decisions influence the circumstances of life. This context puts limits on opportunities and constrains choices, leading to an accumulation of negative life experiences and stress, which cause or exacerbate the effects of mental illness. Socioeconomic status has a profound influence on individual mental health. Studies of depression identify social contributors. Finally, stigma itself may be considered a social determinant of mental health.

Web Links

From Opium to Opioids: A Look at British Columbia's Illicit Drug History
http://toronto.citynews.ca/2017/04/13/from-opium-to-opioids-examining-british-columbias-long-history-with-drugs/

Mental Health: The New Frontier for the Welfare State
www.youtube.com/watch?v=fDE45HqcX2A

How Economic Inequality Harms Societies | Richard Wilkinson
www.youtube.com/watch?v=cZ7LzE3u7Bw

Key Terms

Ottawa Charter   82
Latent transmission   82
Pathway transmission   82
Cumulative transmission   82
Cultural/behavioral   82
Materialist/structuralist   82
Health disparities   82
New Deal reforms   83
Beveridge Report   84
Great Society legislation   84
Social democratic   85
Conservative   85
Liberal   85
Neoliberal   85
Positive mental health surveillance indicator framework   86
Adverse experiences   86
Socioeconomic status   86
Social capital   87
Status anxiety   87
Neo-materialism   87

References

Abel-Smith, B. (1992). The Beveridge report: Its origins and outcomes. *International Social Security Review, 45*(1–2), 5–16.

Ahnquist, J., Wamala, S. P., & Lindstrom, M. (2012). Social determinants of health—a question of social or economic capital? Interaction effects of socioeconomic factors on health outcomes. *Social Science & Medicine, 74*(6), 930–939.

Alber, J. (2017). Government responses to the challenge of unemployment: The development of unemployment insurance in Western Europe. In *Development of welfare states in Europe and America* (pp. 151–184). London: Routledge.

Allen, J., Balfour, R., Bell, R., & Marmot, M. (2014). Social determinants of mental health. *International Review of Psychiatry, 26*(4), 392–407.

American Psychological Association. (2018). *Office on socioeconomic status*. Retrieved from www.apa.org/pi/ses/resources/index.aspx

Arts, W., & Gelissen, J. (2002). Three worlds of welfare capitalism or more? A state-of-the-art report. *Journal of European Social Policy, 12*(2), 137–158.

Baker, M. (1997). *The restructuring of the Canadian welfare state: Ideology and policy* (No. 0077). Kensington, Australia: University of New South Wales, Social Policy Research Centre.

Barer, M. (Ed.). (2017). *Why are some people healthy and others not?* London: Routledge.

Barnett, P. A., & Gotlib, I. H. (1988). Psychosocial functioning and depression: Distinguishing among antecedents, concomitants, and consequences. *Psychological Bulletin, 104*(1), 97.

Bartolomucci, A., Palanza, P., Sacerdote, P., Panerai, A. E., Sgoifo, A., Dantzer, R., & Parmigiani, S. (2005). Social factors and individual vulnerability to chronic stress exposure. *Neuroscience & Biobehavioral Reviews, 29*(1), 67–81.

Baum, F. (2016). *The new public health* (4th ed.). Oxford: Oxford University Press.

Bell, C. N., Thorpe, R. J., & LaVeist, T. A. (2010). Race/ethnicity and hypertension: The role of social support. *American Journal of Hypertension, 23*(5), 534–540.

Benzeval, M., Judge, K., & Whitehead, M. (1995). *Tackling inequalities in health: An agenda for action* (p. xxi). London: King's Fund.

Bergqvist K, Yngwe MA, & Lundberg O. (2013). Understanding the role of welfare state characteristics for health and inequalities—an analytical review. *BMC Public Health, 27*(13), 1234.

Braveman, P., & Gruskin, S. (2003). Defining equity in health. *Journal of Epidemiology & Community Health, 57*(4), 254–258.

Carson, N., Cook, B., & Alegría, M. (2010). Social determinants of mental health treatment among Haitian, African American and white youth in community health centers. *Journal of Health Care for the Poor and Underserved, 21*(2 Suppl), 32.

Compton, M. T., & Shim, R. S. (2015). The social determinants of mental health. *Focus, 13*(4), 419–425.

Ferrera, M., & Rhodes, M. (2013). *Recasting European welfare states*. London: Routledge.

Fisher, M., & Baum, F. (2010). The social determinants of mental health: implications for research and health promotion. *Australian and New Zealand Journal of Psychiatry, 44*(12), 1057–1063.

Flora, P. (2017). *Development of welfare states in Europe and America*. London: Routledge.

Gagné, T., & Lapalme, J. (2017). 1986: Ottawa and onwards. *The Lancet Public Health, 2*(2), e71.

Giroux, H. A. (2018). *Terror of neoliberalism: Authoritarianism and the eclipse of democracy*. London: Routledge.

Hatzenbuehler, M. L. (2014). Structural stigma and the health of lesbian, gay, and bisexual populations. *Current Directions in Psychological Science, 23*(2), 127–132.

Hatzenbuehler, M. L. (2016). Structural stigma: Research evidence and implications for psychological science. *American Psychologist, 71*(8), 742.

Hatzenbuehler, M. L., Phelan, J. C., & Link, B. G. (2013, May). *American Journal of Public Health, 103*(5), 813–821.

Hertzman, C. (2012). Putting the concept of biological embedding in historical perspective. *Proceedings of the National Academy of Sciences, 109*(S2), 17160–17167.

Irwin, A., & Scali, E. (2007). Action on the social determinants of health: A historical perspective. *Global Public Health, 2*(3), 235–256. doi:10.1080/17441690601106304

Jacobs, L. R., & Mettler, S. (2018). When and how new policy creates new politics: Examining the feedback effects of the affordable care act on public opinion. *Perspectives on Politics, 16*(2), 345–363.

Layte, R. (2011). The association between income inequality and mental health: Testing status anxiety, social capital, and neo-materialist explanations. *European Sociological Review*, jcr012.

Link, B., & Hatzenbuehler, M. L. (2016). Stigma as an unrecognized determinant of population health: Research and policy implications. *Journal of Health Politics, Policy and Law, 41*(4), 653–673.

Lundberg, O., Yngwe, M. Å., Bergqvist, K., & Sjoberg, O. (2016).

Mackenbach, J. P., Stirbu, I., Roskam, A. J. R., Schaap, M. M., Menvielle, G., Leinsalu, M., & Kunst, A. E. (2008). Socioeconomic inequalities in health in 22 European countries. *New England Journal of Medicine, 358*(23), 2468–2481.

Marmot, M., & Bell, R. (2012). Fair society, healthy lives. *Public Health, 126*, S4–S10.

Mawani, F. N. (2008). Social determinants of depression among immigrant and refugee women. *Working with Immigrant Women: Issues and Strategies for Mental Health Professionals*, 67–87.

Morel, N., Palier, B., & Palme, J. (Eds.). (2012). *Towards a social investment welfare state? Ideas, policies and challenges*. Chicago, IL: Policy Press.

Myers, H. F. (2009). Ethnicity-and socio-economic status-related stresses in context: An integrative review and conceptual model. *Journal of Behavioral Medicine, 32*(1), 9–19.

National Academies of Sciences, Engineering, and Medicine. (2017). *Communities in action: Pathways to health equity*. New York: National Academies Press.

OEDC. (2016). *OEDC Family database*. Retrieved from November 11, 2018, from http://www.oecd.org/els/family/database.htm

Orpana, H., Vachon, J., Dykxhoorn, J., McRae, L., & Jayaraman, G. (2016). Monitoring positive mental health and its determinants in Canada: The development of the positive mental health surveillance indicator framework. *Health Promotion and Chronic Disease Prevention in Canada: Research, Policy and Practice, 36*(1), 1.

Petersen, P. E. (1990). Social inequalities in dental health. *Community Dentistry and Oral Epidemiology, 18*(3), 153–158.

Phelan, J. C., Link, B. G., & Tehranifar, P. (2010). Social conditions as fundamental causes of health inequalities: Theory, evidence, and policy implications. *Journal of Health and Social Behavior, 51*(S1), S28–S40.

Pickett, K. E., & Wilkinson, R. G. (2010). Inequality: An underacknowledged source of mental illness and distress. *The British Journal of Psychiatry, 197*(6), 426–428.

Porter, D. (2005). *Health, civilization and the state: A history of public health from ancient to modern times.* London: Routledge.

Prüss-Üstün, A., & Neira, M. (2016). *Preventing disease through healthy environments: A global assessment of the burden of disease from environmental risks.* Geneva: World Health Organization.

Puig-Barrachina, V., Malmusi, D., Martínez, J. M., & Benach, J. (2011). Monitoring social determinants of health inequalities: The impact of unemployment among vulnerable groups. *International Journal of Health Services, 41*(3), 459–482.

Raphael, D. (2006). Social determinants of health: Present status, unanswered questions, and future directions. *International Journal of Health Services, 36*(4), 651–677.

Reuben, A., Moffitt, T. E., Caspi, A., Belsky, D. W., Harrington, H., Schroeder, F., . . . Danese, A. (2016). Lest we forget: Comparing retrospective and prospective assessments of adverse childhood experiences in the prediction of adult health. *Journal of Child Psychology and Psychiatry, 57*(10), 1103–1112.

Richardson, J. P. (2017). *"The most complete experiment in army hygiene": British military reform in sanitation from the Crimea to India, a comparative account of sanitary reform in the 19th century.* Canterbury, NZ: University of Catnerbury.

Ringen, S. (2017). *The possibility of politics: A study in the political economy of the welfare state.* London: Routledge.

Rosenfield, P. L. (1985). *The contribution of social and political factors to good health.* New York: The Rockefeller Foundation.

Rosenquist, J. N., Fowler, J. H., & Christakis, N. A. (2011). Social network determinants of depression. *Molecular Psychiatry, 16*(3), 273.

Saint-Arnaud, S., & Bernard, P. (2003). Convergence or resilience? A hierarchical cluster analysis of the welfare regimes in advanced countries. *Current Sociology, 51*(5), 499–527.

Schrecker, T., & Bambra, C. (2015). *How politics makes us sick: Neoliberal epidemics.* New York: Springer.

Schulman, B. J. (2001). *The seventies: The great shift in American culture, society, and politics.* New York: Simon and Schuster.

Schwartz, S. H., Caprara, G. V., Vecchione, M., Bain, P., Bianchi, G., Caprara, M. G., . . . Mamali, C. (2014). Basic personal values underlie and give coherence to political values: A cross national study in 15 countries. *Political Behavior, 36*(4), 899–930.

Shediac-Rizkallah, M. C., & Bone, L. R. (1998). Planning for the sustainability of community-based health programs: Conceptual frameworks and future directions for research, practice and policy. *Health Education Research, 13*(1), 87–108.

Sherraden, M., & Gilbert, N. (2016). *Assets and the poor: New American welfare policy.* London: Routledge.

Skocpol, T. (1987). America's incomplete welfare state: The limits of new deal reforms and the origins of the present crisis. *Stagnation and Renewal in Social Policy: The Rise and Fall of Policy Regimes,* 35–58.

Stone, M. N. (1979). The plumbing paradox: American attitudes toward late nineteenth-century domestic sanitary arrangements. *Winterthur Portfolio, 14*(3), 283–309.

Streeck, W., & Trampusch, C. (2005). Economic reform and the political economy of the German welfare state. *German Politics, 14*(2), 174–195.

Uutela, A. (2010). Economic crisis and mental health. *Current Opinion in Psychiatry, 23*(2), 127–130.

Van Lente, E., Barry, M. M., Molcho, M., Morgan, K., Watson, D., Harrington, J., & McGee, H. (2012). Measuring population mental health and social well-being. *International Journal of Public Health, 57*(2), 421–430.

Vecchione, M., Schwartz, S. H., Caprara, G. V., Schoen, H., Cieciuch, J., Silvester, J., . . . Mamali, C. (2015). Personal values and political activism: A cross-national study. *British Journal of Psychology, 106*(1), 84–106.

Whitehead, M., Judge, K., & Benzeval, M. (Eds.). (1995). *Tackling inequalities in health: An agenda for action*. London: King's Fund Centre.

Wilkinson, R. G., & Marmot, M. (Eds.). (2003). *Social determinants of health: The solid facts*. Geneva: World Health Organization.

World Health Organization. (2015). *World report on ageing and health*. New York: World Health Organization.

World Health Organization and Calouste Gulbenkian Foundation. (2014). *Social determinants of mental health*. Geneva: World Health Organization, 2014.

Zelizer, J. E. (2015). *The fierce urgency of now: Lyndon Johnson, congress, and the battle for the Great Society*. New York: Penguin.

Ziliak, J. P. (2015). *Temporary assistance for needy families* (No. w21038). Washington, DC: National Bureau of Economic Research.

Discussion Questions

1. Which positive mental health factors can you identify for yourself at individual, family, community and society levels? In what ways have they had positive effects? Are there factors that you can address within your work with clients, as a professional and as a citizen?

2. What political ideology or ideologies do you most strongly value? How does this connect with your professional practice? Are the connections explicit? Could the values conflict with the values of your profession or clients?

3. In what ways can social investment assist the efforts of counselors and psychotherapists to promote mental health and manage illness? In what ways does it run counter to our efforts? How could that change?

6

ASSESSMENT FOR PERSONAL CHANGE

In this chapter, the emphasis is on identity and its development, as well as its imposition or claim by counselors, psychotherapists and clients. Typically, assessment focuses on intrapsychic deficits that have a biological or psychological origin as well as on their course and potential to change. From an anti-oppressive perspective, the emphasis is on social location of self. Categories of difference coexist, intersect and interact as well as modify over time among therapists and clients. Experiences of oppression occur through institutionalized and implicit messages about identities as well as traumatic events. Oppression may also be appropriated, allowing one to identify with a privileged group. Experiences of privilege are rarely challenged but are a source of relevant clinical content because of the limitations on experience. In this chapter, an AO perspective on assessment is offered to supplement and broaden existing practice. Considerations about problems, causes and solutions, internal and external attribution and personal and community resolution are offered.

What is an AO perspective on assessment and why is it valuable?

- Traditionally, assessment is a series of observations and judgments about a client. Questions and observations by the counselor and psychotherapist to the following are emphasized: What is the problem? Why does it exist? What is the way forward?
- Typically, the practitioner and profession determine what is identified and how it is interpreted. This includes whether and which instruments are used, criteria for their judgments, conclusions and recommendations that follow. From an AO perspective, the therapist's power is explicit and, as a result, carries with it a heightened level of responsibility for its use and representation.

- Professional decision-making is influenced by personal and professional assumptions, expectations and past experience. Professional training teaches customs (such as acceptable practices), standards (including professional and workplace rules) and guidelines (such as ethical principles). From an AO perspective, self-understanding and awareness about what is important leads to a more accurate understanding of a client's experiences of privilege and oppression.
- Privilege does not guarantee a good life, happiness or well-being. However, it carries substantial psychological (as well as other) advantages. For example, it takes a lot less mental, emotional, social and political energy and effort to carry out the activities of daily living, let alone processing and addressing problematic symptoms, than for anyone who is not similarly privileged. For those of the majority and dominant culture, there is obvious consistency between sense of self and messages of "normal" (i.e. frequent) and "appropriate" (i.e. customary). As a result, privilege offers a less demanding and more forgiving existence as well as a clear and attainable path forward.
- Oppression is the weight of accumulated mental, emotional, social and political forces resulting from membership in a group other than the dominant majority. Group membership does matter. In counseling and psychotherapy, identity reflects a sense of self, roles, expectations and affiliations as well as an indicator of relative starting point and trajectory.
- An AO perspective requires awareness about one's own identities and being a professional within webs of privilege and oppression. Clients are also recognized in general as self-defining people within webs of oppression and privilege. Finally, it is essential to recognize privilege and oppression as interacting forces, with absolute and relative effects on opportunities and outcomes for each client.

Chapter Outline

Identity and Development

Identity is a product of interaction between the person and their social world (Schmitz & Tyler, 2018). Social forces are historical and contemporary and include the meaning of unchangeable as well as changeable features that are chosen or prescribed within a particular context (Galliher, McLean, & Syed, 2017). Major aspects of identity are located in societal functions—usually expected by others—and the internal expectations of self-including categories (e.g. Black or white) and roles (e.g. student and teacher), with different connections to psychological outcomes (e.g. emotion in these relationships—e.g. when self-verification fails) (Syed, 2017). **Group identity** provides a reference point for comparison of self as well as a sense of comfort, belonging and support (Hogg & Terry, 2014). Membership influences individuals through modeling and reinforcement of attitudes and behaviors.

Several models of identity development are in use. These models center on racial, ethnic and sociopolitical identities. Major conceptualizations include Cross' People of Color Racial Identity Model, Nadal's Filipino American Identity Development, Berry's Ethnic Minority Identity Development, Poston's Biracial Identity Development, Helms' White Racial Identity Model, Renn's Identity Patterns approach, Sellers' Multidimensional Model and finally, Crenshaw's Intersectional approach.

The **People of Color Racial Identity Model** (Cross, 1985) of identity development includes five stages: pre-encounter, encounter, immersion/emersion, internalization and internalization/commitment. In **pre-encounter**, there is a distancing from one's own race to connect with others of the majority race. In **encounter**, there is the awareness that being one of the majority race is not possible and realization that is affected by racism. In **immersion/emersion**, symbols of one's own race and distance from the majority race are pursued. In **internalization**, a secure racial identity forms a basis from which one can connect with others from the majority race. Finally, in **internalization/ commitment**, a plan for action as well as recognition of race as one way, and not the only way, of understanding difference are evidenced.

Nadal's **Filipino American Identity Development** is an ethnicity-based view of identity and change over time (2004). It includes six stages: awareness, assimilation, social political awakening, pan-ethnic Asian American consciousness, ethnocentric realization and incorporation. In **awareness**, there is a very partial view of Filipino culture because it is all one has been exposed to. **Assimilation** to a dominant culture is a preference for values and customs of the dominant culture over traditional ones. **Social political awakening** marks growing awareness of racial oppression and identification with Filipino culture. In **pan-ethnic Asian American consciousness**, there is an affiliation with other Asian Americans for organization and power. **Ethnocentric realization** is recognition that one is not only Asian American and that the label itself has limits. Finally, in **incorporation**, identity is no longer about existing in relation to the mainstream but in having pride in one's own culture.

Ethnic Minority Identity Development (Berry, 1993) is a description of four acculturation strategies by those who identify as members of a non-dominant culture. In **assimilation**, an individual withdraws from traditional culture to identify with the host culture. In **separation**, one maintains traditional culture and rejects the host culture. In **marginalization**, the individual rejects both traditional and host cultures. **Integration** is where an individual recognizes identity as a combination of traditional and host cultures.

Biracial Identity Development (Poston, 1990) includes five distinct stages. These stages include personal identity, choice of group characterization, enmeshment/denial, appreciation and integration. One's **personal identity** is a product of early life influences, including friends, family and media representations. **Choice of group characterization** occurs due to pressure to select one ethnic or racial group above another. **Enmeshment/denial** is a response to guilt over leaving one group out of personal identity. In this stage, the individual chooses both and denies differences between them. In **appreciation**, one begins to appreciate the group that has had limited emphasis on in earlier stages and becomes more connected to it. Finally, **integration** is when an individual can still identify primarily with one race or ethnicity as well as appreciate how the individual is part of another ethnic or racial identity.

In the **White Racial Identity Model** (Helms, 1990), two main stages are **Abandonment of Racism** and **Defining a Non-Racist White Identity**. There are three sub-stages within each. In Abandonment of Racism, one begins to understand the salience of race and its relevance to power. In this stage, a person moves through **contact** (i.e. no sense of sociopolitical context of race), **disintegration** (i.e. seeing racism in self or witnessing it in others) and **reintegration** (i.e. returning to pro-white attitudes to deal with dissonance). In Evolution of a Non-Racist Identity, one begins to "be white without also being bad, evil, or racist" (Helms, 1992, p. 61). The sub-stages include **pseudo-independence** (i.e. motivated but limited awareness and paternalistic), **immersion/emersion** (i.e. finding a meaningful meaning for whiteness) and **autonomy** (i.e. accepting whiteness and part played in racial oppression).

Identity Patterns (Renn, 2000) is based on studies with biracial and multiracial postsecondary students in the US. Different profiles were revealed, including mono-racial, multiple mono-racial, multiracial, extra-racial and situational. **Mono-racial** identity is a choice of one background to identify with. **Multiple mono-racial** identities refer to different identifications depending on what one is doing and with whom. **Multiracial identity** is a blend of the ethnic compositions into something "new". **Extra-racial identity** is based on a rejection of the racial identity idea because of its social construction and origins in dominant, European history. **Situational identity** is a sense of identity that is more fluid with different aspects more or less salient in different contexts.

In the **Multidimensional Model** (Sellers et al., 1998), salience, centrality, regard and ideology reflect the nature and degree of personal connection to racial identity and values about diversity. **Racial salience** refers to the degree to which racial identity is important to self-concept at a time and place. **Racial centrality** is the degree to which racial identity is important to self-image. **Racial regard** is one's regard for their own race, both public (e.g. how others view people of my racial identity) and private (e.g. how I feel about my own racial identity). **Racial ideology** refers to how people of the same race should act, including **nationalist** (i.e. us and them, we cannot live in harmony because of differences), **oppressed minority** (i.e. the same forces that oppress my group have oppressed other groups as well), **assimilation** (i.e. degree to which working with the system to achieve economic and political goals is desirable/possible) and **humanist** (i.e. people of my own racial identity have much in common with members of the dominant race).

Intersectionality was named by Kimberle Crenshaw (1988). Her analysis illustrates how race, class and gender interact and affect the ways that women of color experience oppression. For example, at times a woman of color may have similar experiences oppression as men of color such as overrepresentation in justice system (McIntosh & McQueen, 2018). At other times she may have experiences of oppression as a woman of color such as race-based sterilization (Kirkup, 2018). The latter condition is **double discrimination** (Cole, 2009). Categories of difference can be added, including age, class, (dis)ability, sexual orientations and religion. Each includes a form of oppression, with privileged and disadvantaged statuses corresponding with differential experiences (see Table 6.1).

TABLE 6.1 Oppression and Privilege

	Gender	Race	Ethnicity	Age	Class	Ability	Sexuality	Religion
Form of oppression	sexism	racism	ethnocentrism	ageism	classism	ableism	heterosexism	exclusivism
Privileged status	masculine	white	European	young	upper and middle class	without disability	heterosexual	Christian
Diminished status	feminine	non-white	non-European	old	working and lower class	with disability	LGBTQ2+	non-Christian
Contributed to by …	unjust treatment, fear, sadness, anger, loss, superiority and 'right', vilification and condemnation, colonization, imperialism, genocide and eugenics							
Rationalized by …	being 'less than', 'deficient', 'incomplete', 'weak', 'unnatural', 'immoral', 'savage'							
Evidenced by …	exclusion, exploitation, dismissal, ownership, rape, murder							

In addition to intersectionality, shifting contexts (Harper & Schneider, 2003) and internalized and externalized identities (Madigan, 1996) exemplify how the same person may be oppressed in some contexts and privileged in others.

Identities can be complex. They have personal meanings as well as social statuses. They can be useful as well as potentially problematic. Errors that clinicians can make fall into several categories, including overgeneralizing, essentializing, pathologizing and assimilationism (Shin, 2015). In **overgeneralizing**, an identity category is used to homogenize members of a particular group. **Essentializing** refers to the potential for culture-based theories and practices to reinforce the hierarchies of difference they are meant to challenge. **Pathologizing** refers to an equation of 'different' with 'pathological'. **Assimilationism** refers to a perception that one who is different than the dominant group has a goal of becoming like the dominant group (Shin, 2015).

Privilege and Oppression

Privilege may be defined as "any entitlement, sanction, power, immunity, and advantage or right granted or conferred by the dominant group to a person or group solely by birthright membership in prescribed identities" (Black & Stone, 2005, p. 245). Privilege is responsible for oppression, and oppression allows privilege to continue. The two are inseparable as co-dependent structural forces (Bell & Adams, 2016).

Those who experience oppression know very well about its effects. There is a long history of social action undertaken by a range of groups and collectives to express and advance their social power in the interests of political change. While those who have experienced oppression know about privilege, many with privilege have little understanding of oppression (Branscombe, Schmitt, & Schiffhauer, 2007). Three processes that permit privilege to maintain itself are normalcy, neutrality and "the other".

One way that privilege reinforces itself is through self-definition as **natural** (Cappellari, 2016). That is, what is dominant is typical, expected and idealized. These qualities are represented in images of success and embodiment of values, beliefs and traditions based on the views of a group of people who are in positions of power. An extension of this is reflected in social norms, economic processes and political opportunities as "natural" according to the views of those who promote them (Herrera, 2017). These patterns are produced by those who have the greatest influence to advance their interests. Because for many the status quo is the way things are, there is a tendency to work within it, accept it and believe that it is not only normal but natural.

Another way that privilege reinforces itself is through the portrayal of **neutrality** (Parker, 2015). The scientific method is a foundation of psychology and its applications. It produces results that have tremendous social value. However, it cannot claim moral or political neutrality. Psychology, as it is studied and practiced in the United States and Canada, draws heavily from a Euro-American, positivist, natural science approach, based on measurable units with evidence from replicated studies of behavior (Naidoo, 1996). In research, "truth" may be a product of scientific deduction (e.g. quantitative research methods) as well as constructivist induction (e.g. qualitative research methods). It should, however, never be conflated with what is "right".

Finally, "**the other**" refers to a judgment elevating self over other (Challis, 2017). Differentiating and distancing are necessary in counseling and psychotherapy to maintain appropriate boundaries. However, devaluing of another is highly problematic (Avdi, 2017). This may be expressed in a perception that self is the standard by which others are defined and therefore treated with the justification that such use is "for the good" of "the other" (Grey, 2016). Devaluing is rooted in fear. It is based on a judgment by a dominant culture of whether one does or does not belong.

Challenging Privilege

Why would someone confront their own privilege? In addition to **moral obligation** (Crimston, Hornsey, Bain, & Bastian, 2018) and **social responsibility** (Walsh, 2015), one might consider the benefits of experience and expression as opportunities for growth. For example, men who have to be stereotypically "masculine" miss out on emotionality, caring and gentility. As they let go of the beliefs about what a man must be, they can become more open to influence, more willing to listen and more egalitarian in their relationships. Professionals who draw on knowledge based exclusively in Western ideas miss out on the wisdom of other psychologies and healing traditions from other cultures.

Because many of us hold both privilege and disadvantage, there are opportunities to challenge oppression from a privileged position (Shin, Ezeofor, Smith, Welch, & Goodrich, 2016). Awareness, as a first step toward change, is generated through consciousness raising. Development of a critical consciousness (Sidanius & Pratto, 2003) includes recognition of **individual** (e.g. attitudes and beliefs that devalue a social group may be conscious and preconscious, active and passive), **sociocultural** (e.g. norms, rituals, music, art, language support the belief that one group is superior) and **institutional** (e.g. laws, customs lead to differential access to resources and outcomes accepted by most as "the way things are") layers (see Kirby, 2016).

Challenging a privileged identity is difficult (Estrada, Singh, & Harper, 2017). Resistance to challenge often invokes defensiveness, avoidance and aggressiveness. Reception to challenge begins with awareness. Awareness usually leads to discomfort and distress and invokes guilt and shame, sadness and anger.

Institutionalized Oppression

Oppression is expressed and psychologically experienced through institutionalized oppression, personal experiences that cause distress and affect mental health and an internalization of stereotypes and negative messages.

Institutions are stable arrangements in education, health, justice and social services, as well as in governments and the media. Institutionalized oppression refers to the systematic mistreatment of a social identity group. "**Institutionalized oppression** creates a system of invisible barriers limiting people based on their membership in unfavored social identity groups. The barriers are only invisible to those 'seemingly' unaffected by it" (Tri-County Domestic and Sexual Violence Intervention Network, 2018).

Institutionalized oppression is evident in policies. For example, overrepresentation in justice systems is an often-cited example. On June 14, 2018, it was reported in a national Canadian newspaper that "Nearly half of youth incarcerated across Canada are Indigenous: Statistics Canada" (Malone, 2018). Several federal holidays in the United States are markers of colonization (i.e. Columbus Day) and Christian faith (i.e. Christmas and Thanksgiving). In Canada, several holidays are Christian, including Christmas, Thanksgiving, Good Friday and Easter Monday.

Other examples of institutionalized oppression include practices that are less obvious but powerful in the human services. For example, expecting members of oppressed groups to teach privileged groups about oppressive behaviors (Garran, Aymer, Gelman, & Miller, 2015); privileged groups not taking responsibility for learning how actions rooted in privilege cause harm (Trepagnier, 2017); assuming that white staff can meet the needs of all people, but staff of color can only meet the needs of other people of color; "redevelopment" of urban neighborhoods, making them unaffordable for low income residents who had been living there; graduation rate differentials by race, ethnicity, ability and class; and gender differences in income for the same work.

Institutionalized oppression can also be created through political whim. President Donald Trump announced on June 20, 2018 that the federal government of the United States would no longer separate children from their parents at the Mexico border. This came as images of the approximately 2,000 detained children, including crying and distressed infants, drew widespread media attention. This coverage of the consequences of his "zero-tolerance" immigration policy to prosecute every individual who crosses the border illegally led the president of the American Academy of Pediatrics two days earlier to publicly state that this policy amounted to child abuse (Kraft, 2018). Criticism also came from high-profile members of the Republican party, including Laura Bush, wife of former President George W. Bush, who wrote that "these images are eerily reminiscent of the Japanese American internment camps of World War II, now considered to have been one of the most shameful episodes in US history" (2018).

Discrimination and Traumatic Effects

Survey questions measuring two types of discrimination illustrate effects of this form of oppression. The questions used in this survey were adapted from the

Everyday Discrimination Scale and Major Experiences of Discrimination Scale (Williams, 2016). As you read them, consider your own responses. Consider the responses of others you know. What psychological effects would you expect from these experiences? Would fear be one of them?

Q1: In your day-to-day life, how often have any of the following things happened to you?

- *You are treated with less courtesy or respect than other people.*
- *You receive poorer service than other people at restaurants or stores.*
- *People act as if they think you are not smart.*
- *People act as if they are afraid of you.*
- *You are threatened or harassed.*

Frequency:

- never
- less than once a year
- a few times a year
- a few times a month
- at least once a week
- almost everyday

Q2: In the following questions, we are interested in the way other people have treated you or your *beliefs* about how other people have treated you. Can you tell me if *any* of the following has ever happened to you:

- *Have you ever been unfairly fired from a job?*
- *Have you ever been unfairly denied a promotion?*
- *For unfair reasons, have you ever not been hired for a job?*
- *Have you ever been unfairly stopped, searched, questioned, physically threatened or abused by the police?*
- *Have you ever been unfairly discouraged by a teacher or advisor from continuing your education?*
- *Have you ever been unfairly prevented from moving into a neighborhood because the landlord or a realtor refused to sell or rent you a house or apartment?*
- *Have you ever moved into a neighborhood where neighbors made life difficult for you or your family?*
- *Have you ever been treated unfairly when receiving health care?*
- *Have you ever been treated unfairly while using transportation (e.g. buses, taxis, trains, at an airport, etc.)?*

Traumatic effects are increasingly recognized as outcomes of institutional policies and practices as well as discriminatory interpersonal encounters. Trauma occurs as a psychological response to "actual or threatened death, serious injury, or sexual violence" (Center for Substance Abuse Treatment, 2014, p. 7). It can occur through direct exposure, witnessing an event experienced by another or learning about such an event to another. Trauma response symptoms can also result from direct and devastating ethnic or cultural events, vicarious experience or events that are witnessed and micro-aggressions that bring on memories of personal or group trauma that were felt as threatening to life or mental health (Helms, Nicolas, & Green, 2010). Indeed, overlap between experiences of rape victims and victims of racism includes a similar dissociation/shock reaction preventing functional response, as well as a feeling of shame or self-blame for not responding (Janson & Hazler, 2004).

Race-based traumatic injury is a non-pathological accumulation of and reaction to racism stress (Carter, 2007). It is necessary for only the victim and no one else to perceive the event as traumatic (Andrews et al., 2015). Forms of racism stress include avoidance or ostracizing, hostile physical or verbal assaults, harassment and aversive aggression (Polanco-Roman, Danies, & Anglin, 2016). Acute effects include intrusion, avoidance, mood difficulties and arousal. **Intrusions** may be troubling memories, dreams, feeling like events are occurring again, distress when in the presence of cues to the event or physiological reactions. **Avoidance** is trying not to think of/feel/experience it and avoiding reminders. **Mood** difficulties may appear as inability to recall specific aspects of event, negative beliefs about self, distorted beliefs about cause and consequences, persistent emotional state, loss of interest, becoming detached or estranged from others or difficulty experiencing positive feelings. **Arousal** can appear as irritability, recklessness, hypervigilance, exaggerated startle responses and sleep problems. Vulnerability to experiencing trauma is compounded by a disadvantaged social location. Disadvantage is associated with distrust of systems, constant risk and living underground (e.g. who it is safe to tell what) (Keane, Magee, & Kelly, 2016).

Intergenerational trauma is the cumulative psychological wounding of a community. It was initiated with Holocaust survivors in the 1960s seeking treatment in Canada, from which the term "**survivor syndrome**" emerged (Wiseman, Metzl, & Barber, 2006). The grandchildren of survivors were highly overrepresented in clinical samples. Among Indigenous peoples in Canada, there has been attention to the psychological effects of colonial history and the impact of residential schools, where children were removed from their families and communities and placed in European-style classrooms (Quinn, 2007). The parents, their children and communities suffered these effects.

Insidious trauma is not overt or threatening to one's body but violates the spirit and soul of those affected (Root, 1992). Violence against women is high and the effects of feeling unsafe that occur because of it are effects of insidious trauma. Women experience objectification, which is a form of gender-based discrimination, including unwanted advances and body shaming experiences (Brinol, Petty, & Belding, 2017). In some cases, individuals who do not have a trauma history may experience traumatic effects, such as hypervigilance or a numbing out response (Miles-McLean et al., 2015).

Invisibility Syndrome is defined as an inner struggle with the feeling that one's talents, abilities, personality and worth are not valued or even recognized because of prejudice and racism (Franklin, 1999, p. 761). There are seven characteristics of visibility: recognition, satisfaction, validation, legitimacy, respect, dignity and identity (Dowden, Gunby, Warren, & Boston, 2014). Absence renders the individual invisible.

Appropriated Oppression

Appropriated oppression refers to the mastery of judgments that are oppressive to one's own identity while privileging the dominant or majority culture. Appropriated oppression is problematic when it infuses self-perception based on efforts to identify with a privileged group and share in its status with separation of self from membership in a group with an oppressed position (Campón & Carter, 2015). There are five dimensions of appropriated oppression: appropriate negative beliefs, thinking that reinforces negative beliefs, living by dominant group standards, minimizing oppressed groups and having unpleasant emotional reactions (Rangel, 2014).

The following scale is based on a four-factor model of racism associated with anxiety and depression (Rangel, 2014). Consider its relevance based in race, gender, ethnicity, class, ability, sex, family and religion differences. Modified items from the scale follow:

Emotional responses:

- There have been times when I have been embarrassed to be a member of my _____.
- When interacting with other members of my _____, I often feel like I don't fit in.
- I don't really identify with my _____ group's values and beliefs.

Standard of beauty:

- I find persons with/of _____ to be more attractive.
- I find people who don't have _____ to be more attractive.
- Good _____ is better.

Devaluation of own group:

- _____ are better at a lot of things than people of my _____.
- It is a compliment to be told "You don't act like a member of _____".
- I feel that being a member of my _____ group is a shortcoming.

Appropriation of negative stereotypes:

- People of my _____ shouldn't be so sensitive about _____ matters.
- People take _____ jokes too seriously.
- Discrimination is definitely overplayed by some members of my _____.

Each of these beliefs is associated with the placement of lesser value on self as a result of comparisons to an external source. When the references are heavily or exclusively outside of one's own identity and culture, they can weigh on mental health, offering the potential for relief or advancement through imitation.

Activity: Pre-Intake Self-Assessment

Consider the following sociopolitical, contextual and relational factors that inform decisions about problems, causes and solutions.

Identity

What are cultural factors that characterize and influence my sense of self, including self-definition of gender, race, ethnicity, age, class, ability, sexuality and religion? What identities do I claim? What identities do I allow others to give me a "pass" for? Which are privileged in some contexts and oppressed in others and vice versa? How do I handle privilege and oppression in these contexts?

Problem Definition

What is a problem? Is it pathological or non-pathological? What are the advantages and disadvantages to each? See Table 6.2.

What are the benefits and drawbacks of using universal categories of illness based on symptom frequency and duration that cause distress (e.g. DSM-V)? Is the problem better characterized as culturally bound (e.g. ghost sickness)? To what degree is this problem externally imposed (e.g. stress from housing discrimination)?

TABLE 6.2 Benefits and Drawbacks of Diagnosis

	Pros	Cons
Pathological	Formal psychiatric diagnosis	Deficit orientation
	Resource access	Psychobiological origin
	Accommodations	Define self with disorder
	Medication treatment	
Non-Pathological	Normalized	Limited access to health
	External causes formally	resources
	recognized	Limits on accommodations
	Holistic presentation	Potential to underreport severity
		Not medically treatable

Problem Causes

What is "normal"? Is "normal" important?

Purpose of the problem? (maladaptive or adaptive response?)

What does the existence of the problem mean? (informative? nuisance? predictive?)

Why does the problem exist? (internal, e.g. biology, personality, or external, e.g. political, social, economic?)

How much is client determined (by what) and free (to do what)?

How much responsibility for change is personal and collective?

What can the client change? What can others change? Which others?

What can I, as a professional, change?

Inequity Assessment

Assessment is a system of information collection and professional interpretation. It is used to make decisions about the problem and recommend intervention. Often, but not exclusively, the statement of the problem fits a type, category or diagnosis. Choice about the use of interview, observation or testing and test information depends on the purpose and setting. Standardized instruments require evidence to support validity for the particular client and purpose.

Assessment from an AO perspective includes additional considerations that may be applied to the process already in use within a setting. What is suggested is a supplement to the data collected and the way it is interpreted, to guide discussions about the extent to which social inequality constrains opportunities and outcomes as well as their psychological effects. The purpose of this supplement is to consider the impact of sociopolitical forces on the individual and, based on that determination, the degree to which the causes are attributable to personal as well as social forces. It is important that any determination about means and degree of potential for personal change is tempered by explicit recognition of social context and degree to which forces outside of the therapy room constrain a client's potential.

From an AO perspective, assessment and conceptualization include the perceived cause(s) and solution(s) to the problem, including the degree to which the contributors are internally and externally located and produced, as well as recognition that actions to address the problem exist at both personal and community levels. Factors that are relevant to such a determination include the nature of the problem, identity and stress and coping.

Problem Definition

When is something a problem? (e.g. client thinks it is a problem—others in the client's life think it is a problem—counselor thinks it is a problem)

When is something <u>not</u> a problem? (e.g. client doesn't think it is a problem—no one else in the client's life thinks it is a problem—counselor doesn't think it is a problem)

How does the counselor know? (e.g. judgments based in personal experience, engaged citizenship and professional knowledge)

Identities

What is your gender? race? ethnicity? age? education? occupation? sexual orientation? religion? Which are important to you? What makes them important?

Singular or multiple: separation = retain distinctions, intersectional = blending

- Reference groups

    - We all feel privileged in some contexts and disadvantaged in others. What about you as a (___, ___)? In public? In your community? In family? With friends? At work or school? Where do you feel "better than" other people? Where do you feel "equal to" other people? Where do you feel "less than" other people?
    - Where are you included and how? Where are you excluded and how?
    - What are your current and desired levels of engagement, interaction and self-worth?

- Migration history

    - international, national, regional
    - number of years, age, place of origin; stops and transitions
    - adjustment: assimilation, separation, integration, marginalization

Stress

Expectations

- Sociopolitical anxiety

    - What are (___, ___) expected to be like <u>in this society</u>?
    - What are (___, ___) expected to be like <u>in your community</u>?
    - What would you like to be?

- Sociopolitical roles

    - What are (___, ___) supposed to become?
    - How valued are they for their role?

- Sociopolitical regulation of choice (e.g. marriage)

    - What must (___, ___) do to "fit in"?

- Sociopolitical demanding performance (e.g. achieve)
  - What must (___, ___) succeed at?
- Sociopolitical limitations on expression (e.g. dress)
  - What must (___, ___) never do?

Discrimination

- Have you had any of the following experiences because of being a (___, ___) and how often:
  - less respect, poorer service, less courtesy, treated as not as intelligent, people are afraid of you, feel threatened or harassed
  - fired from a job unfairly, denied a promotion, stopped and searched or mistreated by police, discouraged from going on in school, denied a rental property or services of a realtor, neighbors who make it difficult for you and family

Trauma

- Have you experienced direct and devastating events as a (___, ___)?
- Have you witnessed or known someone who experienced direct and devastating events as a (___, ___)?
- Have you experienced smaller events as a (___, ___) that bring on memories of devastating events?
  - acute effects: intrusion, mood, arousal, vulnerability, disadvantage
  - complex effects: sense of self, emotion regulation, re-experiences, feelings about perpetrator, relationships with others, losing clarity, disconnecting or fear
  - delayed effects: oppression, stigmatization and discrimination—may be reflected in a single instance but oftentimes are the cumulative effect of such experiences

Coping

- Difference between how society sees you as a (___, ___) and
  - How you see yourself?
  - How you want to be seen?
- What do you do: resist, accept or ignore? How?
- What would you like to do: resist, accept or ignore? How?

Inequity Formulation

- Identities and reference groups

  - intersections and identifications
  - belongingness (reference groups, community, public)
  - empowerment (self-esteem, self-control, social influence)

- Salience of oppression and privilege

  - internal: beliefs in inferiority and superiority
  - relational: individuals and groups, connections and effects
  - external: societal and community forces as challenges and opportunities

- What client can change for self and others
- What others need to change for client and others

Conclusion

The concept of identity is both sociopolitical and personal. At a personal level, the identifications and intersections of identities are a combination of socially privileged or diminished statuses. From an AO perspective, the privileges as well as disadvantages of the therapist must be well understood. Such understanding situates therapy, the profession and identities within systems of institutionalized oppression. Both institutional oppression and discrimination are explored for their traumatic potential and effects. The existence of appropriated oppression and internalized judgments of self from a dominant cultural view are identified and addressed with a client. An inequality assessment can be used to supplement decision-making about the nature and effects of the problem faced as well as considerations about the locations of responsibility and actions that may be taken.

Web Links

Deconstructing White Privilege
www.youtube.com/watch?v=DwIx3KQer54

Understanding Intergenerational Trauma
www.coursera.org/lecture/aboriginal-education/3-6-interview-with-
    suzanne-stewart-on-intergenerational-trauma-part-1–10–38-fpKfi

Race-Based Trauma
www.youtube.com/watch?v=Xx-a-MDp4ng

Poster in B.C. Schools About White Privilege Hits Nerve With Some Parents www.ctvnews.ca/canada/poster-in-b-c-schools-about-white-privilege-hits-nerve-with-some-parents-1.3835619

'I Chose My Words Very Carefully': Face of Anti-Racism Billboard Responds to Backlash
www.cbc.ca/news/canada/saskatoon/billboard-racism-saskatoon-response-i-am-the-bridge-1.4190540

Canadian Schools Facing Blowback for 'White Privilege' Awareness Campaigns
http://nationalpost.com/news/canada/canadian-schools-facing-blowback-for-white-privilege-awareness-campaigns

Key Terms

Group identity   97
People of Color Racial Identity Model   97
Pre-encounter   97
Encounter   97
Immersion/emersion   97
Internalization   98
Internalization/commitment   98
Filipino American Identity Development   98
Awareness   98
Assimilation   98
Social political awakening   98
Pan-ethnic Asian American consciousness   98
Ethnocentric realization   98
Incorporation   98
Ethnic Minority Identity Development   98
Assimilation   98
Separation   98
Marginalization   98
Integration   98
Biracial Identity Development   98
Personal identity   98
Choice of group characterization   98
Enmeshment/denial   98
Appreciation   98
Integration   98
White Racial Identity Model   98
Abandonment of Racism   98
Evolution of a Non-Racist Identity   98
Contact   98
Disintegration   98

References

Andrews, A. R., Jobe-Shields, L., López, C. M., Metzger, I. W., de Arellano, M. A., Saunders, B., & Kilpatrick, D. G. (2015). Polyvictimization, income, and ethnic differences in trauma-related mental health during adolescence. *Social Psychiatry and Psychiatric Epidemiology, 50*(8), 1223–1234.

Avdi, E. (2017). *Psychology, mental health and distress*. London: Red Globe Press.

Bell, L. A., & Adams, M. (2016). Theoretical foundations for social justice education. In *Teaching for diversity and social justice* (pp. 21–44). London: Routledge.

Berry, J. W. (1993). Ethnic identity in plural societies. *Ethnic Identity: Formation and Transmission among Hispanics and other Minorities*, 271–296.

Black, L. L., & Stone, D. (2005). Expanding the definition of privilege: The concept of social privilege. *Journal of Multicultural Counseling and Development, 33*(4), 243–255.

Branscombe, N. R., Schmitt, M. T., & Schiffhauer, K. (2007). Racial attitudes in response to thoughts of white privilege. *European Journal of Social Psychology, 37*(2), 203–215.

Brinol, P., Petty, R. E., & Belding, J. (2017). Objectification of people and thoughts: An attitude change perspective. *British Journal of Social Psychology, 56*(2), 233–249.

Bush, L. (2018). *Separating children from their parents at the border "breaks my heart"*. Retrieved from www.washingtonpost.com/opinions/laura-bush-separating-children-from-their-parents-at-the-border-breaks-my-heart/2018/06/17/f2df517a-7287-11e8-9780-b1dd6a09b549_story.html?noredirect=on&utm_term=.67908f89c099

Campón, R. R., & Carter, R. T. (2015). The appropriated racial oppression scale: Development and preliminary validation. *Cultural Diversity and Ethnic Minority Psychology, 21*(4), 497.

Cappellari, L. (2016). *Income inequality and social origins*. Bonn, Germany: IZA World of Labor.

Center for Substance Abuse Treatment. (2014). *Trauma-informed care in behavioral health services*. Rockville, MD: Substance Abuse and Mental Health Services Administration.

Challis, E. (2017). *What can and cannot be said: Discourses of spirituality and religion in clinical psychology*.

Cole, E. R. (2009). Intersectionality and research in psychology. *American Psychologist. 64*(3), 170–180.

Crenshaw, K. W. (1988). Race, reform, and retrenchment: Transformation and legitimation in antidiscrimination law. *Harvard Law Review*, 1331–1387.

Crimston, D., Hornsey, M. J., Bain, P. G., & Bastian, B. (2018). Toward a psychology of moral expansiveness. *Current Directions in Psychological Science, 27*(1), 14–19.

Cross, W. E. (1985). Black identity: Rediscovering the distinction between personal identity and reference group orientation. *Beginnings: The Social and Affective Development of Black Children*, 155–171.

Dowden, A. R., Gunby, J. D., Warren, J. M., & Boston, Q. (2014). A phenomenological analysis of invisibility among African-American males: Implications for clinical practice and client retention. *The Professional Counselor, 4*(1), 58–70.

Estrada, D., Singh, A. A., & Harper, A. J. (2017). Becoming and ally: Personal, clinical and school-based social justice interventions. *Affirmative Counseling with LGBTQI+ People*, 343–358.

Franklin, A. J. (1999). Invisibility syndrome and racial identity development in psychotherapy and counseling African American men. *The Counseling Psychologist, 27*(6), 761–793.

Galliher, R. V., McLean, K. C., & Syed, M. (2017). An integrated developmental model for studying identity content in context. *Developmental Psychology, 53*(11), 2011.

Garran, A. M., Aymer, S., Gelman, C. R., & Miller, J. L. (2015). Team-teaching anti-oppression with diverse faculty: Challenges and opportunities. *Social Work Education, 34*(7), 799–814.

Grey, F. (2016). Benevolent othering: Speaking positively about mental health service users. *Philosophy, Psychiatry, & Psychology, 23*(3), 241–251.

Harper, G. W., & Schneider, M. (2003). Oppression and discrimination among lesbian, gay, bisexual, and transgendered people and communities: A challenge for community psychology. *American Journal of Community Psychology, 31*(3–4), 243–252.

Helms, J. E. (1990). *Black and white racial identity: Theory, research, and practice*. Winnipeg, MB: Greenwood Press.

Helms, J. E. (1992). *A race is a nice thing to have: A guide to being a white person or understanding the white persons in your life*. Topeka, Kansas: Content Communications.

Helms, J. E., Nicolas, G., & Green, C. E. (2010). Racism and ethnoviolence as trauma: Enhancing professional training. *Traumatology, 16*(4), 53.

Herrera, J. A. C. (2017). Inequality as determinant of the persistence of poverty. In *Poverty, inequality and policy*. Retrieved November 16, from https://www.intechopen.com/books/poverty-inequality-and-policy/inequality-as-determinant-of-the-persistence-of-poverty

Hogg, M. A., & Terry, D. J. (2014). *Social identity processes in organizational contexts*. London: Psychology Press.

Janson, G. R., & Hazler, R. J. (2004). Trauma reactions of bystanders and victims to repetitive abuse experiences. *Violence and Victims, 19*(2), 239.

Keane, C. A., Magee, C. A., & Kelly, P. J. (2016). Is there a complex trauma experience typology for Australians experiencing extreme social disadvantage and low housing stability? *Child Abuse & Neglect, 61*, 43–54.

Kirby, B. R. (2016). *Teacher to teacher: White culturally relevant educators' attempts to foster their White colleagues towards critical consciousness of race* (Doctoral dissertation), The University of Utah.

Kirkup. K. (2018). *Indigenous women coerced into sterilizations across Canada: Senator*. Retrieved November 16, from https://www.cbc.ca/news/politics/sterilization-indigenous-1.4902303

Kraft, C. (2018). *AAP statement on executive order on family separation*. Retrieved from www.aap.org/en-us/about-the-aap/aap-press-room/Pages/AAP-Statement-on-Executive-Order-on-Family-Separation.aspx

Madigan, S. (1996). The politics of identity: Considering community discourse in the externalizing of internalized problem conversations. *Journal of Systemic Therapies, 15*(1), 47–62.

Malone, K. (2018). *Nearly half of youth incarcerated across Canada are Indigenous: Statistics Canada*. Retrieved from www.theglobeandmail.com/canada/article-nearly-half-of-youth-incarcerated-across-canada-are-indigenous/

McIntosh, E., & McQueen, A. (2018). *Overrepresentation of Indigenous people in Canada's prisons persists amid drop in overall incarceration*. Retrieved November 16, from https://www.thestar.com/news/canada/2018/06/19/overrepresentation-of-indigenous-people-in-canadas-prisons-persists-amid-drop-in-overall-incarceration.html

Miles-McLean, H., Liss, M., Erchull, M. J., Robertson, C. M., Hagerman, C., Gnoleba, M. A., & Papp, L. J. (2015). "Stop looking at me!" interpersonal sexual objectification as a source of insidious trauma. *Psychology of Women Quarterly, 39*(3), 363–374.

Nadal, K. L. (2004). Pilipino American identity development model. *Journal of Multicultural Counseling and Development, 32*(1), 45–62.

Naidoo, A. V. (1996). Challenging the hegemony of Eurocentric psychology. *Journal of Community and Health Sciences, 2*(2), 9–16. Systems of Privilege: Intersections, Awareness, and Applications.

Parker, I. (2015). Towards critical psychotherapy and counselling: What can we learn from critical psychology (and Political Economy)? In *Critical psychotherapy, psychoanalysis and counselling* (pp. 41–52). London: Palgrave Macmillan.

Polanco-Roman, L., Danies, A., & Anglin, D. M. (2016). Racial discrimination as race-based trauma, coping strategies, and dissociative symptoms among emerging adults. *Psychological Trauma: Theory, Research, Practice, and Policy, 8*(5), 609.

Poston, W. C. (1990). The biracial identity development model: A needed addition. *Journal of Counseling & Development, 69*(2), 152–155.

Quinn, A. (2007). Reflections on intergenerational trauma: Healing as a critical intervention. *First Peoples Child & Family Review, 3*(4), 72–82.

Rangel, R. (2014). *The appropriated racial oppression scale development and initial validation.* New York: Columbia University.

Renn, K. A. (2000). Patterns of situational identity among biracial and multiracial college students. *The Review of Higher Education, 23*(4), 399–420.

Root, M. P. (1992). Reconstructing the impact of trauma on personality. *Personality and Psychopathology: Feminist Reappraisals*, 229–265.

Schmitz, R. M., & Tyler, K. A. (2018). LGBTQ+ young adults on the street and on campus: Identity as a product of social context. *Journal of Homosexuality, 65*(2), 197–223.

Sellers, R. M., Shelton, J. N., Cooke, D. Y., Chavous, T. M., Rowley, S. A. J., & Smith, M. A. A. (1998). Multidimensional model of racial identity: Assumptions, findings, and future directions. *African American Identity Development*, 275–299.

Shin, R. Q. (2015). The application of critical consciousness and intersectionality as tools for decolonizing racial/ethnic identity development models in the fields of counseling and psychology. In *Decolonizing "multicultural" counseling through social justice* (pp. 11–22). New York, NY: Springer.

Shin, R. Q., Ezeofor, I., Smith, L. C., Welch, J. C., & Goodrich, K. M. (2016). The development and validation of the Contemporary Critical Consciousness Measure. *Journal of Counseling Psychology, 63*(2), 210–223.

Sidanius, J., & Pratto, F. (2003). Social dominance theory and the dynamics of inequality: A reply to Schmitt, Branscombe, & Kappen and Wilson & Liu. *British Journal of Social Psychology, 42*(2), 207–213.

Syed, M. (2017). Identity integration across cultural transitions: Bridging individual and societal change. *Journal of Psychology in Africa, 27*(2), 105–114.

Trepagnier, B. (2017). *Silent racism: How well-meaning white people perpetuate the racial divide.* London: Routledge.

Tri-County Domestic and Sexual Violence Intervention Network. (2018). *Institutionalized oppression.* Retrieved from www.pcc.edu/illumination/wp-content/uploads/sites/54/2018/05/institutionalized-oppression-definitions.pdf

Walsh, R. T. (2015). Bending the arc of North American psychologists' moral universe toward communicative ethics and social justice. *Journal of Theoretical and Philosophical Psychology, 35*(2), 90.

Williams, C. (2016). *Measuring discrimination resource.* Retrieved from https://scholar.harvard.edu/files/davidrwilliams/files/measuring_discrimination_resource_june_2016.pdf

Wiseman, H., Metzl, E., & Barber, J. P. (2006). Anger, guilt, and intergenerational communication of trauma in the interpersonal narratives of second generation Holocaust survivors. *American Journal of Orthopsychiatry, 76*(2), 176.

Discussion Questions

1. How do you feel about the concept of white privilege? Do you believe that it has an effect on mental health? Why or why not? Can white privilege be used to address social inequality? How so?

2. Is depression following traumatic identity-based (e.g. hate crime) victimization a personal, relational and social problem? In what ways? Where does responsibility for the act lie? Where does responsibility for healing lie? What is the role of the therapist in such situations?

3. How do you characterize your own identities? In what ways do you have privilege and disadvantage? How can you use your own experiences of oppression and advantage therapeutically with clients who have experienced either or both?

7

INTERVENTION FOR PERSONAL CHANGE

In this chapter, connections between oppression and mental health are the basis for approaching individual change through critical consciousness. Critical consciousness is essential for both therapists and clients as a means of generating and maintaining insight into the nature and effects of structural forces on sense of self, with accepting and enhancing features for some and limiting and abusing features for others based on artificial social categories of difference. Critical consciousness is based on self-awareness within an unfair sociopolitical environment. Self-awareness may be enhanced through identity location and its development from acceptance to challenge and transformation.

Therapeutic efforts to enhance awareness can occur from the personal to structural and structural to personal. Using this perspective, the origin and outcomes of approaches to therapy may be considered. Traditional healing looks to the culture of origin for solutions to a culturally located problem. In contrast, western talk therapies emphasize discrete aspects of self with little attention to personal experience of an unjust context as contributors to the problems. Many additional culturally based assumptions are made (e.g. **individualism**). From an AO perspective, cultural assumptions are recognized, removing those that are problematic for the individual client. In addition, professionals are aware of their views concerning the purpose of counseling and psychotherapy in an unequal society.

Specific actions for personal change to address the psychopathology of oppression may be considered. Oppression is an external force that can become internalized and through that process lead to appropriated oppression. In addition, the experiences of oppression are located in hostile contexts and are stressful experiences that take an emotional toll on an individual. This understanding has implications for the therapeutic relationship, where sensitivity to degree of threat and control as well as emotional responses to disadvantage are important considerations. Anxiety and depression are clinical manifestations of these experiences.

What is an AO perspective on intervention?

- Traditionally, counseling and psychotherapy interventions are about client change. A question, "what creates the problem?", becomes answerable with "how does the client contribute to this problem?" Circumstances of the client's life are typically not evaluated or considered targets for change.
- From an AO perspective, additional questions may be asked by practitioners. Is the problem something they too have experienced? How do privilege and oppression play a role in its creation or maintenance? How does the problem manifest in the client's political, economic and social circumstances? What are the alterable contributors that operate outside of the client? What are the alterable contributors within the client and their immediate relationships?
- Intervention from an AO perspective may include individual, relational and community elements. Its purpose may be personal change or change to circumstances. Personal change is for the purpose of changing circumstances.
- An essential ingredient in counseling and psychotherapy from an AO perspective is critical consciousness. The extent to which this is integrated into the therapy depends on the therapist's level of personal and professional engagement in the practice. It is an ongoing, lifelong process. It requires openness to challenging one's own training and experience against limits of personal self-awareness.
- Critical consciousness provides analytic tools and methods to promote sensitivity of one's own oppression and privilege as well as processes of liberation. It is a commitment to constant evaluation of self in society, professionally and personally. It is a process, not a state, predicated on understanding one's own privilege and oppression as well as that of the client.

Chapter Outline

Oppression is the product of unjust political, economic and social structures and practices. It is a cause of mental illness and reduced well-being. From an AO perspective, harmful conditions and the potential for their reproduction within the therapy setting are considered. Critical consciousness is a fundamental means by which oppression may be identified and actions to challenge it taken. Therapists and clients may reach limits to personal change within conditions that cause, exacerbate and maintain the difficulties. Yet, without awareness of structural forces, content that ignores or denies the experience or impact of racism, sexism and other forms of disadvantage will be implicit or explicit. Additionally, structural forces embedded within the organization, therapy itself or professional therapist power imbalances between different groups may inhibit healthy change.

Critical Consciousness

Critical consciousness is as much a spiritual, moral and philosophical process as it is logical and emotional. It is about locating one's place in the cosmology as well as being accountable to self and others (Kumagai & Lypson, 2009). In *The Hungry Spirit*, Handy (2008) wrote

> capitalism (is) . . . a philosophy designed to deliver the means but not necessarily the point in life. Such redefinition would allow it to avoid the frequent criticism that communism had a cause for all—namely the liberation from poverty, the certainty of work, and a home for everyone—but no mechanism to deliver it, while capitalism had the mechanism, but a cause that only worked for a few.
>
> *(p. 59)*

Critical consciousness provides a means by which to promote mental health through mechanisms that challenge inequity.

Privilege and oppression are **primary, secondary** or **tertiary** contributors to personal and social problems. Structural inequality is created and maintained through norms, organizations, policies and individual behaviors. As noted by Freire (2000), critical consciousness is "the ability to perceive social, political, and economic contradictions and to take action against the oppressive elements of reality" (p. 35). It is the critiquing of beliefs and assumptions through the lens of social justice values, ideals and vision that makes consciousness *critical*. Mezirow (1981, p. 13) talks about "being aware of our awareness" of power and privilege.

Critical consciousness includes reflection, motivation and action. Existing measures of **critical reflection** (Thomas et al., 2014; McWhirter & McWhirter, 2016; Diemer, Rapa, Park, & Perry, 2017) focus on perceived inequality (e.g. critical awareness and analysis about inequities based on education and employment) and egalitarianism (e.g. equal treatment of all people would lead to fewer problems) and policies based on this idea. **Critical motivation** has been measured as agency (e.g. capable and motivated to make change happen). **Critical action** has been measured in behavior (e.g. responding to unfair interpersonal treatment) and sociopolitical participation (e.g. involvement in social action, groups that promote justice).

Development

Freire's stages of critical consciousness offer a progression for therapists and clients. There are five steps: naiveté, acceptance, naming and resistance, redefinition and reflection and multi-perspective integration (Freire, 1985). **Naiveté** is an unawareness of self as a cultural person, one's cultural identity as similar to and different from others. This corresponds to Freire's notion of **magical consciousness** (Roberts, 2016), which can be advanced through a description of experience. **Acceptance** is a state of early awareness of difference and lack of fairness that may be passive (i.e. business as usual) or active (i.e. active efforts to maintain the status quo between self and others). This corresponds with Freire's notion of **naive consciousness** (Freire, 1998), which can be nudged forward through contradicting experiences with contextual issues. **Naming and resistance** includes a labeling of the differences between identities and their relative status in society. For Freire, this is the beginning of critical consciousness, which can be promoted by an examination of and reflection on contradictions, resulting in anger. **Redefinition and reflection** is the explicit attention to the sociopolitical hierarchies with situation of self that can be encouraged through emotional pride in self and culture as well as an examination of self-in-relation. **Multi-perspective integration** is where it is possible to view the societal context as well as personal identities and the relationships between the two.

Efforts to promote critical consciousness among youth for therapeutic purposes follow a similar progression across five stages: acritical, adaptive, pre-critical, critical and liberation (Watts, Williams, & Jagers, 2003). In the **acritical** stage, either nothing is wrong or what is wrong is people's own fault. In the **adaptive** stage, there is inequality, but it cannot be changed, so one must take matters into one's own hands to get a fair share. In the **pre-critical** stage, one is starting to question whether the system can change. In the **critical** stage, there is an openness to learning about oppression and injustice, liberation and equity. It is concluded that social change is warranted. In **liberation**, one sees oppression and liberation. Liberation actions are pursued.

Activity: Connecting the Personal and Structural

From a structural view, mental health may be understood as a subject. Questions for exploration may include: What makes people healthy? What makes people unwell? Recognition of differences may be promoted through questions about reasons underlying differences. For example: Why are some people healthier than others? Personalizing the issues may further develop an awareness, with such questions as: What happens in your family that makes some more or less well than others? What happens in your community? Nation?

Identities and their intersections may be identified. For example, what kinds of people have an easier time being successful? What kinds of people have the hardest time being successful? Do you think that some people have more chances in life than others? Who are they? Are you the same or different than those people? How so? Why do some people have more life chances than others? Why do some people have fewer life chances than others?

Considering the categories of gender, sexuality, race, ethnicity, age, class, ability and religion, who, within each, are the socially privileged and the socially disadvantaged? Who among us has better life chances? Worse life chances?

Why does this occur?

Messages from television, advertisements, news and treatment in hospital, restaurant, stores?

Politics (who is elected, who votes, what policies/laws/rules, what programs for who)?

Social (who we (don't) hang out with, who is in the neighborhood, things we do with other people)?

Economic (how people dress, talk, what things they have (or not), school, job, money)?

Where do you see yourself within the categories? Which apply? Which do not? In which other ways do you see your own privilege or disadvantage relative to others (Table 7.1)?

To further explore social identity and social location, several questions may be asked (Kosutic et al., 2009). What are your markers of social advantage and disadvantage? How have you experienced or benefitted from others' marginalization? What has it been like to be the oppressor and the oppressed in a particular context? What messages did you receive about your social identity growing up, as an adult? How do you feel about interacting with those who have similar identities? What about those with different identities? What pride or shame experiences do you have with your identities? Which are easier/more difficult to "own"? How do migration and colonization experiences affect identities?

TABLE 7.1 Social Advantage and Disadvantage

	Gender	Race	Ethnicity	Age	Class	Ability	Sexuality	Religion	??	??
Advantage										
Disadvantage										

Theories of Psychotherapy

Psychotherapy is a political venture (Schmid, 2012). "Psychotherapy as politics means realizing the prevailing conditions, the established political culture (polity), in order to stand up for our image of the human being with its values (policy) in an appropriate and adequate way (politics), aiming at a change of the political culture (policy)". From an AO perspective, the sociopolitical context is always a contributor to personal, familial and community health. The degree to which emphasis is placed on the need for change by the individual, family or community is a fundamental determination.

Theories of counseling and psychotherapy offer a range of methods for promoting or restoring mental health. As presented in Chapter 4, the techniques matter less than the confidence and comfort of the therapist and client in a process. The cultural power of healing is immense. It is essential to recognize the great value of culturally based and traditional healing, how these may replace or complement counseling and psychotherapy practice and how to collaborate or refer as appropriate.

Theories can be grouped into three broad types: problem-solving, empowerment and social change (Payne, 2015). In **problem-solving** (psychodynamic, systems, ecological, cognitive behavioral) theories, the emphasis is on the individual to challenge the self in relation to an oppressive force within or outside. In **empowerment** (humanist, strengths, narratives) theories, the emphasis is on building the self in relation to an oppressive force within or outside. In **social change** (critical, feminist, anti-discriminatory) theories, the emphasis is on mobilizing the self in relation to an oppressive external force. Each has a place in practice from an AO perspective because each offers a means by which personal healing takes place and confronts external challenges.

A comparative analysis of humanism, existentialism, behaviorism and psychoanalysis highlights some differences and similarities in assumptions (Hurley, 2010). These therapies may be recast to consider the individual as well as the context, discrete aspects of self as well as its wholeness, our uniqueness as well as commonalities and pursuit of personal as well as social change (Tateo & Marsico, 2013).

Humanism is based on **symbolic interactionism** and focuses on the meaning created through interpersonal interactions, while **existentialism** is based theoretically on existential philosophies and authenticity created through exercise of choice. While both place the needs of the individual above the needs of society and put great emphasis on free will, humanism is overt in focus while existentialism is covert in focus.

Behaviorism is rooted in **positivism** and focuses on stimulus or behavior and response, while in **psychoanalysis**, the basis is in **structural determinism** and the focus is on insight into unconscious forces. While both are **deterministic**

views, behaviorism is overt and places society above the individual, while psychoanalysis is covert and places the individual above the needs of society.

A humanistic criticism of behaviorism is that it focuses only on mechanics, that existentialism misses the importance of being together and that psychoanalysis is highly constraining. An existential criticism of behaviorism is that it views people in mechanistic terms, that humanism misses the importance of personal responsibility and that psychoanalysis does not see authenticity. A behavioral critique of humanism is that there is no basis in science, that existentialism is far too mystical and that psychodynamic practitioners fail to notice what is obvious. Psychoanalytic criticism of behaviorism is that it is superficial, that humanism is naive, and that existentialism misses the point.

Activity: Beliefs About Counseling and Psychotherapy

What are motives for practicing counseling and psychotherapy?

(e.g. personal experiences of marginalization, painful childhood, psychological mindedness, being a confidant to others, having a mentor, having been in therapy, a need to help others, wanting to understand others, wanting safe intimacy, intellectual stimulation, self-growth and healing)

What is the purpose of counseling and psychotherapy?

- Less sick? More well?
- Contribute to economy?
- Perform a role? Be yourself?
- Individualize? Conform?
- Personal expression? Harmonious relationships?
- Self-actualize? Serve others?
- Accept? Avoid? Change?

What contributes to the problem?

- Childhood experiences?
- Irrational thoughts?
- Personal meaning?
- Family or community life?
- Socioeconomic or political context?

Mechanisms of change?

- Social action?
- Personal insight?
- Positive consequences?
- Belonging?

How do we know what helps?

- Evidence?
- Feel better?

What prevents one from seeking and benefitting?

- Stigma of having a problem?
- Cannot solve on own?
- Expression of illness, pain?
- Previous experiences with counseling and psychotherapy?
- Healers, therapists, already sought?
- Expected treatment?
- Control of outcome?
- Therapist having power over?
- Hopefulness, belief and faith?
- Interpersonal and intrapersonal attributions?

Treatment of Psychopathology of Oppression

Social, political and economic norms, messages and sanctions provide a context within which psychopathology emerges and is sustained. These circumstances produce forces that criticize, belittle, devalue or render the self as invisible. From an AO perspective, the therapy process includes understanding and challenging a pattern of self-blame for issues created by unjust systems within an unfair society (i.e. they are not inherent or unchangeable) and moving towards a more appropriate and healthy view of oneself as worthy of dignity and respect, inclusion and equity.

Treatment begins with self-understanding of oppressive circumstances (Freire's "**read**" of circumstance) with the purpose of changing those circumstances (Freire's "**write**" of present and future). It requires self-challenging of an identity that is oppressed as an adaptive response to unfairness. The focus is on critical interpretation of personal experiences within those structures (Watts & Hipolito-Delgado, 2015).

Critical consciousness reveals problematic self-judgements associated with identity (Lipscomb & Ashley, 2017). Empowerment is important in relation to oppressive external influences with personal agency. In the following illustrations, two mechanisms by which oppressive systems influence personal experience are considered: experiences with prejudice and discrimination and internalization of negative images and stereotypes.

Experiences with (active and passive) prejudice and discrimination (individual, societal and institutional) lead to distress affecting mental health (Feagin & Cobas, 2015). Internalization of negative images and stereotypes lead to distress affecting mental health (Ashcroft, Griffiths, & Tiffin, 2013). In order to appreciate choices made by a client, therapists need to know their own experiences and beliefs with acceptance and resistance of unwanted and unjust pressure to conform to someone else's views of them.

In **acceptance**, there may be an adaptive belief that it is easier or better to internalize oppressive views of self (Malott & Schaefle, 2015). One may act internally and externally to create distance from oppressed identities as well as negatively judge oneself and others with those oppressed identities. A **deferred** viewpoint may include efforts to assimilate, look, act and become separate from an oppressed identity. Confidence in having shed the oppressed identity determines how authentically one may come to view self from the privileged status.

In **resistance**, there may be an adaptive belief that it is worth pushing back against external views of self (Tourse, Hamilton-Mason, & Wewiorski, 2018). One may act internally and externally to own and engage with oppressed identities as well as positively judge oneself and others with those oppressed identities. There may be efforts to accept, look, act and be one with an oppressed identity. Confidence in self as one who owns an oppressed identity determines how much strength in potential or actualized pride in the identity is likely.

In **ambivalence**, there may be efforts to embrace as well as distance the self from an oppressed identity, depending on feelings about oneself or the context(s) within which one is situated. Confidence in clarity about where and when determines how authentically one may view oneself from a privileged identity status and possess pride in an oppressed identity (Hasford, 2016). A **mixed** viewpoint may be based in adaptive beliefs that accepting some identities and resisting others reflects a more advantageous or authentic view of self. One may act internally and externally to distance oneself from or engage with oppressed identities as well as to judge oneself and others positively and negatively.

Therapeutic Alliance

The concepts of **pre-countertransference** and **pre-transference** exist on the part of the therapist and client; each makes assumptions about the other in relation to their previous experiences and beliefs (Eleftheriadou, 2010). Self-awareness guards against predetermining qualities of the problems and potential solutions as well as styles and approaches to take in the therapy (Marecek, 2017). Inquiring about these may become part of the therapy process itself.

Cultural empathy (Ridley & Lingle, 1996) concerns the degree to which one can situate the self in a context of another's worldview, belief values and traditions. From an AO perspective, what is of importance is the perception of client and therapist concerning the qualities that differentiate relative status between the two. While understanding the other and differences from oneself is important, similarities may also carry a great deal of weight in the relationship (Behn, Davanzo, & Errázuriz, 2018).

Particularities of the therapeutic relationship may give rise to different expectations between parties. It is important to be seen as an empathetic person, with some sense of mutuality and an openness to sharing of power and authority (Shonfeld-Ringel, 2001). Issues of boundaries, self-disclosure, neutrality, the significance/importance of the therapist in therapy (transference), the importance of insight, personal experience, directedness, length of time, client knowledge/ therapist knowledge and cost are all have cultural as well as professional and personal meanings to be negotiated (e.g. Levitt et al., 2016).

There are often tensions in an alliance (Safran, Muran, & Shaker, 2014). As a therapist or client, drawing closer to one cause/issue/group puts distance between it and the others. There is also the balance between individual and collective interests. For the therapist, agency/identity in face of contextual demands creates tensions between being non-judgmental and having clear personal values, perspective-taking and honoring differences, self-interest and moral commitments and support and overprotectiveness (DeTurk, 2011).

Consider an individual's resistance to challenging appropriated and internalized oppression. What is appropriate for the therapist to engage in if the client does not seek to alter what should not (to the therapist) be acceptable? To illustrate this idea, consider the following public statement made by American musician Kanye West. In a recent interview (CNN, 2018), Mr. West was quoted as saying that "When you hear about slavery for 400 years . . . For 400 years? That sounds like a choice". This was followed by the comment that "You were there for 400 years and it's all of y'all. It's like we're mentally imprisoned". One response was an altered photo of Mr. West with white skin and the caption "The new Kanye well all white now way to go dude" (Snoop Dogg, 2018).

Depression

From an AO perspective, **social rank** is a fundamental contributor to personal experience. In therapy and daily life, it exists as a distinct factor in perception and problem-solving (Kraus, Tan & Tannenbaum, 2013). We tend to associate in highly bounded systems differentiated by rank. Examples of this are neighborhoods and schools, clubs and jobs. **Cross-rank interactions** are low frequency events, and because of this we tend to have greater fear associated with them. Rank is also easily and reliably ascertained by others socially (Kraus & Mendes, 2014). Every time a person engages in a behavior that is associated with another social rank, that person is providing information to others.

One's perception of acting from a higher rank contributes to enhanced confidence in prediction, control and influence on one's environment (Kraus & Keltner, 2013). Belief in a lower rank means less value and less ability to manipulate one's environment. High rank is associated with autonomy, freedom and control (Rubin et al., 2014). Low rank is associated with constraint, helplessness and uncertainty. Low rank is more sensitive to threat but is less active in response. High rank is less sensitive to threat but is active in response (Kraus & Mendes, 2014). Lower rank has more need for others. High rank means less need for others. Low rank is more able to recognize others' emotions and act in support and in prosocial ways. High rank is less aware and more focused on self and others' capabilities to lift themselves up. Greater inequality and more relative comparison produce greater effects of difference. In a context of unfairness, low rank responds with guilt or shame as well as lower likelihood to act on behalf of self (Kraus, Park, & Tan, 2017).

Social comparisons associated with depression can be addressed from a problem-solving approach such as **cognitive-behavioral therapy** (David & Derthick, 2014). Core beliefs lead to low confidence and avoidance or learned helplessness and depression. It is essential to locate evidence contradicting thoughts about _____ people (like oneself) by learning about struggles and successes for the group as well as against forces of oppression. The important point is that while oppression remains it need not result in hopelessness. The approach is pragmatic, not idealistic. It leaves room for more work to be done to counteract oppressive external forces.

Social comparisons associated with depression may also be addressed from an empowerment approach, such as **narrative therapy** (Gergen, 2006). The case description of depression as "The Pig" is as follows: "stupid, lazy, crazy, sick, ugly, bad and deserves to die" (Aldarondo, 2013). An important feature of this approach is to locate the external messages. In this case, depression was also thought of as "the internalized police officer that keeps US in our place". A new narrative about the police officer who keeps THEM in their place may be constructed as a means to enforce distinctions between oppressive (unhealthy) and egalitarian (healthy) messengers and messages.

Social comparisons associated with depression may also be addressed through a social change approach such as **postcolonial feminism** (Lykes & Moane, 2009). From a feminist view, decolonization is an essential process for addressing depression. Critical consciousness may take the form of recognition of structures (i.e. patriarchy) that organize society, facilitate the "use" of some by others and diminish personal agency. These forces contribute to a social position and a personal view from the position of helplessness and personal failing. Terminology that situates the mood problem politically (e.g. "post colonization stress disorder", "colonized mentality", "racial terrorism", "cultural Stockholm syndrome", "ethnocultural allodynia") is a basic step toward reclaiming personal dignity and mastery. Recovery is rooted in reconnection and transformation through group action (Comas-Diaz, 2007).

Conclusion

Critical consciousness is a means to sensitize therapies to the forces of oppression. Major theories of counseling and psychotherapy focus on problem-solving, empowerment and social change.The clinical problem of appropriated oppression can be addressed through counseling and psychotherapy. However, the conditions of life continue unaltered. These causes are left unaddressed and require a response. Improvements to mental health made through personal change are continually challenged by external forces. Oftentimes personal change is a necessary step for engagement in community change that holds the potential to buffer negative effects.

Web Links

Cracking the Codes
www.youtube.com/watch?v=cVvKy1pWHvI

My Experience With Internalized Oppression
www.youtube.com/watch?v=7QHGzfORZTM

Mental Health Treatment, Culture & Social Justice
www.youtube.com/watch?v=NvR9El_SwPM

Cultural Competence in Trauma Treatment
www.youtube.com/watch?v=gc9Sb8z7NoU

The Critical Psychotherapy Network
https://criticalpsychotherapy.wordpress.com

Centre for Diversity in Counseling and Psychotherapy
www.oise.utoronto.ca/cdcp/

Cultural Humility
www.youtube.com/watch?v=Ww_ml21L7Ns

Collaboration & Accountability
https://dulwichcentre.com.au/lessons/collaboration-accountability/

Key Terms

Individualism   118
Primary   120
Secondary   120
Tertiary   120
Critical reflection   120
Critical motivation   120
Critical action   121
Naiveté   121
Magical consciousness   121
Acceptance   121

References

Aldarondo, E. (2013). Radical psychiatry: An approach to personal and political change. In *Advancing social justice through clinical practice* (pp. 89–114). London: Routledge.

Ashcroft, B., Griffiths, G., & Tiffin, H. (2013). *Post-colonial studies: The key concepts*. London: Routledge.

Behn, A., Davanzo, A., & Errázuriz, P. (2018). Client and therapist match on gender, age, and income: Does match within the therapeutic dyad predict early growth in the therapeutic alliance? *Journal of Clinical Psychology, 74*(9), 1403–1421.

CNN. (2018). *Kanye West says 400 years of slavery was a choice*. Retrieved from https://wtvr.com/2018/05/01/kanye-west-says-400-years-of-slavery-was-a-choice/

Carter, R. T. (2007). Racism and psychological and emotional injury: Recognizing and assessing race-based traumatic stress. *The Counseling Psychologist, 35*(1), 13–105.

Comas-Diaz, L. (2007). Ethnopolitical psychology: Healing and transformation. In E. Aldarondo (Ed.), *Advancing social justice through clinical practice* (pp. 91–118). Mahwah, NJ: Lawrence Erlbaum.

David, E. J. R., & Derthick, A. O. (2014). What is internalized oppression, and so what. *Internalized Oppression: The Psychology of Marginalized Groups*, 1–30.

DeTurk, S. (2011). Allies in action: The communicative experiences of people who challenge social injustice on behalf of others. *Communication Quarterly, 59*(5), 569–590. doi: 10.1080/01463373.2011.614209

Diemer, M. A., Rapa, L. J., Park, C. J., & Perry, J. C. (2017). Development and validation of the critical consciousness scale. *Youth & Society, 49*(4), 461–483.

Eleftheriadou, Z. (2010). *Psychotherapy and culture: Weaving inner and outer worlds*. London: Karnac Books.

Feagin, J. R., & Cobas, J. A. (2015). *Latinos facing racism: Discrimination, resistance, and endurance*. London: Routledge.

Freire, P. (1985). *The politics of education: Culture, power, and liberation*. Westport, CN: Greenwood Publishing Group.

Freire, P. (1998). Cultural action and conscientization. *Harvard Educational Review, 68*(4), 499.

Freire, P. (2000). *Pedagogy of freedom: Ethics, democracy, and civic courage*. Lanham, MD: Rowman & Littlefield Publishers.

Gergen, K. J. (2006). *Therapeutic realities: Collaboration, oppression, and relational flow*. Chagrin Fall, ID: Taos Institute.

Handy, C. (2008). *The hungry spirit: New thinking for a new world*. New York: Random House.

Hasford, J. (2016). Dominant cultural narratives, racism, and resistance in the workplace: A study of the experiences of young Black Canadians. *American Journal of Community Psychology, 57*(1–2), 158–170.

Hurley, G. (2010). *Recollections of our past*. Canadian Counselling Psychology Conference, Montreal, QC.

Kosutic, I., Garcia, M., Graves, T., Barnett, F., Hall, J., Haley, E., . . . Kaiser, B. (2009). The critical genogram: A tool for promoting critical consciousness. *Journal of Feminist Family Therapy, 21*(3), 151–176.

Kraus, M. W., & Keltner, D. (2013). Social class rank, essentialism, and punitive judgment. *Journal of Personality and Social Psychology, 105*(2), 247.

Kraus, M. W., & Mendes, W. B. (2014). Sartorial symbols of social class elicit class-consistent behavioral and physiological responses: A dyadic approach. *Journal of Experimental Psychology: General, 143*(6), 2330.

Kraus, M. W., Park, J. W., & Tan, J. J. (2017). Signs of social class: The experience of economic inequality in everyday life. *Perspectives on Psychological Science, 12*(3), 422–435.

Kraus, M. W., Tan, J. J., & Tannenbaum, M. B. (2013). The social ladder: A rank-based perspective on social class. *Psychological Inquiry, 24*(2), 81–96.

Kumagai, A. K., & Lypson, M. L. (2009). Beyond cultural competence: Critical consciousness, social justice, and multicultural education. *Academic Medicine, 84*(6), 782–787.

Levitt, H. M., Minami, T., Greenspan, S. B., Puckett, J. A., Henretty, J. R., Reich, C. M., & Berman, J. S. (2016). How therapist self-disclosure relates to alliance and outcomes: A naturalistic study. *Counselling Psychology Quarterly, 29*(1), 7–28.

Lipscomb, A. E., & Ashley, W. (2017). Colorful disclosures: Identifying identity-based differences and enhancing critical consciousness in supervision. *Smith College Studies in Social Work, 87*(2–3), 220–237.

Lykes, M. B., & Moane, G. (2009). Editors' introduction: Whither feminist liberation psychology? Critical explorations of feminist and liberation psychologies for a globalizing world. *Feminism & Psychology*, *19*(3), 283–297.

Malott, K. M., & Schaefle, S. (2015). Addressing clients' experiences of racism: A model for clinical practice. *Journal of Counseling & Development*, *93*(3), 361–369.

Marecek, J. (2017). Blowing in the wind: '70s questions for millennial therapists. *Women & Therapy*, *40*(3–4), 406–417.

McWhirter, E. H., & McWhirter, B. T. (2016). Critical consciousness and vocational development among Latina/o high school youth: Initial development and testing of a measure. *Journal of Career Assessment*, *26*(3).

Mezirow, J. (1981). A critical theory of adult learning and education. *Adult Education*, *32*(1), 3–24.

Payne, M. (2015). *Modern social work theory*. Oxford: Oxford University Press.

Ridley, C. R., & Lingle, D. W. (1996). Cultural empathy in multicultural counseling: A multidimensional process model. In P. B. Pedersen, J. G. Draguns, W. J. Lonner, & J. E. Trimble (Eds.), *Counseling across cultures* (pp. 21–46). Thousand Oaks, CA, US: Sage Publications, Inc.

Roberts, F. D. (2016). *Paternalism in early Victorian England*. London: Routledge.

Rubin, M., Denson, N., Kilpatrick, S., Matthews, K. E., Stehlik, T., & Zyngier, D. (2014). "I Am Working-Class" subjective self-definition as a missing measure of social class and socioeconomic status in higher education research. *Educational Researcher*, *43*(4), 196–200.

Safran, J. D., Muran, J. C., & Shaker, A. (2014). Research on therapeutic impasses and ruptures in the therapeutic alliance. *Contemporary Psychoanalysis*, *50*(1–2), 211–232.

Schmid, P. F. (2012). Psychotherapy is political or it is not psychotherapy: The person-centered approach as an essentially political venture. *Person-Centered & Experiential Psychotherapies*, *11*(2), 95–108.

Shonfeld-Ringel, S. (2001). A re-conceptualization of the working alliance in cross-cultural practice with non-western clients: Integrating relational perspectives and multicultural theories. *Clinical Social Work Journal*, *29*(1), 53–63.

Snoop Dogg. (2018). *The new Kanye well all white now way to go dude*. Retrieved from https://imgur.com/gallery/eIHbKtt

Tateo, L., & Marsico, G. (2013). The self as tension of wholeness and emptiness. *Interacções*, *9*(24).

Thomas, A. J., Barrie, R., Brunner, J., Clawson, A., Hewitt, A., Jeremie-Brink, G., & Rowe-Johnson, M. (2014). Assessing critical consciousness in youth and young adults. *Journal of Research on Adolescence*, *24*(3), 485–496.

Tourse, R. W., Hamilton-Mason, J., & Wewiorski, N. J. (2018). Deconstruction of racism. In *Systemic racism in the United States* (pp. 129–147). Cham: Springer.

Watts, R. J., & Hipolito-Delgado, C. P. (2015). Thinking ourselves to liberation? Advancing sociopolitical action in critical consciousness. *The Urban Review*, *47*(5), 847–867.

Watts, R. J., Williams, N. C., & Jagers, R. J. (2003). Sociopolitical development. *American Journal of Community Psychology*, *31*, 185–194.

Discussion Questions

1. Can you identify values and thoughts you carry about race, age, ethnicity, disability, sexuality, gender, class and religion that place one group in a higher social status than others? Where do these come from? How do you know when you are acting on them? What would it take to be aware of their emergence in your practice, personal life and civic responsibilities?

2. In what ways have you become aware of feeling inferior based on a quality of yourself that is less valued in society? Where do these feelings rise to the surface? Where are they dormant? In what settings do they become irrelevant?

3. When you think about your counseling and psychotherapy practice orientation, how prominent are considerations to fairness and equity? In what ways can you or do you incorporate them specifically into practice? Are there ways you could become more deliberate about this with your clients? What benefits and drawbacks are associated with a more formally stated stance on equity?

8

BRIDGING PERSONAL AND COMMUNITY CHANGE

In this chapter, the focus is on alliance building and maintenance. Allies use their privilege to challenge oppression. They engage in deliberate political acts that conflict with the structures, systems and processes that grant and protect their own privilege. Being an ally may mean action in solidarity with a formal partnership for change to benefit those who experience oppression. Adherents often find it necessity to engage in supportive efforts to strengthen community building and in actions that represent collective needs for social and political change. Activities may include witnessing and acting within systems of support, as well as actively promoting group formation or coalition building. Case networking, outreach and advocacy are additional and more familiar means by which professionals may become familiar with and take action to address structures and processes that sustain disadvantage.

What is an AO perspective on bridging personal and community change?

- Problems brought to counseling and psychotherapy are typically defined as intra or interpersonal in nature. The environment is not viewed as a target of change. While the mutual influence of people and their contexts is understood, the practical efforts of counselors and psychotherapists center on the person and their immediate relationships.
- Bridging is a process and practice of connecting personal struggles with community issues. From an AO perspective, conditions reinforcing or exacerbating the problem are important considerations. Because a personal struggle has both internal and external dimensions, its resolution is simultaneously a personal and collective responsibility. If collective responsibility is not activated, there is a hard limit on personal change.

- Efforts have been made to document practices that explicitly bridge personal and community issues. They start from the personal and move into the community. Professional practices that are associated with being an ally may include advocacy, case management and outreach.

Chapter Outline

Sue (2017) describes ally behavior by offering an analogy from Tatum (2001, pp. 11–12) of a motorized walkway. Active racism, sexism, ethnocentrism, ageism, classism, ableism, heterosexism and religious exclusivism are what happens when one walks quickly on the walkway, in the direction it is headed. Passive behavior is standing still on the walkway and following those ahead. The only way to avoid going in the same direction as the others is to walk in the opposite direction, at a speed faster than the walkway itself. There are four types of behavior: **active supremacists**, who walk quickly forward; **unintentional supremacists**, who follow the direction of the walkway; **non-supremacists**, who do not walk at all; and **anti-supremacists**, who walk in the opposite direction or disrupt the mechanics of the walkway.

Allies possess several characteristics (Spanierman & Smith, 2017). They understand privilege that arises from racism, sexism, ethnocentrism, ageism, classism, ableism, heterosexism and religious exclusivism. They self-reflect on their own beliefs and actions and use their privilege to promote equity. Allies take action to interrupt racism, sexism, ethnocentrism, ageism, classism, ableism, heterosexism and religious exclusivism. They build coalitions with organizations and groups and rise against forces that silence allies. They emphasize the importance of understanding systemic issues and make a commitment to dismantling ways of privileged thinking, biases and beliefs (Patton & Bondi, 2015). Their motives may be **altruistic** (e.g. knowing about and challenging their and others' privilege) or stem from **self-interest** (e.g. helping out people with whom one has personal relationships) and a desire for **social justice** (e.g. working in partnership and building coalitions) (Patton & Bondi, 2015)

Anyone can be an ally. From an AO perspective, oppression affects us all. There is little value in ranking depths of oppression. That practice only recreates a hierarchy and removes the responsibility of the majority culture from the competition by pitting disadvantaged groups against each other. Affiliations may be expressed as levels of self-interest: the individual who is "me"; the coalition that is "you and me", which benefits us both; and the society that is "us", which benefits us all (Reason & Davis, 2005). A **universalist stance** has been described in the following way:

> Once we realize that there are very few pure victims or oppressors, and that each one of us derives varying amounts of penalty and privilege from the multiple systems of oppression that frame our lives, then we will be in a position to see the need for new ways of thought and action... [without which we remain] locked in a dangerous dance of competing for attention, resources and theoretical supremacy.
>
> *(Collins, 2003, p. 332)*

Allies With Privilege

Privileged status is conferred, but hierarchical values, beliefs and practices are assumed. Each individual possesses a choice to accept or challenge hierarchical organization and to choose "equal" or equitable treatment of others with or without regard for social identities. Privilege can be used to send a message to others with privileged identities about the problems of inequity and inaction. In this way, a privileged identity need not be used to justify the status quo or create further distance between identities. Daily acts may include speaking up to family members and coworkers, teaching about it and advocating in everyday settings (Neville, Worthington, & Spanierman, 2001). Criticism of the status quo often means being self-critical. It is a lifetime commitment to maintain self-awareness, critical monitoring and action. As new awareness emerges, guilt and failure may as well. Many who identify as anti-privileged also feel outside of their identity groups (Case, 2007).

While a privileged status offers many advantages, it does not automatically result in a "good life". Privilege is not about being wealthy or happy or successful. It is about having more and better opportunities and other advantages that are maintained at the expense of groups who have fewer (Ancis & Szymanski, 2001). Personal awareness, spiritual healing and charitable actions are positive but not in and of themselves disruptive to systems, such as school, workplace, welfare and justice, or to policies that are oppressive (Kendall, 2012).

Holding privileged status while valuing equity produces tension that does not go away. However, the position of privilege provides access to its challenge. By challenging, however, one is also challenging their own identity (DeTurk, 2011). Because "judgments about what is 'just', 'fair', or 'deserved' are central social judgments that lie at the heart of people's feelings, attitudes, and behaviors in their interactions with others" (Tyler & Smith, 1998, p. 595), support from like-minded others is essential. Affiliations with others who hold privilege and choose to challenge the structures that perpetuate it offer essential support for what is often a very isolating experience (Lupfer, Weeks, Doan, & Houston, 2000).

Allies for Social Change

A conceptual model for the development of privilege into social change (Watts, & Abdul-Adil, 1998) includes five stages: acritical, adaptive, pre-critical, critical and liberation. In the **acritical** stage, an individual views opportunities and privileges as distributed in a fair way and according to what is deserved. In the **adaptive** stage, opportunities and privileges are recognized to be distributed in an unfair way, but the system is believed to be beyond change. Therefore, one must cheat or push to get what is actually deserved. In the **pre-critical** stage, opportunities and privileges are distributed unfairly and systemic change is considered. In the **critical** stage, unfair systemic conditions are problematic and need to be challenged through social change. In the **liberation** stage, social action and community development efforts are engaged.

A practical model for the translation of personal privilege into social change includes a series of ten steps, which the authors describe as a "**confidence-shaking process**" followed by a "**confidence-building process**" (Curry-Stevens, 2007). Confidence shaking includes: awareness of oppression, awareness of oppression as structural and thus enduring and pervasive, locating oneself as oppressed, locating oneself as privileged, understanding the benefits that flow from privilege, understanding oneself as implicated in the oppression of others and understanding oneself as an oppressor. Confidence building steps include: knowing how to intervene, planning actions for departure, finding supportive connections to sustain commitments and declaring intentions for future actions.

A learning strategy approach characterizes the methods of teaching and learning that may occur in this process (Curry-Stevens, 2007). Learners transform in several ways. Spiritually, this change occurs with shift from the recognition of self as individual to self as interdependent. Ideologically, this change occurs in shifting from emphasizing self-interest to what is the common good. Psychologically, the transformation of self-concept as "free" changes to self as "embedded".

Emotionally, this change may occur as a shift from grief, fear and guilt to excitement. Behaviorally, there is a commitment and alteration in the type and amount of support provided. Finally, the process is intellectual and evolves from relearning one's place in the world and the responsibilities that come with it.

An interpersonal communication approach illustrates a means for locating evidence of the transformation of attitudes through personal meaning. Coordinated Management of Meaning (CMM) includes nine interactive layers of meaning (Pearce & Pearce, 2000), including content, sensations, speech act, episode, identity, family, culture, spiritual and political meanings. **Content** refers to the words used; bodily sensations are what one feels, affecting experience. The **speech act** is the meaning of what is said, and the episode is the event in which it occurs. **Identity** includes the personal, professional and autobiographical meanings that one brings to an experience. **Family and culture** refer to meanings within one's family and community. **Spirituality** concerns meanings derived from belief systems, and the political includes global and political issues and meanings.

The Problem of Isolation

A lack of connection with others leads to social and emotional isolation as well as loneliness. Connections are essential for awareness of shared experiences, linked to structural disadvantage and a sense of community. In addition, connections make it possible to take collective action for social change.

Isolation occurs because of unmet social needs (e.g. Fromm-Reichmann, 1959; Weiss, 1973). Needs include attachment, social integration, nurturance, reassurance of worth, alliance or guidance (Weiss, 1987). **Loneliness** is based on the difference between the social relationships we desire and what we actually have. Vigilance to guard against social threats influences perceptions, feelings and how we think as well as our sense of self and what we do (Hawkley & Cacioppo). Such distorted explanations lead to avoidance (Perlman & Peplau, 1982).

However, social connections buffer against life stressors and can, when developed into relationships, provide a sense of security. **Social participation** provides affiliation and opportunities to develop further connections with others and their groups (Haslam, Cruwys, Haslam, Dingle, & Xue-Ling Chang, 2008; Van Zomeren & Iyer, 2009). This strengthens sense of social identity, **belonging** and **inclusion** (Haslam, Cruwys, Haslam, & Dingle, 2016). In addition to direct mental health benefits, indirect benefits of identity and affiliation may contribute to feelings of collective control and influence (Greenaway et al., 2015).

Social Network Assessment

A very common approach to identifying relationships that exist between clients and their communities is known as an **ecomap** (Hartman, 1995). It can be very helpful for therapists to construct such a map for themselves in order to understand their own relationships and to become familiar with the approach before using it with a client.

The purpose of an ecomap is to identify **social networks** of relationships for clients with others. These maps can be used for assessment, progress tracking and goal setting. They can be drawn up by a client, therapist or collaboratively. They can have a preventive or restorative emphasis. There is no single way to draw the maps, and because they are visual, they depend little on verbal skill.

Typically, the person of interest is in the center of the map. All informal and formal entities are positioned around the individual. The distance between the entities and the individual may be a reflection of the closeness of the relationship. Some informal entities include family, friends and neighbors, as well as others that are important or potentially important for a client. Formal components include the organizations and systems that a client has, does or would like to come into contact with. Important issues from an AO perspective are the recognition of perceived status in relation to each of the components (higher, same, lower), extent to which their identities are represented (yes, no) and importance of such matching (none, low, high). Lines can be drawn to represent emotional energy and physical energy and the direction ($\rightarrow$, $\leftarrow$, $\leftrightarrow$).

The value of this activity is to draw attention to the people, groups and organizations to which an individual is connected. This can lead to insight for both professional and client regarding the potential for achieving a place to belong and feel included. The entities that mean the most can be especially helpful for awareness of balance between energy in and out as well as the history, present and future relationship desired. From an AO perspective, the identities with which one identifies and the identities of each entity on the map show the degree to which fitting in is encouraged and supported. The map may be full of entities that do not support the identities of the individual. In this situation, addition of entities that are supportive should be pursued.

Witness Bearing

The use of **reflecting teams** may open possibilities for depth and complexity of experience through a constructive process of responding to a client's story telling (Smith, Jenkins, & Sells, 1995). The content of these processes varies (Smith, Yoshioka, & Winton, 1993). The content may be communicated verbally or nonverbally, about a particular issue or decision as well as more broadly such as a relationship or relationships (Cole, Demeritt, Shatz, & Sapoznik, 2001). It also possible to simply ask the client to tell a story about an experience. Observation may take place behind a one-way glass, in person or via audio or video recording. Participants in the team may be professionals, community members or students (Griffith & Frieden, 2000). There may be as few as two or as many as is appropriate and feasible. What is important is that those on the team are not "experts" and so are not evaluative or interpretive. They are to speak to expressions or images that came to them, identities they speak to and how participants were affected as well as how their lives were changed by the experience. The therapist needs to make sure that the participants are not being clinical and that opportunities for all are protected. The purpose is to come up with a richer story of experience than the client started with (Norman, 2003). The client can use the richness to consider possibilities for the story to be more reflective of the experience.

A variation of this practice includes others who have direct knowledge of a situation for a client and are able to offer support. These others know the client and are able to hear the client's experience and, going forward, offer support. They might be family members, friends or neighbors. Involvement may turn into a **community of care**, which starts with bearing witness to the client, listening with compassion and becoming a source of support within a collective that can take action on the systemic injustices that contribute to the problem (Kotzé, van Duuren, & Small, 2011).

Community Building

Groups with a community-building purpose have been developed for a range of different populations using different modalities. In the counseling and psychotherapy literature, such groups have taken the forms of "friendship" groups, art-based therapy and social action.

The development of women's **friendship groups** was based on common parenting challenges. They drew together individuals with shared interests. The purpose was to create a place where women could have positive social interaction to enhance confidence and interpersonal communication skill (Mentinis, 2015). It was found that group members became more comfortable interacting with each other. They also led to friendships among participants that carried forth into their lives in the community (Newman & Lovell, 1993).

In an art therapy group with adolescent males, the facilitator helped members create a vision of their community. They were asked to use art supplies to construct it as it was and then, later, the community they would like it to be. The differences between "known" and "ideal" communities gave insight into the changes they viewed as important (Slayton, 2012). The group process that individual participants were led through encouraged positive **community building** outside of the therapy.

Creative therapy approaches have been organized around a specific activity. In one group, the medium was sand, and participants were instructed to represent their experiences. The experience had positive effects on anxiety, loneliness and self-expression. Following the end of the formal group, members decided to continue the group themselves for **mutual support** without a therapist facilitator (Jang & Kim, 2012).

A **social action group** for immigrant LGBTQ adults was formed in a counseling center. Its purpose was to connect participants with others interested in public awareness and knowledge of local community issues. The group organized a variety of events, including rallies, speeches, public art displays and performances. They also provided information and connections to legal, social and economic resources (Reading & Rubin, 2011).

Case Networking

A potential role that professionals may take on is networking. The purpose of networking is to maintain connections with other service providers and local agencies that provide information, support and specialized services as well as community groups for self-help, resources and advocacy.

Case networking practices vary considerably in their intensity, frequency and duration, size and location (Clark et al., 2011). The four most common models are Brokerage, Intensive, Strengths-Based and Clinical (Vanderplasschen, Wolf, Rapp, & Broekaert, 2007). In **Brokerage**, the coordination function is brief. The purpose is to empower a client to reach out to appropriate services and resources. In **Intensive**, more involvement and a strong alliance with the client are needed. The purpose is to provide service within the context of a team for client growth. In **Strengths-Based**, a close relationship with the client is needed to provide direct strengths-based service. In addition, service coordination and outreach are included. The most intensive involvement is the **Clinical** model, where a counselor or psychotherapist provides coordination as well as outreach in addition to the therapeutic role.

From an AO perspective, the purpose of case networking is to work at the interface between clients and their environments (Hepworth, Rooney, Rooney, Strom-Gottfried, & Larsen, 2006, p. 451). It requires a broadening of the role. It is essential that case networking practice center on changing the social situation and not the individual to adapt to existing circumstances. The purpose is to improving a client's control over effects of the circumstances rather than just coping with them (Fook, 1993). In terms of activities, case networking includes resource use, providing empathy and support. However, in traditional case networking, the emphasis is on skill development, while in **radical case networking** the emphasis is on education (Fook, 1993). Another difference concerns the traditional emphasis on **client self-awareness**; in radical networking, the emphasis is on **client critical awareness** (Fook, 1993).

Outreach

Another potential role that therapists may engage in is outreach. This typically means meeting clients where they are physically and geographically (Chung, Bemak, & Grabosky, 2011). Often, this is done in addition to or instead of meeting in a professional office. The purpose is to make services more accessible (Chung & Bemak, 2008).

Four types of outreach include domiciliary, detached, peripatetic and satellite (Rhodes, 1996). **Domiciliary** outreach refers to a service provided in the home of a client. **Detached** outreach is undertaken in public environments with individuals, and **peripatetic** outreach is undertaken at public or private environments with organizations. **Satellite** outreach is where services are provided at a dedicated alternate site.

Reaching out to connect with people who can engage with the service breaks down barriers to access. The traveling therapist can be convenient for clients. It also can help a professional see the context within which a client lives and, through new partnerships with other community agencies, bring services to where people are (Aldarondo & Straus, 1994). However, it is a challenge to deliver service outside of the office because of possible distractions in the environment or lack of privacy, a lack of professional support and supervision, isolation, role confusion and blurred boundaries. Professional education and support around boundaries, managing countertransference, self-disclosure, dual relationships and safety are necessary (Rogers, 2014).

Advocacy

There are several forms of advocacy. One distinction can be made between issue and cause-based advocacy (Dalrymple & Boylan, 2013). In **issue-based** advocacy, efforts may be made on behalf of an individual or a group. Therapists need to be aware of the local agencies, organizations and groups that represent the issues that clients bring into therapy and connect individuals with those groups. In such cases, it is helpful for the facilitation of access by a client to have preexisting relationships with the group. It is essential to recognize when a client is ready and not ready for advocacy. Pressure to advocate when unwanted is oppressive and a misuse of the therapist's power.

In **cause-based** advocacy, efforts are made across individuals and groups with a systemic emphasis. Therapists may develop partnerships as appropriate (Ali & Lees, 2013). In some cases, it can be helpful to bring people together to advocate for a specific need. In one model (Hof, Dinsmore, Barber, Suhr, & Scofield, 2009), a structured procedure provides seven steps for a collaborative process on advocacy that can be used with clients, community groups and professionals. First, target needs of an underrepresented group and what professional advocacy would be for them. Second, respond to these needs by identifying competencies that need to be developed. The third step is to articulate a plan to accomplish social and professional advocacy. In the fourth and fifth steps, the plan is implemented with professional networking. The sixth and seventh steps are to evaluate the training and retarget efforts to address unmet needs.

Another distinction may be made between active and passive activism (Dalrymple & Boylan, 2013). In **active**, the individual or group advocated for is a citizen and capable of speaking for themselves. In **passive**, the individual needs protection and the therapist speaks on behalf of them. In some cases of passive activism, the decision is relatively easy. For example, an infant's needs in a family cannot be represented by the child. However, in many cases, the decision should be made by the professional and client. The power differential is necessary to understand. The potential advantages and disadvantages of advocacy on behalf of the professional or on the part of the client are best considered together. It is also important that the professional knows why advocacy is necessary and that it is only for the client's benefit (Lewis et al., 2011).

Finally, another distinction can be made between **internal** and **external advocacy**. Internal advocacy is from inside the system and external is from outside the system. Internal advocacy is an underrecognized form of change. Therapists who are employed by organizations are in a position to advocate within that system. Therapists who are registered are in a position to advocate within their professions (Lewis, Ratts, Paladino & Toporek, 2011). One format for considering organizational change is through the concept of **organizational critical consciousness** (Evans et al., 2014). In this model, critical consciousness at an organizational level determines the degree of awareness and potential for change in response to advocacy for client needs (see Table 8.1). A major distinction in this model is the degree to which there is awareness versus the degree to which the practice has changed in response. A divide between knowledge and action can provide motivation for change. A lack of knowledge suggests that the process should begin with considering the issues.

Competencies

The American Counseling Association has a series of six competencies for advocacy (Ratts, DeKruyf & Chen-Hayes, 2007). **Empowerment counselor competencies** are based on the recognition of client and student counselor strengths. **Client advocacy competencies** focus on knowing the resources available and making a plan with a client to address challenges to access. **Community collaboration counselor competencies** include the need to have alliances with

TABLE 8.1 Critical Consciousness and Critical Practice

		Critical Practice	
		low	high
Critical consciousness	high	"ideology–practice divide"	deliberate critical practice
	low	traditional services	instinctive critical practice

other community groups that are promoting positive change. **Systems advocacy counselor competencies** refer to the ability to look more broadly at environmental factors that affect development of clients and students. **Public information counselor competencies** include outreach efforts to promote better awareness of the effects of oppression and the means by which it can be challenged. **Social/political advocacy** means taking direct action to challenge existing political, social and economic barriers to full inclusion.

Strategies

For professionals themselves, it is important to recognize the need to take chances to become an advocate and that we have more commonalities with clients than differences. Professionals can use their titles, share personal experiences and educate themselves and others. We should also make efforts to understand each client from the viewpoint of that client's community, and also be active in our communities and a model self-advocacy.

With clients, advocacy may include learning about a culture, celebrating its strengths, visiting a community or home outside of office hours, building confidence and knowledge of one's rights and teaching assertiveness. Advocacy on behalf of clients could include giving testimony to decision-makers, lobbying individual policymakers, litigation and representing a client in an administrative hearing. Additional examples include facilitating client access to information, mediating between clients and institutions and negotiating with outside agencies and institutions to provide better services for clients.

At a community level (Lewis et al., 2011), advocacy centers on working with systems, educating and becoming known. Specific strategies might include educating the public on an issue, conducting issue research, organizing coalitions, influencing media coverage of an issue, mobilizing constituent support and political campaigning. Collaborating with other professionals and across disciplines, sharing information and advocating for needed services are also possibilities. Within one's own agency and clients, this may include influencing administrative policies, arguing for better services, pushing for increased client rights and negotiating with other agencies for access and services (Brown & Hannis, 2012).

Conclusion

Allies possess a commitment to fairness and equity. This stance is expressed within counseling and psychotherapy itself as well as in an awareness of structural privilege and oppression that permeates their own as well as clients' daily lives. From an AO perspective, professionals express this by working on themselves to self-monitor their actions and delve deeper into their motives and values. They choose to disrupt oppressive policies and practices in their professions and workplaces. With clients, they consider approaches to promoting connections for support and solidarity with community groups and organizations. These efforts may involve others in their therapy to bear witness and group practices that create feelings of belonging through collective shared experience. Case networking is a method by which therapists may connect clients with professional, self-help and activist communities of support. Outreach is a means through which to connect that offers potential advantages for a client who might otherwise face multiple barriers to meeting a therapist. Advocacy offers many potential ways to support a specific client as well as groups of similarly affected individuals or entire communities that have faced disadvantage. The purpose of advocacy is to promote change that assists members of groups affected by oppressive forces challenge and to alter the conditions and circumstances of their disadvantage with their strengths.

Web Links

Guide to Allyship
www.guidetoallyship.com

Becoming an Ally
www.becominganally.ca/Becoming_an_Ally/Home.html

Advocacy in Action
https://ct.counseling.org/2014/04/advocacy-in-action/

Advocacy Competencies
www.counseling.org/Resources/Competencies/Advocacy_Competencies.pdf

10 Things All 'Allies' Need to Know
https://everydayfeminism.com/2013/11/things-allies-need-to-know/

Key Terms

Active supremacists 135
Unintentional supremacists 135
Non-supremacists 135
Anti-supremacists 135
Altruistic 136
Self-interest 136
Social justice 136
Universalist stance 136
Acritical 137
Adaptive 137
Pre-critical 137
Critical 137
Liberation 137
Confidence-shaking process 137

References

Aldarondo, E., & Straus, M. A. (1994). Screening for physical violence in couple therapy: Methodological, practical, and ethical considerations. *Family Process, 33*(4), 425–439.

Ali, A., & Lees, K. E. (2013). The therapist as advocate: Anti-oppression advocacy in psychological practice. *Journal of Clinical Psychology, 69*(2), 162–171.

Ancis, J. R., & Szymanski, D. M. (2001). Awareness of white privilege among white counseling trainees. *The Counseling Psychologist, 29*(4), 548–569.

Brown, J., & Hannis, D. (2012). *Community development in Canada*. Toronto, ON: Pearson Higher Ed.

Case, K. A. (2007). Raising white privilege awareness and reducing racial prejudice: Assessing diversity course effectiveness. *Teaching of Psychology, 34*(4), 231–235.

Chung, R. C. Y., & Bemak, F. P. (2008). *Social justice counseling: The next steps beyond multiculturalism* (p. 88, Kindle ed.). New York: Sage Publications.

Chung, R. C. Y., Bemak, F. P., & Grabosky, T. K. (2011). Multicultural-social justice leadership strategies: Counseling and advocacy with immigrants. *Journal for Social Action in Counseling and Psychology, 3*(1), 57–69.

Clark, C. R., Baril, N., Hall, A., Kunicki, M., Johnson, N., Soukup, J., . . . Bigby, J. (2011). Case management intervention in cervical cancer prevention: The Boston REACH coalition women's health demonstration project. *Progress in Community Health Partnerships: Research, Education, and Action, 5*(3), 235–247.

Cole, P. M., Demeritt, L. A., Shatz, K., & Sapoznik, M. (2001). Getting personal on reflecting teams. *Journal of Systematic Therapies, 20*(2), 74–87.

Collins, P. H. (2003). Toward an Afrocentric feminist epistemology. In *Turning points in qualitative research: Tying knots in a handkerchief*. New York: Rowan & Littlefield.

Curry-Stevens, A. (2007). New forms of transformative education: Pedagogy for the privileged. *Journal of Transformative Education, 5*(1), 33–58.

Dalrymple, J., & Boylan, J. (2013). *Effective advocacy in social work*. New York: Sage Publications.

DeTurk, S. (2011). Allies in action: The communicative experiences of people who challenge social injustice on behalf of others. *Communication Quarterly, 59*(5), 569–590.

Evans, S. D., Kivell, N., Haarlammert, M., Malhotra, K., & Rosen, A. (2014). Critical community practice: An introduction to the special section. *Journal for Social Action in Counseling and Psychology, 6*(1), 1.

Fook, J. (1993). *Radical casework: A theory of practice*. London: Allen & Unwin.

Greenaway, K. H., Haslam, S. A., Cruwys, T., Branscombe, N. R., Ysseldyk, R., & Heldreth, C. (2015). From "we" to "me": Group identification enhances perceived personal control with consequences for health and well-being. *Journal of Personality and Social Psychology, 109*(1), 53.

Griffith, B. A., & Frieden, G. (2000). Facilitating reflective thinking in counselor education. *Counselor Education and Supervision, 40*(2), 82–93.

Halevy, J. (1998). A genogram with an attitude. *Journal of Marital and Family Therapy, 24*(2), 233–242.

Hartman, A. (1995). Diagrammatic assessment of family relationships. *Families in Society, 76*(2), 111–122.

Haslam, C., Cruwys, T., Haslam, S. A., Dingle, G., & Chang, M. X. L. (2016). Groups 4 Health: Evidence that a social-identity intervention that builds and strengthens social group membership improves mental health. *Journal of Affective Disorders, 194*, 188–195.

Hawkley, L. C., & Cacioppo, J. T. (2010). Loneliness matters: A theoretical and empirical review of consequences and mechanisms. *Annals of Behavioral Medicine*, *40*(2), 218–227.

Hepworth, D. H., Rooney, R. H., Rooney, G. D., Strom-Gottfried, K., & Larsen, J. (2006). *Direct social work practice: Theory and skills*. Belmont, CA: Cengage Learning.

Hof, D. D., Dinsmore, J. A., Barber, S., Suhr, R., & Scofield, T. R. (2009). Advocacy: The TRAINER model. *Journal for Social Action in Counseling and Psychology*, *2*(1), 15–28.

Jang, M., & Kim, Y. H. (2012). The effect of group sandplay therapy on the social anxiety, loneliness and self-expression of migrant women in international marriages in South Korea. *The Arts in Psychotherapy*, *39*(1), 38–41.

Kendall, F. (2012). *Understanding white privilege: Creating pathways to authentic relationships across race*. London: Routledge.

Kotzé, E., van Duuren, L., & Small, J. (2011). Three wise young men, a cyber community and music—counseling as social action: Storying a community of care in the aftermath of violence. *Australian and New Zealand Journal of Family Therapy*, *32*(3), 194–207.

Lewis, J. A., Ratts, M. J., Paladino, D. A., & Toporek, R. L. (2011). Social justice counseling and advocacy: Developing new leadership roles and competencies. *Journal for Social Action in Counseling and Psychology*, *3*(1), 5–16.

Lupfer, M. B., Weeks, K. P., Doan, K. A., & Houston, D. A. (2000). Folk conceptions of fairness and unfairness. *European Journal of Social Psychology*, *30*(3), 405–428.

Mentinis, M. (2015). Friendship: Towards a radical grammar of relating. *Theory & Psychology*, *25*(1), 63–79.

Neville, H. A., Worthington, R. L., & Spanierman, L. B. (2001). Race, power, and multicultural counseling psychology: Understanding white privilege and color-blind racial attitudes. In J. G. Ponterotto, J. M. Casas, L. A. Suzuki, & C. M. Alexander (Eds.), *Handbook of multicultural counseling* (pp. 257–288). Thousand Oaks, CA, US: Sage Publications, Inc.

Newman, J. A., & Lovell, M. (1993). A description of a supervisory group for group counselors. *Counselor Education and Supervision*, *33*(1), 22–31.

Norman, H. (2003). Solution-focused reflecting teams. *Handbook of Solution-Focused Therapy*, 156–167.

Patton, L. D., & Bondi, S. (2015). Nice white men or social justice allies? Using critical race theory to examine how white male faculty and administrators engage in ally work. *Race Ethnicity and Education*, *18*(4), 488–514.

Pearce, W. B., & Pearce, K. A. (2000). Extending the theory of the Coordinated Management of Meaning (CMM) through a community dialogue process. *Communication Theory*, *10*(4), 405–423.

Perlman, D., & Peplau, L. A. (1982). Theoretical approaches to loneliness. *Loneliness: A Sourcebook of Current Theory, Research and Therapy*, 123–134.

Prilleltensky, I., & Gonick, L. (1996). Polities change, oppression remains: On the psychology and politics of oppression. *Political Psychology*, 127–148.

Ratts, M. J., DeKruyf, L., & Chen-Hayes, S. F. (2007). The ACA advocacy competencies: A social justice advocacy framework for professional school counselors. *Professional School Counseling*, *11*(2). doi:10.1080/2156759X0701100203.

Reading, R., & Rubin, L. R. (2011). Advocacy and empowerment: Group therapy for LGBT asylum seekers. *Traumatology*, *17*(2), 86–98.

Reason, R. D., & Davis, T. L. (2005). Antecedents, precursors, and concurrent concepts in the development of social justice attitudes and actions. *New Directions for Student Services*, *110*, 5–15.

Reichmann, F. F. (1959). Loneliness. *Psychiatry*, *22*(1), 1–15.

Rhodes, T. (1996). *Outreach work with drug users: Principles and practice*. Bonn, Germany: Council of Europe.

Rogers, S. (2014). The moving psychoanalytic frame: Ethical challenges for community practitioners. *International Journal of Applied Psychoanalytic Studies, 11*(2), 151–162.

Smith, T. E., Yoshioka, M., & Winton, M. (1993). A qualitative understanding of reflecting teams I: Client perspectives. *Journal of Systemic Therapies, 12*(3), 28–43.

Spanierman, L. B., & Smith, L. (2017). Roles and responsibilities of white allies: Implications for research, teaching, and practice. *The Counseling Psychologist, 45*(5), 606–617.

Sue, D. W. (2017). The challenges of becoming a white ally. *The Counseling Psychologist, 45*(5), 706–716.

Smith, T. E., Jenkins, D., & Sells, S. P. (1995). Reflecting teams: Voices of diversity. *Journal of Family Psychotherapy, 6*(2), 49–70.

Slayton, S. C. (2012). Building community as social action: An art therapy group with adolescent males. *The Arts in Psychotherapy, 39*(3), 179–185.

Tatum, B. D. (2001). Defining racism: Can we talk. *Race, Class, and Gender in the United States: An Integrated Study, 100*, 107.

Tyler, T. R., & Smith, H. J. (1998). Social justice and social movements. In D. T. Gilbert, S. T. Fiske & G. Lindzey (Eds.), *The handbook of social psychology* (Vol. 2, pp. 595–629). New York: McGraw-Hill.

Vanderplasschen, W., Wolf, J., Rapp, R. C., & Broekaert, E. (2007). Effectiveness of different models of case management for substance-abusing populations. *Journal of Psychoactive Drugs, 39*(1), 81–95.

Van Zomeren, M., & Iyer, A. (2009). Introduction to the social and psychological dynamics of collective action. *Journal of Social Issues, 65*(4), 645–660.

Watts, R., & Abdul-Adil, J. (1998). Sociopolitical development as an antidote for oppression: Theory and action. *American Journal of Community Psychology, 26*, 255–272.

Weiss, R. S. (1973). *Loneliness: The experience of emotional and social isolation*. Cambridge, MA, US: The MIT Press.

Weiss, R. S. (1987). Reflections on the present state of loneliness research. *Journal of Social Behavior and Personality, 2*(2), 1.

Discussion Questions

1. Many of us are familiar with the role of scientist–practitioner. What are the pros and cons of identification of self as scientist–practitioner–advocate or counselor–advocate–scholar? (Counseling for Multiculturalism and Social Justice, Chapter 4)

2. In a practice that has been called a Genogram-with-an-Attitude (Halevy, 1998), therapists are asked to draw their family members connected by lines between each. In each relationship, recall memories of episodes in which race, gender, class, sexual orientation, religion, ethnicity, ability, appearance, or age were a focus. What was said? How did you feel? What did you do? What messages did you receive from this?

3. An advocate role puts the therapist in a powerful position. How do you know when this is appropriate? Consider the possibility that sometimes clients are not ready, sometimes practitioners do not see it as part of their role and that it doesn't always work. Who are you doing it for (self or client)?

4. What are some potential downsides of taking an activist stance in your organization or workplace? How can these be overcome?

9

ASSESSMENT FOR COMMUNITY CHANGE

In this chapter, the restorative, supportive and activist functions of communities are considered as assets for personal and social change. Community assessment may be incorporated with or on behalf of clients. It is useful to build knowledge and capacity for change that benefits members of groups experiencing oppression.

From an AO perspective, professional awareness of individuals—including both self and clients—within the context of communities can be useful for raising potential support and collective influence for groups facing structural disadvantage. Communities can be viewed as functional, conflicted or marginalizing. In response to each of these dynamics, different ways to engage and mobilize support are possible. Professionals providing counseling and psychotherapy can support and extend the benefits of their clients' personal changes by engaging in community action. This requires awareness of self as one who can access and contribute to broad-based change through the use of personal and professional resources. Careful consideration of the type and degree of involvement is essential for embarking on this work.

What is community assessment and why is it valuable from an AO perspective?

• Community assessment is not typically considered in counseling and psychotherapy. Traditionally, assessment is a series of observations and judgments about a client. Professionals' questions and observations are the focus. In the case of community assessment, the observations and judgments are about a community. From an AO perspective, community members' perceptions are important. For example: What is the problem? Is it a neighborhood, community or societal problem? Why does it exist?

- Assessment can be very influential. Assessors determine what measures are used, the criteria for their judgments, conclusions and recommendations. From an AO perspective, the power differential is explicit, and appropriate use is for maximum client group benefit. Self-awareness about what matters personally as well as professionally permits a more accurate understanding of clients and their experiences within communities.
- Assessment that does not account for the client's resources and barriers in the community leaves that individual solely responsible for the totality of their mental health. A professional's perceptions of "normal" and "appropriate" for a community influence judgment about what is healthy and unhealthy, as well as the type and amount of change possible to benefit a client and others of the same identity groups.
- An AO perspective requires professionals to have knowledge of the specific community as well as critical awareness of structural forces that operate within society and impact on that community. Knowledge of the client requires understanding factors that hinder, facilitate, fit and balance individuals with their communities. There is always a connection between personal and social, economic and political forces.

Chapter Outline

Policies

"**Good society**" has different meanings for different people. In relation to inequity and diversity, Canada's **cultural mosaic** focuses on differentiation, while in the United States, the **melting pot** emphasizes uniformity (Skerrett, 2008). These ideals refer to desirable outcomes of equivalence or equality. However, both nations demonstrate increasing social, political and economic inequality.

Social policies are what governments do about social problems. They are oriented toward improving wellness or addressing disadvantage. They may be in the broad areas of social, political, and economic affairs. They authorize the creation, maintenance and functions of public institutions. Policies organize the institutions. They determine who can access what, when and for what purpose. They have a major impact on community life.

There is significant distance between government policy and community life. The creation of policy is often criticized as uninformed by the daily life experiences of the people who are most directly affected by it. A recent addition to the literature on public policy is **community engagement** which refers to the connections that government has with its citizens. This idea can be leveraged to the benefit of community groups who want a voice and want to influence policy decisions at election time as well as between elections.

"Community engagement refers to the connections between the governments, citizens and communities on a range of policy, program and service issues" (Queensland Government, 2006, p. 5). Three levels of engagement in this model include: information (government communicates to residents), consultation (residents give government feedback on specific issues determined by government) and **active participation** (residents have influence on policy, but government holds final say).

A different model of community engagement concerns the power or influence that community members have. These levels (Government of Manchester, 2006) include: informing people (providing information to residents); researching needs, priorities and attitudes (using research to understand the issues); consulting and learning (obtaining views of residents on an issue); involving communities (bringing residents into the decision-making); devolving decisions (providing support for the community to make decisions for themselves); and supporting hands-on community decision (supporting developing plans put in place by themselves).

Devolving decisions can be very responsive to a community. However, if the process is not supported with funding and expertise, the resulting instability will consume the efforts. Under the guise of giving greater control over decisions to the community, governments can, by relinquishing responsibility for that function, conserve their own resources. One major benefit of community ownership is local control. Often, however, there is a lack of support and ongoing resources to properly administer it.

In order to influence policy, it is important to become knowledgeable about the particular policies themselves as well as their creation. Theories of policy creation include institutional, rational, garbage can, incremental, process, elite and public choice theories (Sabatier, 1999). **Institutional theories** indicate that the government's job is to create, enact and enforce policies. A **rational theory** concerning policy creation is a judgment of the best sociopolitical and economic cost-to-benefit ratio. A **garbage can theory** is very practical. Policies are created by throwing every problem and solution together and the mix is what decides. **Incremental theories** include the same policies with small changes with each iteration over time. Mixed scanning is a combination of rational and incremental theories, with solutions generated by trial and error. **Process theory** starts with a problem, from which potential policy solutions are considered, and is followed by selection and evaluation. In **elite theory**, a small group decides and disseminates policies to the masses. In **public choice theory**, collective decisions by those who are interested and together based on individual needs find collective solution.

Communities

Community may be defined as "the combination and interrelationships of geographic, locational and non-locational units, systems, and characteristics that provide relevance and growth to individuals, groups and organizations" (Galbraith, 1990, p. 5). It has also been defined as "a human system of more than two people in which the members interact personally over time, in which behavior and activity are guided by collectively-evolved norms or collective decisions, and from which members may freely secede" (Boothroyd & Davis, 1993, p. 105). In a more action-oriented definition, it has been called "a collection of people who have become aware of some problem or some broad goal, who have gone through a process of learning about themselves and about their environment, and have formulated a group objective" (Roberts, 1979, p. 10). As such, community is far more than dress, food, language, music, literature, games, rituals, visual art and festivals. It includes norms, beliefs, communication styles, values, method of handling emotions, notions of time, notions of modesty, how physical space is handled, competition and cooperation and sense of ethics.

Assets

Forces that strengthen communities include active voluntary organizations, community centers, a common need or enemy, good transportation and balanced land use (Brown & Hannis, 2012). Forces that challenge communities include lack of collective history, stigma, high mobility, fragmentation, lack of services, lack of decision-making authority and lack of boundaries (Brown & Hannis, 2012). Types of communities include **Gemeinschaft** (pre-industrial) and **Gesellschaft** (modern) (translation in 1957). There are also geographic, function attribute and interest (Lee, 1986) communities. Communities have different patterns of production, distribution and consumption as well as socialization, social control, participation and mutual support.

Capital is an important concept for studying communities. There are two major types of capital: physical and social (Aldrich & Meyer, 2015). **Physical capital** refers to the local natural and built resources that exist and can be accessed by community members. **Social capital** has two subtypes: bonding and bridging (Leung, Chin & Petrescu-Prahova, 2016). Bonding social capital is what brings individuals together as a group. Bridging social capital is what connects groups to each other.

Power is another fundamental concept in community change. Power may be defined as the capacity to move people in a desired direction to accomplish some end (Homan, 2010). It depends on social context and includes other people, time, place and purpose. It can be positive (e.g. collaboration, nobleness, cooperation) and negative (e.g. dominance, manipulation, coercion). There are different types of power in groups (Northouse, 2018), including: **reward** (i.e. to reinforce), **coercive** (i.e. to punish), **legitimate** (i.e. a right to position of influence), **referent** (i.e. how well-liked a person is), **expert** (i.e. technical expertise), and **informational** (i.e. control and access to information).

Roles

There are also roles in communities that hold power, including public officials, funders, private organizations, professionals, families of well-connected people, grassroots organizations, local leaders, business owners and service providers. Individuals in these roles control different forms of power (Homan, 2010), such as information, money, laws, customs, constituencies, natural resources, goods and services, network participation and illegal actions.

Each of us is a part of multiple communities, including our neighborhoods, professional organizations and work locations as well as interest memberships and activities outside of work with family or on our own. In some communities we are **insiders**, and in other communities we are **outsiders** (Merriam et al., 2001). This is an important distinction that also has the potential to blur depending on context and application. The perceptions of others in a group are important as one's status may influence the degree to which one is accepted on their own merits or viewed in terms of their associations, past or present, as one who is part of or external to the community and its goals.

Boundaries, a concept very familiar to professionals providing counseling and psychotherapy, also has a meaning in community life. The lines of separation between self and another individual in a therapy setting applies to self in relation to a group as well as a group in relation to another group (Suleiman & Agat-Galili, 2015). A community that is very differentiated and possibly fragmented has limited solidarity, but a community with a great deal of solidarity has strong boundaries and differentiation from other groups. Professionals, by virtue of their training, carry "baggage" into their community connections, which can be positive and negative (LeCroix, Goodrum, Hufstetler, & Armistead, 2017). There are multiple reasons for this, but of some importance are the ways people in the community have interacted with professionals, including researchers, in the past and how they have been left feeling by these interactions.

Theories of Change

Myths about community change include the following: it is easy, anyone can do it, services are well funded, communities are democratic, communities speak with one voice, change is easy to measure, solutions are easy to find and implement and change processes are the same in all communities (Brown & Hannis, 2012).

Broad-based sociological theories refer to the major dimensions of societal harmony and tension (Hustedde & Ganowicz, 2002). **Functionalists** consider a society much like a watch with parts that work together. From a conflict perspective, society is divided. Functionalists, such as the French sociologist Emile Durkheim (1858–1917) consider society to be comprised of individual functions (Gorski, 2017), while **conflict theorists**—such as the socialist Karl Marx (1818–1883)—see society as competitive (Simon, 2016). **Symbolic interactionists** view society more as a collection of meanings that are created and maintained by individuals. Symbolic interactionists, such as the German sociologist Max Weber (1864–1920), view society as a function of interactions and the meanings attached to them (Rock, 2016).

For symbolic interactionists, change centers on the development of consensus among a critical mass of the problems and strategies to address them. It is a positive, slow and measured process. From a functionalist perspective, change also requires consensus but centers on a function that is not being addressed, and only to the degree that it restores functioning of the system. It is a deficit approach, restoring balance and resisting change from the outside. From a conflict view, change is based on fairness and receipt of opportunity or outcome in equal measure to other groups. Change is ongoing, inevitable and often radical.

Psychological theories of practice were not developed with an explicit recognition of sociopolitical community life. It is important to note that, as was identified in Chapter 7, the theory of psychotherapy that one considers appropriate for addressing appropriated oppression or to target social isolation, as in Chapter 8, need not be problematic from the perspective of a conflict of interactionist view of society.

There are theories of psychotherapy that fit more clearly within each of the three views presented (see Table 9.1). These three broad schools of thought include problem-solving, social change and empowerment (Jun, 2018). In problem-solving, a likely fit with a functionalist view of society, there are systems

TABLE 9.1 Theoretical Underpinnings of Individual and Community Change

Symbolic Interactionism	Functionalism	Conflict
• society as a collection of meanings that are created and maintained by individuals • German sociologist Max Weber (1864–1920) • society is a function of interactions and the meanings attached to them	• society much like a watch with parts that work together • French sociologist Emile Durkheim (1858–1917) • society is comprised of individual functions	• society is divided based on the inequality that exists • socialist Karl Marx (1818–1883) • society is competitive
• change centers on development of consensus among a critical mass of the problems and strategies to address them • positive, slow and measured process	• change also requires consensus but centers on a function that is not being addressed, and only to the degree that it restores functioning of the system • a deficit approach, to restore balance and resist change from outside	• change is based on fairness and receipt of opportunity or outcome in equal measure to other groups • ongoing, inevitable and often radical
Empowerment Theories	**Problem-Solving Theories**	**Social Action Theories**
In empowerment, which is a closer fit with an interactionist perspective, emphasis is on strengths, solutions, narrative, advocacy, macro practice, humanism, existentialism and spiritualism	In problem-solving, a likely fit with a functionalist view of society, there are systems and ecological, psychodynamic, cognitive behavioral, crisis and task centered approaches	In social change, a likely fit with a conflict perspective, include feminist, critical and anti-discriminatory approaches.
Locality Development	**Social Planning**	**Social Action**
• emphasis on self-help • focus is on broad-based social and economic progress • partnership with power structure	• emphasis on rational, technical problem-solving • focus is on social problems • sponsorship by the power structure	• emphasis on redistribution of power and resources • focus is on social justice issues • variable orientation to power structure

and ecological, psychodynamic, cognitive behavioral, crisis and task centered approaches. Social change, a likely fit with a conflict perspective, includes feminist, critical and anti-discriminatory approaches. In empowerment, which is a closer fit with an interactionist perspective, the emphasis is on strengths, solutions, narrative, advocacy, macro practice, humanism, existentialism and spiritualism.

Activity: Pre-Engagement Self-Assessment

Prior to engaging with a new or unfamiliar community, it may be helpful to reflect on personal and professional experiences and expectations.

Identity and Community

What are the identities I claim?

What communities am I a part of?

What influences stability and change in those communities?

What are my community experiences with participation, mutual support and social control?

What roles do governments, charities and families play in those communities?

Are my identities elevated or diminished within the community to be engaged with?

Problems and Solutions

What is(are) the problem(s)? According to who?

What is(are) the perceived cause(s) and solution(s) for each?

Which causes are internally and externally (to the community) located and produced?

What solutions to address the problem exist at community and systemic levels?

Degree of Involvement

How do I want to be involved?

Consider: amount and type of involvement, degrees of control and responsibility for collective effort

- Staying informed through news and professional communications?
- Doing things to support causes or organizations in an unacknowledged way?
- Becoming involved in a personal way where one is seen and named?
- Becoming involved in meetings and public efforts?
- Organizing or becoming a member of a board?

Community Assessment

Most community assessments have a specific purpose. Some different purposes include (Hashagen, 2002): **public participation** (government opinion polls), **assets and social economy** (community assets with control and benefit over those assets), **community democracy** (another layer of government within the community), **identity** (finding and expressing a voice), **popular education** (enhancing skills of community members) and **service development** (identifying service needs or responding to service gaps).

It is also helpful to collect information in a way that conveys **responsibility** (e.g. due diligence to ensure different views are represented), **credibility** (e.g. important sources such as census data and key informants are incorporated), **versatility** (e.g. the data can be used to profile the community for different purposes) and **accountability** (e.g. performing the collection and analysis as required by funders or other stakeholders).

Both **primary sources** (e.g. community members' perspectives) and **secondary sources** (e.g. census data) should be used. In addition, the power sources and structure of the community are important to recognize. The following guide may be useful to identify relevant information.

Physical

Sources: government documents, census, planning reports (city, county, province/state, national), observations, consultations with key informants

Boundaries: What are the boundaries of the community? When did the boundaries first appear? What was the purpose of the boundaries at the time?

Governance: What local formal and informal governance exists in the community? What layers of formal and informal governance is the community subsumed within?

Historical: Who were the founders of the community? What was the vision the founders had for the community? What efforts have been made, and by whom, to change the boundaries and why? What natural resources existed within the boundaries? Who owned the resources?

Present: What physical landmarks characterize the community today? What physical resources exist within the community (both manmade and naturally occurring)? For example, housing, schools, government offices, local businesses, human services, food sources, financial institutions; also green space, play space, meeting space, transportation within and between community and outside. Finally, what climate-related, natural resource-related, size-related and location-related issues are pressing for the community?

Economic

Sources: government documents, census, planning reports (city, county, province/state, federal), observations, consultations with key informants).

Present: What are the conduits for income into the community? What are the conduits for income out of the community? Where is political power located internally (informal and formal)? Where is political power located externally (informal and formal)? What is the ethnic or religious leadership? What advocacy organizations or groups exist?

Social

Sources: government documents, census, planning reports (city, county, province/state, federal), observations, consultations with key informants

Demographics: population size, mobility (within and outside of community)? Age of population, family status, children, ethnicities, religions? Income sources and amounts?

Participation: community organizations? Forms of communication used (newsletters, newspapers, Internet)? Festivals, celebrations?

Historical: "founding" interests of the community? Is this contested? Which interests have been prominent over time? Which interests have been marginalized over time? Which interests are most prominent in the present?

Present: What social functions characterize the community today? What social resources exist within the community? For example, formal and informal cooperatives, gatherings, associations, and clubs. What age-related, ethnicity-related, and class-related issues are pressing for the community?

Stakeholders: it can be helpful to consider communities as comprised of different stakeholder groups all within an arena of action (Homan, 2010). There is a **benefit system**, which includes the members who will benefit in some way from the proposed change. There is an **action system**, which includes all members who will be engaged in some form of activity to create the change. Finally, the **target system** is the members who will need to change in response to the actions taken.

Inequity Formulation

In sum, there are aspects for any community assessment that reflect the sources, strength and distribution of influence within and between the community, other communities and institutions. The degree of support for any potential change is measured in roles, resources and social capital. The following are categories for consideration in such an analysis of community disadvantage and potential strengths to be mobilized for progressive change.

- Stakeholders

  - identities
  - boundaries
  - participation
  - power

- Salience of oppression and privilege

  - internal: social, economic and physical capital and gaps
  - external: social, economic and physical capital and gaps

- 'Theory' of why the problem exists to inform 'theory' of action

  - approaches: problem-solving, social change, empowerment
  - sites: personal, family, workplace or school, community, nation

- What community can change (and needs for itself to undertake)
- What community needs others to change

Conclusion

From an AO perspective, there are always connections between individual mental health, community well-being and structural advantage or disadvantage. An assessment of the community or communities in which a client participates is necessary to recognize the facilitators and barriers that exist in daily life. While a full community assessment is well beyond what many therapists would be expected to engage in, a critical appraisal of the practical realities and their structural origins is helpful for both to make connections and identify points where investment in change is most helpful. A theory that includes the role of forces outside of the individual client offers opportunities for action in ways that are personally empowering, socially responsible and politically active.

Web Links

Everything You Need to Know About This Year's Women's March
http://time.com/5107988/womens-march-2018-las-vegas-chicago-new-york/

Guiding Vision and Definition of Principles
https://static1.squarespace.com/static/584086c7be6594762f5ec56e/t/587ffb
20579fb3554668c111/1484782369253/WMW+Guiding+Vision+%26+
Definition+of+Principles.pdf

Women's March Mission
www.womensmarch.com/mission/

What Is Social Capital?
https://sustainingcommunity.wordpress.com/2011/04/03/what-is-social-capital/

Key Terms

References

Aldrich, D. P., & Meyer, M. A. (2015). Social capital and community resilience. *American Behavioral Scientist, 59*(2), 254–269.

Boothroyd, P., & Davis, H. C. (1993). Community economic development: Three approaches. *Journal of Planning Education and Research, 12*(3), 230–240.

Brown, J., & Hannis, D. (2012). *Community development in Canada.* Toronto, ON: Pearson Higher Ed.

Galbraith, M. W. (1990). The nature of community and adult education. In M. W. Galbraith (Ed.), *Education through community organizations* (pp. 3–11). San Francisco: Jossey-Bass.

Gorski, P. S. (2017). Recovered goods: Durkheimian sociology as virtue ethics. In *Varieties of virtue ethics* (pp. 181–198). London: Palgrave Macmillan.

Government of Manchester. (2006). *Understanding community engagement: Principles and tools.* Retrieved June 7, 2006, from www.manchester.gov.uk/bestvalue/pdf/area/community. pdf#search='Principles%20of% 20%20Community%20Engagement'

Hashagen, S. (2002). *Models of community engagement.* Glasgow: Scottish Community Development Centre.

Homan, M. (2010). *Promoting community change: Making it happen in the real world.* Pacific Grove, CA: Brooks, Cole.

Hustedde, R. J., & Ganowicz, J. (2002). The basics: What's essential about theory for community development practice? *Community Development, 33*(1), 1–19.

Jun, H. (2018). *Social justice, multicultural counseling, and practice: Beyond a conventional approach.* New York: Springer.

LeCroix, R. H., Goodrum, N. M., Hufstetler, S., & Armistead, L. P. (2017). Community data collection with children of mothers living with HIV: Boundaries of the researcher role. *American Journal of Community Psychology, 60*(3–4), 368–374.

Lee, B. (1986). *Pragmatics of community organization.* Mississauga, ON: Common Act Press.

Leung, M. R., Chin, J. J., & Petrescu-Prahova, M. (2016). Involving immigrant religious organizations in HIV/AIDS prevention: The role of bonding and bridging social capital. *Social Science & Medicine, 162*, 201–209.

Merriam, S. B., Johnson-Bailey, J., Lee, M. Y., Kee, Y., Ntseane, G., & Muhamad, M. (2001). Power and positionality: Negotiating insider/outsider status within and across cultures. *International Journal of Lifelong Education, 20*(5), 405–416.

Northouse, P. G. (2018). *Leadership: Theory and practice.* New York: Sage Publications.

Queensland Government. (2006). *Engaging Queenslanders: An introduction to community engagement.* Retrieved from http://time.com/5107988/womens-march-2018-las-vegas-chicago-new-york/

Roberts, H. (1979). *Community development: Learning and action.* Toronto, ON: University of Toronto Press.

Rock, P. (2016). *Making of symbolic interactionism.* New York: Springer.

Sabatier, P. A. (1999). The need for better theories. *Theories of the Policy Process, 2*, 3–17.

Simon, R. M. (2016). The conflict paradigm in sociology and the study of social inequality: Paradox and possibility. *Theory in Action, 9*(1), 1.

Skerrett, A. (2008). Racializing educational change: Melting pot and mosaic influences on educational policy and practice. *Journal of Educational Change, 9*(3), 261–280.

Suleiman, R., & Agat-Galili, Y. (2015). Sleeping on the enemy's couch: Psychotherapy across ethnic boundaries in Israel. *Peace and Conflict: Journal of Peace Psychology, 21*(2), 187.

Discussion Questions

1. Neoliberalism and globalization have together been described as "capitalism without borders". These benefit the most affluent in all nations through deregulation of markets, state retrenchment and wealth accumulation. In what ways do these forces affect you as a citizen and professional? How do these affect the lives of individual clients? (See Vicente Navarro (ed.) *Neoliberalism, Globalization, and Inequalities: Consequences for Health and Quality of Life*.)

2. Public policy has an effect on inequality. There is less differentiation when left-leaning politics are influential because of higher public access to income and services, union activity and proportional participation in elections. Neoliberal policies promote competition, tax reductions, and reduce reliance on public institutions. In what ways can these forces be activated and leveraged by ourselves or our clients for therapeutic benefit?

3. Given a mismatch between clients' personal needs and available resources in the community, does the role of the therapist shift toward assisting with personal readiness to engage with community resources and assisting with the location of those resources? Why or why not?

10

INTERVENTION FOR COMMUNITY CHANGE

In this chapter, an overview of community change approaches is described. From an AO perspective, community change may be viewed as a process of building support to mobilize strengths held by individuals facing systematic disadvantage. The outcomes of mobilization may include social support, as well as targeted local change or advocacy on behalf of a group or entire community. The efforts can lead to organization development and localized service delivery as well as political representation and social action against a negative outside influence. Although community change does not often directly change government policy, it is a building block of power that can combine with other efforts, such as coalition-building, to produce major change. At a local level, community change is a strong force of support and service.

There are three main approaches to community change: local social networking and support, technical problem-solving for issues at a community level and social action, which is a formal stance against or in support of an issue, event or practice. In each of these approaches, local, credible and influential leadership is especially important. Efforts for community change often relate to employment, housing and the local economy. The process depends on an organizer to initiate and assume initial leadership.

Critical consciousness is a basic means by which to create awareness of structural determinates of personal problems and insight into goals and means available for local change to buffer or challenge those forces. A community meeting is often used to bring together stakeholders to consider shared problems and solutions. Information gathering may occur in advance of as well as following the meeting. Goals and a communications strategy should be set so that progress can be monitored and information shared with constituents.

The most common outcomes of community change are organization and program development. Organizations are formal entities that have membership and leadership with vision, mission, objectives and activities. Programs, in contrast, are more specific and intended to reach a particular group for a purpose that is important to the organization within which they are housed.

What is community intervention and why is it valuable from an AO perspective?

- It is recognized that for individuals facing disadvantage there is constant pressure to adapt, avoid or resist structural forces that define what is socially "acceptable" and "successful" according to the dominant culture. For privileged identities, this pressure to conform does not exist, because one is "normal" relative to social standards set by privileged others like oneself.

- Counseling and psychotherapy interventions focus on client change. From an AO perspective, however, the question "how can the social, economic and political structures that create the problem effectively challenged?" is asked alongside "what the client can do about the problem?" Additionally, the circumstances of a client's life are explicitly identified and considered as targets for change.

- From an AO perspective, counseling and psychotherapy include critical self-reflection of the practitioner on experiences in their own lives, as well as how political, economic and social circumstances manifest in barriers to community, family and personal well-being for themselves and their clients. Intervention from an AO perspective includes community organization for social change. There is always a need to confront privilege to promote equity and social justice.

- Communities facing disadvantage have problems, but the abilities, capacities, strengths and resiliencies collectively held are the keys to positive change.

Chapter Outline

Approaches to Community Change

The 1960s and 1970s were the heydays of community intervention. However, there was no analysis of the scientific literature until the 1990s. Jack Rothman (1996) has written extensively about approaches to community change. He proposed three main approaches: locality development, social planning and social action.

In **locality development**, there is an emphasis on self-help and broad-based social and economic progress. Typically, the efforts undertaken within this approach partner with the power structure. A critical factor in the success of this approach is leadership development. The leader's primary purpose is to engage members. The main benefits of this approach are a reduction in isolation and loneliness, cultivation of local leadership and building of personal, interpersonal and collective power. The internal power structure that is created can communicate with external power structures (Green & Haines, 2015). A drawback of this approach is the local focus, which has limited reach to regional or national levels. These efforts do not directly challenge inequality, structural oppression or wealth distribution or address complex issues like unemployment.

In **social planning**, the emphasis is on rational and technical problem-solving that has at its base a specific social problem to be solved. Typically, in these efforts the relationship with the power structure is sponsorship. Efforts from this approach tend to have a linear procedure following steps for the exploration, engagement and evaluation of specific and measurable change. An example (Weil, 2014) of stages includes: preparation, needs assessment, policy development, program development, implementation and monitoring and evaluation. Some benefits of this approach include the credibility of an expert who is very involved in the process, the specificity of the issues and sophistication of the analysis and the evidence it produces. Potential drawbacks are the technical nature, which may be beyond what is necessary and potentially overshoot the effects of more general but broader issues, as well as the political nature of the evidence and predetermination of the desired results.

In **social action**, the emphasis is on redistribution of resources and power with a focus on issues of social justice. Efforts within this approach have a variable orientation to the power structure. A process is typically followed in order to prepare an effort to confront an interest or position represented by another group. An example (Cameron & Kerans, 1985) of such a process includes defining, researching and formulating an action goal, developing a method and evaluating the action. Major benefits of efforts within this approach are that the effort to thwart a common enemy can be fun, energizing and socially cohesive. The actions themselves might be gritty and aggressive but allowable in the service of a heightened moral purpose. Results are often immediate, and with success the confidence of the group is heightened. One potential downside is that the result often alienates the opposition, making potential future collaboration difficult. The process requires a charismatic leader and committed group. Finally, if the tactics are "fun", sometimes the act itself, rather than the change pursued, becomes focal.

Types of Community Change

Examples of community change efforts more prominently in use today center on the distinction between power-based and program-based development (Stoecker, 2012). In **power-based development**, the purpose is specific change to a circumstance or position that is untenable for a particular group. In **program-based development**, the purpose is to develop collaborations and networks that produce change within existing structures. Program-based efforts commonly in use primarily include employment development, neighborhood development, community-based housing and social enterprise (Loewen, Cates, & Chorney, 2003). In **employment development**, efforts made are with both prospective employees and employers to improve opportunities for individuals looking for work as well as with recruitment and retention of those individuals with employers. In **neighborhood development**, a social community within a geographic area is the basis for group-building to strengthen connections and create local governance. In **community-based housing**, both the physical and social aspects of housing for individuals and families who have few or no options are pursued to create local opportunities. In **social enterprise**, the emphasis is on building businesses that meet a social need, such as local employment, decent employment and goods and services that are needed locally but not available.

Tactics of Community Change

Four strategies include confrontation, negotiation, collaboration and cooptation (Homan, 2010). In **confrontation**, the purpose is to use force to pressure an opposing group or organization to accept an agreement. The use of confrontation will often have the effect of irritating the other side and can possibly provoke retaliation. It is useful when there is a very clear target for change, when a compromise is unlikely and when they are not expecting it. It shows the groups willingness to challenge an opponent to a contest from which there will be a winner and a loser. Some of the benefits include solidifying support on your side for the issue, drawing public attention to the issue and your group and displaying the resources your group has. One major potential downside is that the members of one's group can lose confidence and cohesion if the contest is drawn out or if retaliation threats or actions are substantial. Such actions can also create long-term enemies and result in defeat. Some examples of conflict tactics include personalizing the issue, freezing the target, having an "accountability" meeting, being disruptive, lawsuits, cutting off support and civil disobedience (Alinsky, 1971).

In **negotiation**, the purpose is to create an agreement that both sides can accept. It is a useful tactic to consider when it seems that your group does not have the strength or means to win a confrontation (Walls, 2015). It is also useful in terms of potential for finding a compromise and avoiding win/lose scenarios. There may be benefits to your group in relation to some of the other side's positions, and it is also possible for groundwork for a closer working relationship or smoother negotiations in the future to be put down in the process. The tactic allows for a better chance of making progress and avoiding conflict. It is more "professional" in the sense that the process can be formalized, entered into and withdrawn from and can involve a neutral third party if necessary. There are two main types of negotiations: positional and principled (Homan, 2010). In **positional negotiation**, there is typically more tension between the groups and positions, so interests are hidden, while in **principled negotiation**, there is more goodwill and positions are outlined so that both sides' interests can be advanced. Major benefits include potential for future work together and potential to get "something", though not everything. A downside is that in negotiation it is possible to give away too much, to focus on small things instead of the big issues and to feel like or be seen as losing if some significant gains are not made through the process. Some examples include making agreements, clarifying ownership, acknowledging the partner's involvement, offering rewards to a partner, taking on a fair share of the work and getting to know each other personally.

The purpose of **collaboration** is to generate an outcome that is the joint product of efforts on both sides. It is beneficial when there are commonalities between the groups and some confidence that both share enough common interest and desire to work together (Christens & Speer, 2015). Another possibility is that the groups are looking to develop a more formal working relationship on the issue at hand as well as other issues in the future. Oftentimes, the government or private organizations requires some form of collaboration for grant funding. The benefits are that the groups receive something that neither could achieve on their own, there is potential to develop a longer-term relationship and interdependence may be facilitated through the process (Holgate, 2015). One drawback is that the groups may still have significant differences outside of the issue. In addition, relationships require effort in and of themselves, take time and go through ups and downs. They also have an impact on the independence of the groups.

Cooptation is a tactic to incorporate one group into another (Fields, 2015). It begins with a formal alliance; as the partnership grows, one side grows in power while the other side loses relative power. It can be useful when a group wants specialized information or resources that another holds. It may also be useful when a group wants to influence another group but not in a confrontational way. Major benefits may include silencing a critic by bringing that critic inside the group, learning about the other side with only a small investment and positioning both sides on the same side for a specific purpose. A potential drawback is that this takes a long time to develop and opens up knowledge and connections about the group's structure and operations to the other group.

Process of Community Change

A process for facilitating community change includes the important elements of preparation, organization and building momentum as well as taking and sustaining action. From an AO perspective, counselors and psychotherapists may be involved in a myriad of ways, such as awareness of the types of efforts underway, efforts that could be undertaken to support social networks and collective efforts to combat structural oppression of clients. Preparation for the organizer includes recognition of how involved to be and how one's role and influence may change over time as the effort develops. The benefits and drawbacks of involvement should be considered as well as the potential for dual relationships with individuals as clients, neighbors and citizens in private and public life.

Considerations about involvement may include time commitment, results orientation, context of the work, the employer and peer evaluations, as well as whether it will be done in addition to or in place of income-generating employment. Good community work takes time, and the energy for community work can be drawn from other activities or, if simply added on, lead to burnout. It is important to anticipate the effects of involvement in the eyes of employers and colleagues because the nature of community work is also very political. There are potential roles as organizers, teachers, coaches, facilitators, advocates, negotiators, brokers and researchers.

There is the potential for dual relationships, because as part of these efforts one may meet up with or be part of groups sharing similar interests (Brown, 2017). Dual roles for many counselors are to some extent unavoidable (e.g. small communities); responsibility is always on the counselor to ensure this occurs and never on the client. The best way to manage dual roles is to prevent them from occurring in the first place.

Organization

Consciousness raising is a basic mechanism underlying effort at this point of the process. Education is an essential means (Bryant & Usher, 2014). However, the ways that education is used vary a great deal in relation to the amount of community involvement in the topics and process as well as the intended outcome. Distinctions can be made between formal adult education, non-formal adult education, community education and radical adult education. **Formal adult education** is the education offered by credit-granting institutions, such as colleges and community schools. **Non-formal adult education** is offered through community networks and mentorships that are not for credit or subject to any accreditation. **Community education** is locally developed and delivered programs and courses through community agencies that have credibility and practical connections to the content and instructors. Finally, **radical adult education** is specific to critical awareness of the problems facing a community or group and the forces that oppress and constrain opportunities and outcomes.

One activity is to have a **community meeting**. The structure can be a one-time only event or a series of events; the event may have a designated speaker or speakers followed by discussion as a large group, or may break out into groups on the same or different topics (Hunter, 2017). The purpose of such a gathering is to bring together stakeholders on an issue, share information and begin to develop connections that can lead into collaborations or partnerships. It is important to be realistic about the outcome of such a gathering. If there is a large or broad representation, the likelihood of consensus is modest. If the stakeholders already know each other and work together with a particular funding opportunity to pursue or a policy issue to address, the chances of consensus may be greater. It is also very helpful to remember that each stakeholder has their own perspective or "lens" which is culturally based and shaped by gender, class, age, ethnicity, and the level of education received. Therefore, those in attendance may not speak with one voice or have a clearly defined understanding of their needs. There are also individuals who tend to dominate in group discussions and those who withdraw. The facilitator or facilitators play a significant role in ensuring that each in attendance has an opportunity to contribute. But there is never an easy answer to the question of to whom one should listen.

Building Momentum

In order for a collective to move forward on a particular issue or issues, there may be work remaining to clarify focus, purpose and strategies. It is helpful to engage with and improve depth of understanding and commitment to the process. This can be pursued through collaborative strengths and needs assessment. From a motivational and community wellness perspective, it is more important for a process to challenge a particular set of circumstances than to focus on the problem and its resolution. Strategically, it is important to consider which positioning of the problem is best for clarifying, giving focus to the effort while encouraging the involvement of most, if not all, members of the community.

For an assessment, it is helpful to have a clear purpose, means and knowledge of the intended audience. Methods can be qualitative or quantitative (Creswell &

Clark, 2017). Often, "**key informants**" are useful, providing in-depth information with limited resource expenditure. In addition, focus groups (Stewart &
Shamdasani, 2014) offer the opportunity to engage broader representation of
the community and stakeholders, to bring them together and to benefit from
dialogue about the issues. In addition, surveys (Ledwith, 2017) provide potentially the broadest reach with relatively fewer resources than interviews. In general, group efforts are less resource-intensive than individual efforts but have the
potential to overrepresent the views of the most vocal. Interviews provide more
depth and surveys provide more breadth of knowledge.

Goal setting is another means of generating momentum. The process of setting
goals should follow from and be supported by the findings of the assessment. The
goals themselves can be immediate, short term and long term. To be useful, they
are best kept concrete and achievable with aspirational statements included as part
of the overall vision of the process.

Taking and Sustaining Action

Decisions about which tasks are undertaken, and how, occur in this component
of the community change process. Effective communication is essential. While it
is important to have ongoing communication among those directly involved in
the effort, communication with other potential stakeholders as well as the broader
communities affected by the process is also vitally important for building support.
Major benefits of making efforts known include letting people know you and the
change effort exist, exposing the issue, educating for action, attracting new support, strengthening the affiliation between existing and potential future members
and promoting the credibility of the issue and proposed change.

Determining who is important to reach can be organized through the consideration of the market, medium and message. The **market** comprises the recipients
of the message, from whom you want a reaction. The **medium** is the technique
or device used to get the message to the market. And, finally, the **message** is what
the market needs to hear to respond (Lefebvre & Flora, 1988). Major outcomes
of efforts over time include mutual support, program planning and organization
building. Mutual support is often a starting point for community change as well
as a prerequisite for program or organization development (Belone et al., 2016).

Development of Organizations and Programs

Two common forms of community change include **organization building** and
program development. In these cases, a power structure is created by the
effort that often requires partnership with a power structure to establish itself.
These efforts may be more general (e.g. community networking), focused (e.g.
employment readiness and support), remedial (e.g. survivors support group) or
preventive (e.g. community clean up). An organization is a formal entity that

can represent the needs of a particular community and exist over the long term. Program development exists within an organization as a direct means to provide a service to a particular group.

Community-Based Organizations

Community organizations have a formalized structure with a purpose, procedures and membership. There are distinct types (Scott & Davis, 2015), including both **temporary** (e.g. responding to a local water crisis) and **ongoing** (e.g. business development) as well as **single issue** (e.g. violence against women) and **multi-issue** (e.g. social development) organizations. Organizations may also be defined in relation to their purposes, including self-help (e.g. mutual support), partnership (e.g. social support), coproduction (e.g. culturally based organizations), pressure (e.g. think-tanks) and protest (e.g. advocacy organizations) (Rubin, Rubin, & Doig, 1992).

Community organizations usually have an immediate and compelling issue in focus. They often start with a group of citizens who all recognize a particular issue or need. They develop over long periods and undergo shifts in priorities and activities. As counselors, we hear experiences that are common among our clients, which lead us to the desire to be involved in a collective effort that makes a difference. It is important to check on the agencies and services that exist to ensure that what you are considering has not already been identified as within the mandate of a government or community group.

One way to start might be to contact an existing organization about an issue that is concerning; this can lead down a fruitful path for collaboration or, at the least, help you determine what your idea could add to the community as a supplement to what already exists. If there is not an organization with a mandate for a particular issue, bringing a selective group of people together is a good way to start. It can be helpful to invite those with expertise and other resources needed to identify and address the issue. From that meeting, setting specific next steps can be helpful to keep motivation and focus. Taking action early can be very helpful for cohesion and confidence. The stages of organizational development are as follows: introduction, initial action, emergence of leadership and structure, letdown and floundering, recommitment and new members, sustained action and, finally, growth/decline/ending.

Community-Based Program Development

There are several considerations for community-based program development within an existing organization. It is helpful to understand the nature and operations of the organization, including the its history, mission, service area, population served, current programs and staffing as well as future plans (O'Neill, Albin, Storey, Horner, & Sprague, 2015). In addition, it is important to understand its funding sources and other agencies providing similar services, as well as its informal contacts and formal connections.

From this knowledge, a more formal assessment can be undertaken. An **organizational assessment** may include the organization's administrative structure and organizational chart with lines between positions. It is important to recognize that an informal structure always exists (Dolgoff & Feldstein, 2012). The organization's resources, including unallocated or allocated funding that is available internally as well as physical space both within and surrounding the building, should be accounted for (Holzemer, Klainberg, Murphy, Rondello, & Smith, 2014). Physical spaces include whether there are relevant spaces for cooking, child minding, reading, prayer and private and large meetings or presentations as well as adequate bathroom facilities or possibly a gymnasium. Equipment and materials are also important to account for. It is also important to know about the administrative, secretarial or professional expertise within the organization. Additionally, the motivation, commitment and support for the idea are good to ascertain.

It is helpful to have a sense of the physical, demographic, institutional and social indicators relevant to the community and potential participants. Consider both the needs and strengths within each of eight areas: physical environment, education facilities and services, transportation sources and adequacy, local and regional government health and social services, businesses and employment opportunities, communication sources and networks and recreation facilities and their use.

Process

Different stakeholders include the potential participants themselves, the sponsoring organization's mission and the mandate of the funder or, oftentimes, funders. Through the assessment process, the preparation, background and skills of service providers within the organization, in relation to the general direction for program development, will be evident. Finally, the border community and its stakeholders, including grassroots activists, neighbors, local politicians and vocal residents, should be consulted. The ways that decisions are made in organizations vary. Different processes have been suggested (Schwenk, 1989), including rational (i.e. the "facts" with logical connections), bureaucratic (i.e. greater decision-making authority resides in higher positions), anarchic (i.e. whoever raises the most fuss at the time) and political (i.e. oftentimes, this is funder-related).

Structure

Types of programs developed by community organizations involved in social justice related efforts may include those with a focus on training or education, information, case management, advocacy, counseling or meeting basic needs for social support and food, clothing or shelter assistance. A key component is the provision of a service that helps not only the participants in attendance but that can also be used by those participants to help others as well. Implicit or explicit theories of change are evident. A **theory of change** includes the framework linking what program participants directly experience in the program to a particular change (Funnell & Rogers, 2011). Programs are often organized around three components. These components include goals, objectives and activities.

Challenges

Potential barriers to service include availability, accessibility, acceptability, affordability, appropriateness and adequacy (Souliotis, Hasardzhiev, & Agapidaki, 2016). Availability refers to the presence or perceived presence of a service. Accessibility includes the ability of potential participants to use services. Acceptability refers to the degree to which participants feel that they can use the services. Affordability of services includes both tangible and intangible costs to participants for use. Appropriateness of services depends on the right kind of assistance for the participants. Finally, adequacy of service refers to the quality and completeness of service for the level of diversity and need.

Conclusion

Communities are a means of support and influence against oppressive structures and forces. Counseling and psychotherapy from an AO perspective attend to the positive functions of belonging and empowerment as well as safety that may be promoted through organizing. The potential for community change, in ways that buffer against or alter economic, social and political forces, helps to locate the contributors to problems faced by clients in a therapeutic setting. There is great political value in becoming involved in community change efforts on behalf of clients as well as the profession or for oneself as citizen.

Web Links

Understanding Community Organizing
www.youtube.com/watch?v=flXHRxc9q1k

Mobilizing the Poor
www.youtube.com/watch?v=PZ9Si5pkAqg

The Antidote to Apathy
www.ted.com/talks/dave_meslin_the_antidote_to_apathy

Settlement Houses Today
www.ifsnetwork.org/ifs/resources/history/settlement-houses-today-their-
    ro:en-us.pdf

Jacob A. Riis Neighborhood Settlement, New York, NY USA

Website: www.facebook.com:443/riissettlement.org/

Centre for Social Justice
www.socialjustice.org

Key Terms

References

Alinsky, S. (1971). *Rules for radicals*. New York, NY: Vintage.
Belone, L., Lucero, J. E., Duran, B., Tafoya, G., Baker, E. A., Chan, D., . . . Wallerstein, N. (2016). Community-based participatory research conceptual model: Community partner consultation and face validity. *Qualitative Health Research, 26*(1), 117–135.

Brown, J. (2017). *Counseling diversity in context.* Toronto, ON: University of Toronto Press.

Bryant, I., & Usher, R. (2014). *Adult education as theory, practice and research: The captive triangle.* London: Routledge.

Cameron, J. G., & Kerans, P. (1985). Social and political action. *An Introduction to Social Work Practice in Canada,* 11.

Christens, B. D., & Speer, P. W. (2015). Community organizing: Practice, research, and policy implications. *Social Issues and Policy Review, 9*(1), 193–222.

Craig Lefebvre, R., & Flora, J. A. (1988). Social marketing and public health intervention. *Health Education Quarterly, 15*(3), 299–315.

Creswell, J. W., & Clark, V. L. P. (2017). *Designing and conducting mixed methods research.* New York: Sage Publications.

Dolgoff, R., & Feldstein, D. (2012). *Understanding social welfare: A search for social justice.* Toronto, ON: Pearson Higher Ed.

Fields, D. (2015). Contesting the financialization of urban space: Community organizations and the struggle to preserve affordable rental housing in New York city. *Journal of Urban Affairs, 37*(2), 144–165.

Funnell, S. C., & Rogers, P. J. (2011). *Purposeful program theory: Effective use of theories of change and logic models* (Vol. 31). New York: John Wiley & Sons, Inc.

Green, G. P., & Haines, A. (2015). *Asset building & community development.* New York: Sage Publications.

Holgate, J. (2015). An international study of trade union involvement in community organizing: Same model, different outcomes. *British Journal of Industrial Relations, 53*(3), 460–483.

Holzemer, S. P., Klainberg, M., Murphy, D. J., Rondello, K. C., & Smith, D. (2014). Precision and principles of community program development. *Community Health Nursing,* 261.

Homan, M. (2010). *Promoting community change: Making it happen in the real world.* Pacific Grove, CA: Brooks, Cole.

Hunter, F. (2017). *Community power structure: A study of decision makers.* Chapel Hill, NC: UNC Press Books.

Ledwith, M. (2017). Emancipatory action research as a critical living praxis: From dominant narratives to counternarrative. In *The Palgrave international handbook of action research* (pp. 49–62). New York, NY: Palgrave Macmillan.

Loewen, G., Cates, P., & Chorney, P. (2003, November 26). *Maintaining momentum—CD/ CED gathering.*

O'Neill, R. E., Albin, R. W., Storey, K., Horner, R. H., & Sprague, J. R. (2015). *Functional assessment and program development.* Toronto, ON: Nelson Education.

Rothman, J. (1996). The interweaving of community intervention approaches. *Journal of Community Practice, 3*(3–4), 69–99.

Rubin, H. J., Rubin, I., & Doig, R. (1992). *Community organizing and development* (p. 3). New York, NY: Palgrave Macmillan.

Schwenk, C. R. (1989). Linking cognitive, organizational and political factors in explaining strategic change. *Journal of Management Studies, 26*(2), 177–187.

Scott, W. R., & Davis, G. F. (2015). *Organizations and organizing: Rational, natural and open systems perspectives.* London: Routledge.

Souliotis, K., Hasardzhiev, S., & Agapidaki, E. (2016). A conceptual framework of mapping access to health care across EU countries: The patient access initiative. *Public Health Genomics, 19*(3), 153–159.

Stewart, D. W., & Shamdasani, P. N. (2014). *Focus groups: Theory and practice* (Vol. 20). New York: Sage Publications.

Stoecker, R. (2012). *Research methods for community change: A project-based approach.* New York: Sage Publications.

Walls, D. S. (2015). *Community organizing.* New York: John Wiley & Sons, Inc.

Weil, M. (2014). *Community practice: Conceptual models.* New York, NY: Routledge.

Discussion Questions

1. Consider the identity intersections in your own life. In which ways are your identities privileged? In which ways are they disadvantaged? How would you define the ideal community for yourself? How close is the imagined community to the kind of community that you live in? What are the similarities and differences? How could you make it more like the kind of community you would like to live in?

2. In what ways can a personal problem be defined as a social problem? Consider the problem of depression within a high poverty community. What are the personal, neighborhood and civic and societal contributors? Define what is going on: Why is it going on? Theory of change? Who or what needs to change? Consider who will do what with community, with government and its systems, with employers.

3. Apply case conceptualization to community-level issues for an individual client. Consider how you might recognize internal community-level contributors and goals (e.g. self-help, resource sharing, local parallel economy), relational contributors and goals (e.g. training, social/economic organization, program development) and external contributors and goals (e.g. representation, coalitions, lobbying).

INDEX

Note: Page numbers in **bold** indicate a table on the corresponding page.

Printed in Great Britain
by Amazon